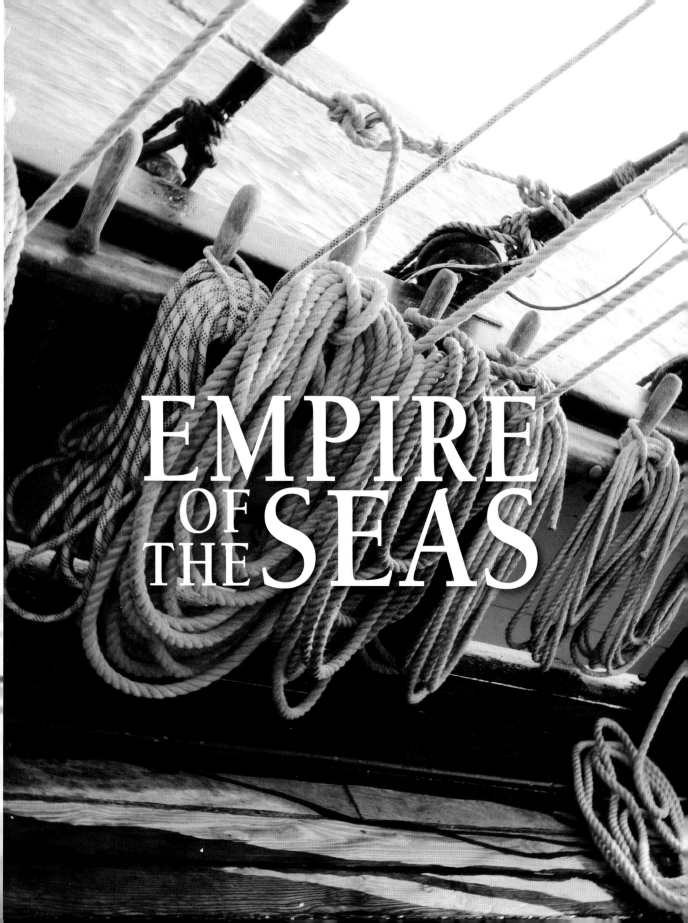

EMPIRE
OF
THE SEAS

BRIAN LAVERY

EMPIRE OF THE SEAS

HOW THE NAVY FORGED THE MODERN WORLD

To accompany the BBC series presented by Dan Snow

CONWAY

© Brian Lavery, 2009

First published in Great Britain in 2009 by
Conway
A Division of Anova Books Ltd
10 Southcombe Street
London W14 0RA
www.anovabooks.com
www.conwaypublishing.com

By arrangement with the BBC

The BBC logo is a trade mark of the British
Broadcasting Corporation and is used under
licence.

BBC logo © BBC 1996

British Library Cataloguing in Publication Data:
A catalogue record for this book is available from
the British Library.

ISBN 9781844861095

Printed and bound by Butler Tanner & Dennis,
Frome, Somerset

Half title page: The *Phoenix* (detail).
Frontispiece: *Matthew* replica.
These pages: Fort Charles, Port Royal, Jamaica.
Page 6: Fire buckets on HMS *Victory*.

CONTENTS

Acknowledgements   7
Introduction   8

Part 1   Heart of Oak

Chapter 1   Defeating the Armada   16
Chapter 2   The Drift to Civil War   32
Chapter 3   Dutch Wars   44
Chapter 4   Reform and Revolution   62

Part 2   The Golden Ocean

Chapter 5   European War   74
Chapter 6   Stability and Stagnation   92
Chapter 7   Broadening Horizons   102
Chapter 8   Defeat into Victory   112

Part 3   High Tide

Chapter 9   The Loss of America   128
Chapter 10   Crisis and Mutiny   146
Chapter 11   Nelson and the New Tactics   164
Chapter 12   The Triumphs and Limitations of Sea Power   182

Part 4   Sea Change

Chapter 13   The Effects of a Long Peace   196
Chapter 14   Steam, Steel and Shellfire   214
Chapter 15   Road to War   234
Chapter 16   The Test of War   250

Notes   265
Bibliography   267
Picture Credits   268
Index   269

ACKNOWLEDGEMENTS

Author's Acknowledgements

This work is influenced by the recent generation of historians, including the late David Lyon and David Syrett, who straddled the eighteenth and the twentieth centuries. Museum personnel include Roger Knight, Simon Stephens, Robert Blyth and Rina Prentice of the National Maritime Museum; Jenny Wraight and Iain Mackenzie, of the Naval Historical Library, and Campbell MacMurray and the late Colin White of the Royal Naval Museum. Academics include Robert Prescott of St Andrews, Eric Grove of Salford, Nicolas Rodger of All Souls Oxford, Andrew Lambert of King's College London, Pat Crimmin of Royal Holloway College and many more.

Much material is from manuscripts in the National Archives, British Library and National Maritime Museum; thanks are due to the staffs of these institutions. For printed books I have used the British Library and the National Maritime Museum, and especially the London Library with its huge range of books for borrowing. Finally my gratitude is due to John Lee at Conway for asking me to write the book and to Alison Moss for editing it so thoroughly and often against the clock as schedules changed rapidly.

Publishers' Acknowledgements

The Publishers would like to thank Brian Lavery for accepting the challenge of writing such an involved text amidst the constantly changing winds of a TV tie-in production. We are also most grateful to Georgie Hewitt, Gemma Wilson, Matthew Jones and Nicki Marshall for their supporting roles in the production of this book. At the BBC we would like to acknowledge the support and encouragement of Dan Snow and all of the 'Empire of the Seas' programme team, namely Catherine Abbot, Marie Baer, Daniel Bankover, Sophie Chapman, Steven Clarke, Dominic Crossley-Holland, Tom Horne, Alexander Leithead, Lisa MacHale, Tom McCarthy, Daniel Mirzoeff, Catherine Sacher, Rosie Schellenberg and Paul Tilzey. For most fair and safe passage we would like to graciously thank Singe Green, Ben Jones and Jo Lovell (*Matthew* replica), Lt Rolf Williams RN and Peter Goodwin (HMS *Victory*), Jane Skinner and Andrew Baines (*Warrior* Preservation Trust), Dave Redhead and his skilful square-rig sailors (brig *Phoenix*/Square Sail shipyard). Such a splendidly illustrated book would not have been possible without Doug McCarthy and his team at the Picture Library of the National Maritime Museum, Greenwich.

INTRODUCTION

THESE PAGES The sixth-rate replica ship *Grand Turk*, used for filming the *Hornblower* television series, passes between the frigate *Lancaster* and the naval supply ship *Wave Ruler* during preparations for the Trafalgar 200 naval review in 2005.

The Royal Navy of today has far more fire power and reach than it ever had in the days of Drake, Nelson, Fisher or Churchill. It now has eighty-eight ships compared with a thousand in the early 1800s and eight thousand during the Second World War, but its smallest patrol boat could take on and destroy the whole of Nelson's fleet, staying upwind and out of range and using its 30mm gun to destroy or incinerate the wooden hulls of its opponents, one by one. The fleet has radar to find the enemy in fog or darkness and sonar that might detect a submarine a hundred miles away. It has aircraft that can find and attack an enemy over hundreds of miles, on land, sea or air. Beyond that its Trident submarines have the awesome energy of thermonuclear weapons, with far more destructive power than all the forces of the Second World War and the ability to destroy most of the world's great cities. Even though it is a long way behind the United States Navy in size and power, and it no longer enjoys the enormous public respect that it once did, it is still a hugely powerful and infinitely flexible force, with ships, aircraft and marines able to operate on, under and above the sea as well as on land.

Yet it was the relatively feeble and vulnerable navies of Drake, Blake, Pepys, Anson and Nelson that became the expression of British power and the object of public affection, and changed Britain and the world in all sorts of subtle and unexpected ways. Nelson's ships were made of wood, highly inflammable and likely to break up very quickly on rocks. Their large crews were often the unwilling victims of the press gang rather than the highly motivated volunteers of today. They could see nothing beyond the horizon or below the surface of the water. Once out of sight of land they had no contact with higher authority ashore. The range of their guns was a few hundred yards at best, and the marines could never move too far inland for fear of losing contact with their parent ships. Their technology might seem primitive from the decks of a modern air-craft carrier, but their ships were the most advanced machines of their day, requiring vast amounts of skill to operate them effectively. For all their faults they were more successful than the ships and crews of other nations, and came to dominate the seas.

The Royal Navy was very successful in saving Britain from invasion, and in protecting its trade and empire. But its world and national role was far wider than that, it was an arbiter of world power and the essential creator and guardian of British democracy.

The paradox is how could an authoritarian organisation like the Royal Navy contribute so strongly to the growth of democracy? Partly it is because a navy needs a great deal of money, not just in the short term to run a military campaign but over many years to build the ships and maintain a core of professional officers and seamen. In the end this money can only be raised with the consent of the people – initially the wealthy classes who will pay the bulk of the taxes, but finally the whole of society as the tax burden is spread. Henry VIII used the windfall of looted monastic

wealth to finance his navy, but Charles I came to grief when he tried to raise money by extra-parliamentary means. After that kings took good care to get parliament on side when expanding the fleet, and Samuel Pepys told the House of Commons in 1677, 'all our safeties are concerned in it'. As the power of the monarch declined, parliament was still consulted when a great expansion was planned, for example with the Naval Defence Act of 1889. A generation later a proportion of power had devolved to the people themselves, when in 1909 they demonstrated in the streets demanding more Dreadnought battleships: 'We want eight and we won't wait!'

Unlike an army, a navy cannot be used to control the people in general, especially when many of its sailors are press-ganged and likely to desert if allowed on shore for any length of time. Parliament had a long memory of Cromwell's Major-Generals who repressed the country in the 1650s and it only passed the Mutiny Act, investing legal authority in army officers, on an annual basis. The naval equivalent, the Articles of War, was permanent. Britain relied more on her navy than any other major nation, and never needed a large army except during the two world wars of the twentieth century. As a result the army was never a major factor in politics in Britain the way it often was in Spain, France, and later Germany. The navy was fully occupied at home and abroad, in peace and in war, and as a group its officers rarely had time or inclination for political affairs.

On board ship, the navy was never quite as authoritarian as legend suggested. The tyranny of Captain Bligh of the *Bounty* was greatly exaggerated in fiction, and was rare in any case. Certainly captains had awesome powers of discipline in their hands, perhaps more than any other individuals in law-abiding society, but they could only operate a ship with a great deal of co-operation from the crew. Shipboard life naturally creates a bond between the members of the ship's company sharing a common purpose, though like any community it has its divisions and differences. It was only with bad man-

LEFT The state coach of Queen Elizabeth II passes out of Trafalgar Square into The Mall, during her coronation in 1953. Since it was built in 1843, the Square has always played an important part in national life, becoming a key location for public celebration and demonstration.

agement outside or inside the ship that these tended to spill over into mutiny. As Admiral Sir Max Horton wrote in 1944, 'no ordinary ship's company will resort to mass indiscipline unless they are labouring under grievances which a reasonable investigation will prove to be well founded.'[1]

BELOW Dan Snow views the Income Tax Act of 1789 at The National Archives during the filming of the BBC series.

The sea has long featured in English literature, though it was some time before it came to centre stage. The first great nautical character is Chaucer's Shipman, based on John Hawley of Dartmouth – 'Of nyce conscience he took no keep'. Shakespeare often used maritime themes, which was perhaps unavoidable in the great port of Elizabethan London. *The Merchant of Venice* is set in the maritime republic, and *The Tempest* is based on the wreck of the *Sea Venture* on the Bahamas in 1609. Daniel Defoe had a varied journalistic career but his lasting fame rests in a single book. *Robinson Crusoe* has some claim to be the first English novel, and it remained highly influential for more than a century. Many young men were inspired to begin a seafaring career after reading it. Tobias Smollett, a naval surgeon, set his novels *Roderick Random* and *Humphrey Clinker* in the dark days of the early Georgian navy, with a portrait of a dilettante captain. 'I found him lolling on a couch with a languishing air, his head supported by his valet-de-chambre who from time to time applied a smelling-bottle to his nose.' Captain Frederick Marryat had served as a midshipman under Thomas Cochrane, and became one of the most popular novelists of the second quarter of the nineteenth century. His naval books tend to centre on the life of a young midshipman and they appealed to the expanding boys' market. His period, the Napoleonic Wars, was taken up a century later by C S Forester with his Hornblower novels. They are

ABOVE Our seafaring past lives on in the Sea Cadets, a uniformed youth organisation modelled on the rank structure of the Royal Navy, which trains young people of 12–18 years in traditional square-rig seamanship. Dating back to 1854, it was originally set up for disadvantaged boys orphaned by the Crimean War by returning sailors.

mostly based on the life of a captain on an independent mission, which allowed him a great deal of initiative in the days before radio. Others followed, most famously Patrick O'Brian. Though he dismissed Forester's work as 'pap', he took up the idea of a frigate captain on detached service and produced a series of books which have gained world fame.

Nowhere in Britain is more than 80 miles from the sea, but spiritually it is often much closer than that. The sea has influenced our vocabulary in well-known phrases such as 'by and large', 'nip and tuck' and perhaps 'chip on his shoulder'. It has influenced our dress, from the sailor's suit worn by the Victorian boy to modern yachting gear and deck shoes. More profoundly, the British sense of liberty has always depended on the country being able to isolate itself

from totalitarian rulers in Europe, from Louis XIV to Hitler, and for this it depends on a strong navy. It was the possession of a large empire that allowed British trade to flourish in the early modern age, and today that is reflected in the diverse population of the country. The empire was not created by the navy, but often defended by it. Largely because of the empire, English is on the way to becoming a universal language. The navy itself has always reflected the class structure of the country, for better or for worse. In the age of sail it was one of the most meritocratic institutions in the world, and men of humble origins like James Cook could rise to command. In Victorian times it turned this on its head, and became one of the most class-bound organisations in the country. It had to spend most of the first half of the twentieth century correcting this. The Royal Navy has also provided the country with many of its heroes, including Drake and Nelson. In addition to them, hundreds of thousands of men served with the fleet over the centuries. This is the story of the effect they had on the world.

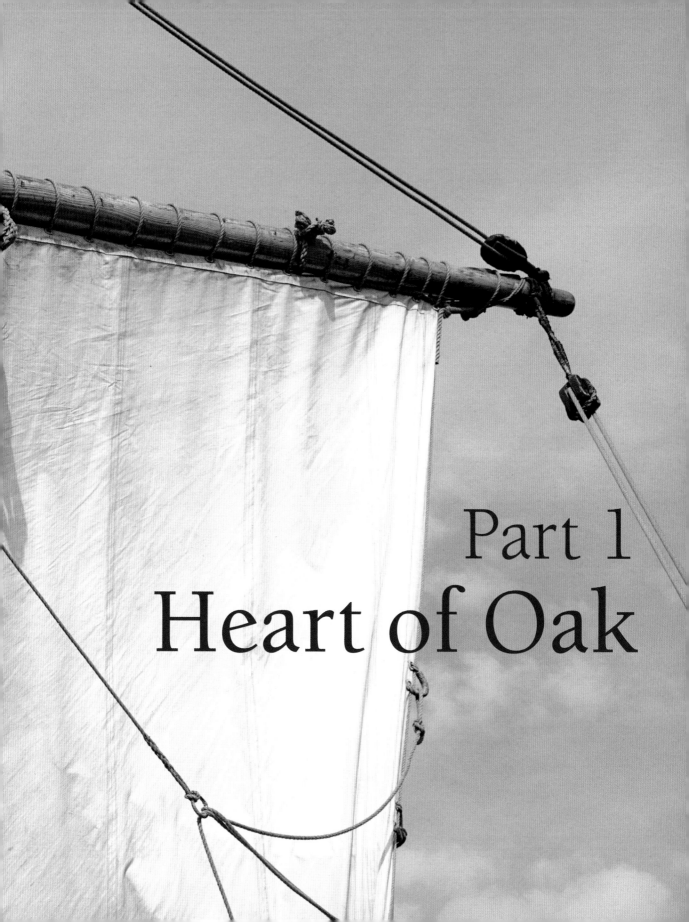

Part 1
Heart of Oak

ANNᵒ DÑI 1581,　　　　　　　　　　ÆTATIS SVÆ 44,

Sʳ Iohn Hawkins

Chapter 1

DEFEATING THE ARMADA

Most of the world's armed forces can trace their beginnings to definite dates. British regiments, including the Royal Marines, use the date of their first raising to establish their seniority, starting with the 'First of Foot', the Royal Scots, founded in 1627. The Royal Air Force has a definite birthday, 1 April 1918, and even a 'father' in Marshal of the Royal Air Force Lord Trenchard. In contrast the Royal Navy has no definite date for its foundation, for it had several births, declines and rebirths over the centuries. King Alfred constructed a fleet of long-ships to fight the Vikings around 900 AD. Three hundred years later King John, as unpopular abroad as he was at home, built a navy of more than 50 ships and developed a base at Portsmouth. Henry V supported his aggressive foreign policy by building a fleet that included the *Grace Dieu* of 1418, by far the largest ship of the day at 1400 tons. After the Protestant Reformation in 1630, Henry VIII needed a fleet to guard his shores against his Catholic neighbours. His cousin James IV of Scotland built the *Great Michael* using 'all the woods in Fife except Falkland Wood, [besides] all the timber that was gotten out of Norway'. Henry had to respond with his own great ship, the *Henri Grace à Dieu*, which was armed with a total of 122 guns (mostly very light) and manned by 349 soldiers, 301 mariners and 49 gunners. He had a total of 58 vessels in 1546, divided into ships, galleasses (rowing ships with a substantial gun armament), and much smaller pinnaces and rowing barges.

Henry's fleet did not collapse on his death, but survived in reduced form during the reigns of his Protestant son Edward and Catholic daughter Mary, so there was an unprecedented period of continuity. Mary had lost Calais to the French so when her sister Elizabeth came to the throne in 1558 she was the first ruler for whom the English Channel was the natural boundary of England. And she used the navy in a genuinely popular campaign against the foreign, Catholic invaders of the Spanish Armada.

Elizabeth did not start as a warlike queen; her policies at home and abroad aimed at reconciliation. But she was gradually sucked into informal war against the mighty power of Spain, largely by private captains such as the cousins John Hawkins and Francis Drake. They in turn had begun by trading in slaves with the Spanish Empire, but were stunned by a surprise attack on their ships at San Juan de Ulúa in Mexico in 1568. After that they waged their own wars against Spanish commerce and in 1577 Drake set off to raid their possessions in the Pacific, with the tacit support of the Queen.

Hawkins and Drake developed into an ideal partnership. Drake was the fighting captain, while

Hawkins went to London and took charge of Elizabeth's own navy. In 1577 he was appointed Treasurer of the Navy, probably at the instigation of Lord Burghley, the Secretary of State and main architect of Elizabeth's policies. Despite opposition from his rival Sir William Winter, who had dominated the Navy Board up until then, Hawkins began a programme of naval reform. He increased the seamen's pay to aid recruiting, and reduced the number of men on each ship to one per two tons, rather than one and a half. He was one of the first naval administrators to pay attention to hygiene, and he may have introduced the hammock on board English ships. Most importantly, he devised a new breed of race-built ship based on the

BELOW Henry VIII's great ship the *Henri Grace à Dieu*, or *Great Harry*, originally built in 1514 and armed with up to 80 guns, mostly small and of many different calibres. The illustration comes from the famous Anthony Roll, a pictorial survey of the King's navy compiled by Anthony Anthony, a clerk in the ordnance office.

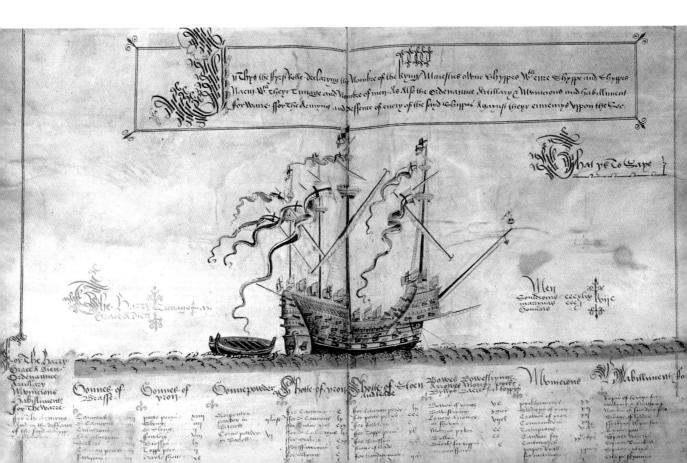

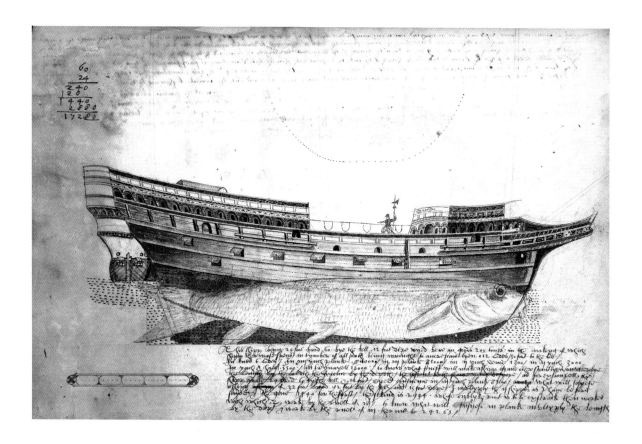

ABOVE A race-built English galleon from Matthew Baker's manuscript of 1586 entitled *Fragments of Ancient English Shipwrighting*, illustrating the theory that the underwater hull should follow that of a fish – although that didn't work very well in practice.

Spanish galleon and Henry VIII's galleasses, but longer in relation to the beam, with lower superstructure, heavier guns mounted lower down and an improved sail plan. Hawkins was able to draw on some very skilled ship designers, such as Mathew Baker, who translated the ideas into reality.

England drifted towards open war with Spain over several years. The religious issue was prominent, for England was a leading protestant power while Spain was by far the most important Catholic one, with her great empire including Portugal, much of Italy, the Philippines and large parts of the American continent. Even if they were not fanatically religious, Elizabeth's subjects craved stability. Over the last decades they had seen Henry VIII break with Rome, then his son Edward impose a more extreme form of Protestantism. When he died his sister Mary reverted to Catholicism and enforced it by burning heretics. Elizabeth offered a moderate and less repressive form of Protestantism. Greed was not compatible with religion, and Drake and Hawkins, Sir Walter Raleigh, Sir Martin Frobisher, Sir Humphrey Gilbert and many others made huge profits from their expeditions. There was further cause for dispute from 1568 when the Dutch revolted against the Spanish and were openly supported by the English. The last straw was the execution of Elizabeth's cousin Mary Queen of Scots in 1587. She was a staunch Catholic, unlike her son James, and she was also heir to the English throne. Her death meant that the Protestant James would inherit if Elizabeth died. In September 1587 King Phillip of Spain issued an order to assemble a fleet, the famous Armada, for the invasion of England. In response, Francis Drake ranged along the coast and had his most notable success at Cadiz, where he destroyed many vessels and took prizes. Drake later claimed that he had 'singed the King of Spain's beard', but perhaps that was not as boastful as it sounded. It was only 16 years since the Battle of Lepanto, after which the Sultan of Turkey had claimed, 'When the Venetians sunk my fleet they only singed my beard. It will grow again. But when I captured Cyprus I cut off one of their arms.'[2] Drake knew that he had humiliated and perhaps frightened the Spanish with his daring, but he had not stopped them in their tracks.

For the first time the 'great gun' was the main weapon of a ship of war. Guns of one kind or another had been carried on board ships since the fifteenth century. Long ships or galleys usually had a heavy gun firing forward. Round ships, usually sailing merchantmen converted for war, often had light guns firing over their sides onto the enemy decks and rigging. The gunport had been invented earlier in the sixteenth century, to allow a gun to be mounted low in the hull of a sailing ship. It could be closed and the gun brought in for reloading or in bad weather. Lighter guns were often built up from several sections held together with hoops, hence the 'barrel' of a gun. They were often breech loading but were only safe because of the poor quality of the powder of the day. Larger guns were cast in iron or bronze. The improvement in gunpowder made it possible for the English to think of using more powerful guns, with longer range. As King Phillip of Spain himself commented using information from his numerous spies,

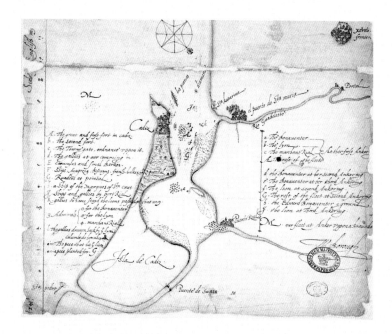

OPPOSITE Theodore de Bry's engraving shows Drake's forces landing in San Domingo in Hispaniola in January 1586 to capture one of the largest settlements in the West Indies.

LEFT Drake's attack on Cadiz in April 1587. Drake entered the port and destroyed 30 Spanish ships, delaying their invasion preparations by a year.

It must be borne in mind that the enemy's object will be to fight at long distance, a consequence of his advantage in artillery ... the aim of our men, on the contrary, must be to bring him to close quarters and grapple with him. ... the enemy employs his artillery ... to deliver his fire low, and sink his opponent's ships.[3]

The Spanish plan was profoundly misconceived. The Armada was to sail up the English Channel to the Netherlands, where it would embark the Duke of Parma's army off the coast; but any serious action by the English or the Dutch would make that impossible. It was said,

Unless God helps us by a miracle the English, who have faster and handier ships than ours, and many more long-range guns, and who know their advantage just as well as we do, will never close with us at all, but stand aloof and knock us to pieces with their culverins, without our being able to do any serious hurt. And so we are sailing against England in the confident hope of a miracle![4]

The Spanish differed from the English in organisation as well as gunnery.

Their soldiers watch and ward, and their officers, in every ship round, as if they were on shore; this is the only task they undergo, except cleaning their arms, wherein they are not over-curious. The gunners are exempted from all labour and care, except about the artillery. ... the mariners are but slaves to the rest, to moil and to toil day and night ... and not suffered to sleep or harbour themselves under the decks. For in fair or foul weather, in storms, sun, or rain, they must pass void of covert or succour.[5]

This was very different from Drake's ideal that the crew should 'all be of a company' and that gentlemen must 'haul and draw with the mariner'.

The Crown had always claimed the right to 'impress' or press seamen into the navy. It was founded on the ancient right of Saxon kings to call any of their subjects to serve in the Fyrd or army, but it was a burden that fell increasingly on seamen over the years as the navy became more important in national defence. In the Middle Ages, when warships were just

Sir Francis Drake (1540? –1596)

Drake was born near Tavistock in Devon, the son of a shearman of woollen cloth and part-time preacher, who had to flee to Kent for a time, where Francis learned sailing on the Medway. Back in Devon he teamed up with this older cousin John Hawkins, who influenced him a great deal. Soon they were involved in trading African slaves with the Spanish colonies in the New World. They made several highly profitable voyages in this way, but it became more problematic as the Spanish Government imposed restrictions. In 1567 they experienced some difficulty in selling the slaves and were on the way home when they stopped to repair their ships at San Juan de Ulúa on the coast of modern Mexico. A Spanish treasure fleet arrived in the port, and after a few days the Spanish mounted a surprise attack on Drake and Hawkins. Both escaped after heavy losses but they had a horrific voyage home in damaged and overcrowded ships. Drake was left with a lasting hatred of the Spanish. Often this seemed to rooted in religion, but there is no sign that he was especially pious in private; the propagandists who later took up his cause found it useful to cast him as the Protestant hero.

Drake got married after his return but did not stay at home for long. After several raids on Spanish possessions and ships, he mounted his most ambitious plan in 1577, perhaps with the support of Sir Francis Walsingham the Secretary of State, and with investment by the Queen herself. He was to sail south, round Cape Horn and raid the rich but poorly guarded Spanish possessions in the Pacific. On the way he beheaded his second-in-command, Thomas Doughty, for alleged mutiny. Losing most of his ships, he was left with the *Pelican*, which he re-named *Golden Hind*, when he passed through the Strait of Magellan and entered the Pacific. He raided various places and attacked a rich galleon, *Nuestra Señora de la Concepción* (not *Cacafuego* as some would have it) even though his crew was reduced to 30 fit men. He landed in California, possibly in what became San Francisco, and returned home across the ocean, perhaps looking for the Manila treasure galleon.

Eventually he arrived home in September 1580, after nearly three years away, becoming the first Englishman to circumnavigate the world. At first the Queen kept her distance for diplomatic reasons, but she, like all the investors, was delighted with the huge wealth that the voyage had brought to them. Drake rose above his humble background by being knighted, becoming a Member of Parliament and buying a former abbey as his home.

He was soon at sea again pursuing various projects against the Spanish, with mixed success. A raid on the West Indies in 1585–6 involved attacks on Hispaniola, Cartagena and Florida, and he brought home settlers from the failing colony of Roanoke in Virginia. By 1587 the threat of war was building (partly due to Drake's activities) and he raided the coasts of Spain and Portugal, which was then under Spanish control. He attacked Cadiz harbour and found easy prey among dangerous waters, destroying around 25 Spanish ships and taking about 172,000 ducats. Off the coast of Portugal he captured the richly laden galleon *San Felipe*, and he gathered a great deal of information about Spanish preparations. On his return he was made second-in-command of the English fleet under Lord Howard of Effingham, for despite his knighthood he was too low-born to take supreme command in those days.

Drake commanded one of the squadrons against the Armada during the latter part of its voyage up the channel, along with Howard, Hawkins and Martin Frobisher. He neglected his fleet duties to capture the *Rosario* and take her into Torbay. He fought well for an hour or so in the battle off Gravelines, but withdrew apparently to protect his valuable captives.

After the Armada campaign Drake led an expedition to Portugal, but he failed to inspire the people to rise against Spanish rule, to take Lisbon or to capture some Spanish galleons off the Azores, possibly due to lack of tactical planning. He spent some time at home until 1595 when he and Hawkins set out a fleet to raid the West Indies and perhaps capture Panama. Hawkins died in the November, and Drake raided Panama before he too died in January 1596. He was buried in at sea in a lead coffin. Legend has it that his drum (still preserved in his home at Buckland Abbey) will beat again if England is in danger.

Drake is full of contradictions as a national hero. He was a model of maritime daring and initiative but his leadership practices and constant disputes with his subordinates left much to be desired, and he never completely gave up piratical practices to focus on

naval tactics. With Hawkins he was instrumental in bringing the English into the slave trade from Africa. Though he came from a humble background himself (or perhaps because of it) he tended to show off his wealth in clothes and entertainment. He often lavished gifts on the wealthier and more aristocratic members of his circle, rather than his own crews. He was a Protestant hero but his own religion was not consistent or enthusiastic.

OPPOSITE Sir Francis Drake in 1591. It shows his coat of arms as a knight and a globe symbolising his circumnavigation.

ABOVE AND BELOW Views of a replica of Drake's ship the *Golden Hind*, which can be seen in St Mary Overie Dock on the south bank of the Thames in London.

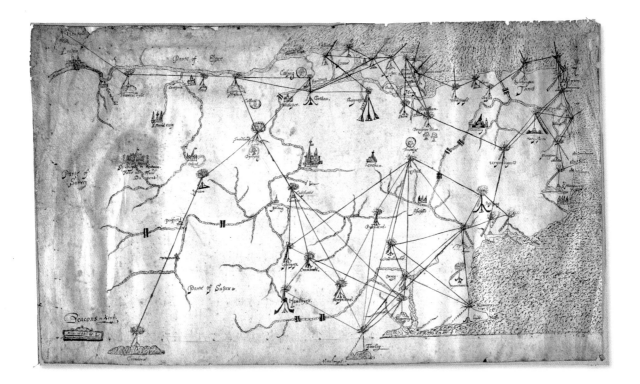

armed merchantmen, the sailors often came with the ship. Later it became common to issue a seaman with a small sum of money, an 'imprest' to retain his services. Thus the process of 'pressing' men into the navy became confused with the verb 'to press' meaning to force. In Henry VIII's time the process was quite mild, the sailors were well paid and wars tended to be short. This began to change in Elizabeth's reign.

After many delays the Armada was sighted from Plymouth on 29 July 1588. According to a later tale Drake was playing bowls at the time and decided to finish his game. This is not implausible, as he would have had to wait for the tide, and in any case his plan was to get behind the Armada and have the wind behind him, the 'weather gage', which would allow him to attack at will. The Spanish had 130 ships carrying nearly 30,000 men arranged in what the English took to be a crescent but was actually a more complex formation. One myth at least can be discounted. The Spanish ships were not huge in comparison with the English. If they did have a few big ships, they were mostly troop transports. If there was any difference in

the smaller ships, it was because of Hawkins' 'race-built' galleons and the discrepancy was not nearly as great as Victorian legend liked to believe.

The English fleet had around 110 ships, but most of these were requisitioned merchantmen of very little power. Drake was only the second-in-command, as an aristocratic leader was considered necessary and Lord Howard of Effingham, the Lord High Admiral, took charge in person. There were many engagements as the English squadrons attempted to use their guns at long range, but they did little damage. There was an engagement off the Isle of Portland, in which the English tactics of 'feather plucking' were shown to be futile. After that the fleet was divided into four squadrons to mount stronger attacks. Two Spanish ships were captured, but only after they had collided with one another. A week after entering the Channel the Spanish anchored off Gravelines and the English launched fireships against them. They were not always an ideal weapon but the Spanish were at anchor and immobile, and their crews greatly feared the terrifying explosion vessels that had been used by the Dutch at

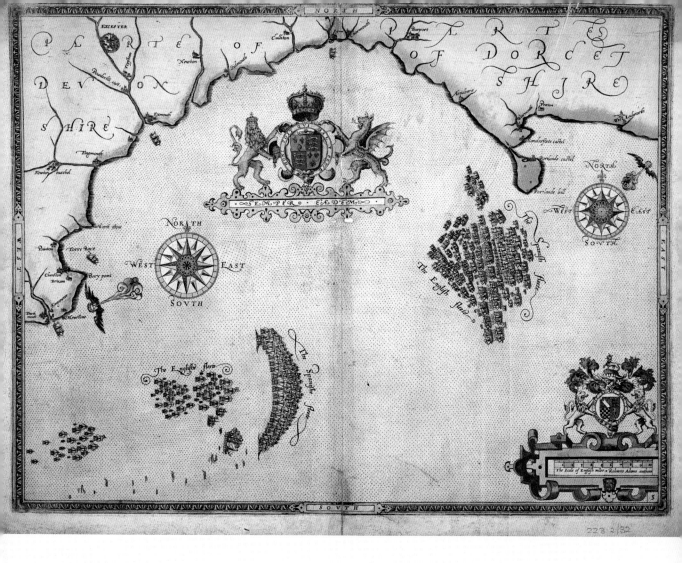

ABOVE Taken from a series of charts based on Lord Howard's account of the attempted invasion by the Spanish Armada, this shows two stages in the campaign. On the left, the English chase the Armada and capture the *San Salvador*. To the right, a major but inconclusive battle develops off Portland Bill.

OPPOSITE The beacon system in Kent, set up in 1585, drawn by William Lambarde. Each was placed on a hilltop and could be lit to give warning of the Armada.

Antwerp three years earlier. The Armada's formation was broken at last, and the English were able to get amongst them, using short-range gunnery this time. The English reloading technique was far better, for the Spanish thought of a broadside as a one-off affair, and could only reload, perhaps from outboard, away from the scene of battle. The Spanish gave up any hope of linking up with Parma's army and the ships headed

home round the north of Scotland where many of them would be wrecked in storms. A week after the Battle of Gravelines Queen Elizabeth added to her legendary fame by addressing her soldiers at Tilbury on the Thames. 'I know that I have the body of a weak and feeble woman, but I have the heart and stomach of a king, and a king of England too; and think foul scorn that Parma or Spain, or any Prince of Europe, should dare to invade the border of my realm.'

It was a great naval victory, which was celebrated in St Paul's Cathedral in November, with church bells ringing throughout the country; and it would remain one of the great events of English history. The English Queen ruled a little more than half an offshore island, with potential enemies to the north and fractious subjects within. To the Spaniards it was a land of heretics and pirates, but it had taken on the greatest empire in the world and defeated it. The victory confirmed English independence and the survival of the Protestant religion in its moderate Elizabethan form, which was to become an essential factor in English and later British identity.

The destruction of the Spanish fleet in 1588 was as much due to bad weather as English action but that did not trouble the Protestants. It only meant that God was on their side, and medals bore the inscription, 'God's wind blew, and they were scattered'. But Drake knew that his long-range tactics had not been as successful as he had hoped and was almost apologetic. 'If I have not performed as much as was looked

OPPOSITE Maritime map of the British Isles, showing the final stages of the campaign and the track of the retreating Spanish Armada around the north of Scotland and west of Ireland, blown by the 'Protestant Wind'. Many of the ships were wrecked in storms.

BELOW The attack of the English fireships off Calais on 7 August 1588, with the larger Spanish ships to the left, the English fleet coming in from the right, and the fireships in the centre.

for, yet I persuade myself his good lordship will confess I have been dutiful.'[6] The great gun as the decisive weapon at sea was nevertheless an English invention, and in later years the fortunes of Britain would depend on it. When the big, heavily gunned ship was threatened by the mine, the torpedo, the submarine and the aeroplane, British sea power would begin to decline – but that would not be for another three centuries.

The victory did not end the war. By the end of 1588 the defects of the naval manning system were beginning to become plain. There had been some warnings in 1587, when the men of the *Golden Lion* had mutinied and complained, 'We were pressed by Her Majesty's press to have her allowance and not to be thus dealt withal; you make no men of us, but beasts.'[7] Even as he was praising the quality of his men in 1588, Lord Howard added, 'it were pity they should lack meat, when they are so desirous to spend [expend] their lives in Her Majesty's service.'[8] By August supplies were falling drastically short. According to Howard,

Sickness and mortality begins wonderfully to grow amongst us; and it is a most pitiful sight to see, here at Margate, how the men, having no place to receive them here, die in the streets ... It is like enough the like infection will grow throughout the most part of our fleet; for they have been so long at sea and have so little shift of apparel, and so few places to provide them of such wants, and no money wherewith to buy it, for some have been – yea the most part – these eight months at sea ... Good my lord, let mariners be prest and sent down as soon as may be; and money to discharge those that be sick here ...[9]

As well as disease, discontent began to spread among the seamen as their pay was delayed. The Queen's treasury had been put under considerable strain. After the windfall from the monasteries had

been exhausted, the Tudor state did not have the financial resources to prosecute a hard and long war without subjecting its seamen to great hardship.

It was certainly a long war, which went on for the rest of Elizabeth's reign, more than 15 years. Year by year fleets were sent out, and year by year the quality and morale of the crews became worse. The first effect was to teach the most qualified seamen to avoid the Royal service – a lesson they were never to forget over the centuries. According to Sir Walter Raleigh, writing early in the next century, 'many times they go with great grudging to serve in His Majesty's ships, as if they were to be slaves in the galleys, for so much do they stand in fear of penury and hunger, the case being clean contrary in all merchants ships'.[10] Furthermore, the actual system of impressment began to break down, with allegations of corruption. According to Raleigh, 'As concerning the musters and presses for sufficient mariners to serve in his majesty's ships, either the care

ABOVE The 'Armada' portrait of Queen Elizabeth, showing an English attack in the Channel on the left, and Spanish shipwrecks on the right. The victory was seen as a combination of English endeavour and God's will.

therein is very little, or the bribery is very great; so that of all other shipping his majesty's are ever the worst manned ... it is grown a proverb among the sailors, that the muster masters do carry the best and ablest men in their pockets.'[11]

Even the seamen who had been recruited were prone to desertion. In 1602 William Monson complained, 'it is an incredible thing to inform your honours of the number of sailors that are run away since our coming home'.[12] He suggested some measures against this, and wrote to 'the chief officers of the towns where any presses have been that if they find any prest men returned from Her Majesty's ships without a discharge under my hand, that they shall apprehend him and cause him to be conveyed to the gaol, to be tried according to the statute'. The Royal orders became more strict, and applied to a wider range of men; in 1599 mariners from ages 16 to 60, instead of 18 to 50, were called, and were 'charged upon pain of death to make their present repair unto Chatham'. Each vice admiral was 'to appoint some discreet and trusty persons to come in their company, to hasten them in coming hither, and see that none of them do run away.'[13]

If people were beginning to lose heart, then the increasing numbers who could read were able to turn to books for inspiration. Richard Hakluyt first published his *Principal Navigations, Voyages, Traffiques and Discoveries of the English Nation* in 1589, followed by a much expanded three-volume edition in 1598–1600. Supported by the Secretary of State, Sir Francis Walsingham, he edited numerous stories of exploration and

ABOVE The frontispiece of *The Mariner's Mirror*, a collection of charts of 1588, showing much detail of navigational instruments, such as the astrolabe and the lead line, and of the Tudor seaman's dress.

bravery by land and sea, confining himself to English voyages and ignoring the contribution of France and Spain to the knowledge of the world. The defeat of the Spanish Armada, though not strictly a voyage of exploration within his terms of reference, was included in the second edition. It soon became the first English publishing phenomenon, a patriotic inspiration for years to come, when English naval power seemed far less heroic and triumphant.

Sailing the *Matthew* Replica, Fifteenth-Century Caravel

In Episode 1 Dan Snow sailed on the *Matthew* replica, to get a sense of what life would have been like on a Tudor ship. 'Sailing one of these things, you're just so struck by the ingenuity ... the combination of wood, rope and a bit of metal, and you can sail to the other side of the world.'

John Cabot set sail from Bristol on the original *Matthew* in 1497 with a crew of 18 men. Their destination was the New World. Letters Patent, granted by Henry VIII, stated that he was to 'seeke out, discover and finde whatsoever iles, countreyes, regions or provinces ...'. Cabot landed in Newfoundland and took possession of it in the name of the King.

The *Matthew* replica is based on the caravel, a typical trading vessel of the period, which would seem to be the right generic type for an explorer with its general characteristics of speed and manoeuvrability. She is three masted with a square rig on the fore and main masts and lateen-rigged mizzen.

The photographs show, anticlockwise from top left, Dan assisting the crew in hoisting the main sail.

BELOW The fleet bringing Prince Charles back from an unsuccessful mission to Spain in 1623, with the *Prince Royal* in the lead and several of the new 'great ships' astern.

Chapter 2
THE DRIFT TO
CIVIL WAR

K ing James VI of Scotland inherited the English throne – as James I – on the death of Queen Elizabeth in 1603. Though Scotland remained a separate state, with its own parliament and navy, it was now accurate to talk of an island kingdom. There would be plenty of Scottish revolts over the next century and a half, but the island was more united than ever before, and this increased the importance of the English navy as the main defence. The new king, however, was a peace-loving man, and soon ended the war with Spain. He carefully avoided involvement in foreign wars for many years, and allowed the navy to fall into decline for the first 15 years of his reign, though in 1610 he did build one very big ship, the *Prince Royal*, the largest of her time and in some senses the first three-decker. In 1618 a commission reported on the state of the navy and 'discovered many imperfections and decays in the former 23 ships of war, two hoys and lighter'. It recommended a restored fleet of four 'ships royal' including the *Prince Royal*, 14 'great ships' which would be the backbone of the fleet, six middling ships, two small and four tiny pinnaces.[14] This programme was largely adhered to over the years.

Though it was not a glorious time for the navy, the early 1600s saw the real birth of the overseas empire. This was largely done through private initiative, and inspired by many different motives. The East India Company made its first voyage in 1601, mainly to break into the rich Dutch spice trade in Indonesia, rather than the sub-continent that would eventually become its home. In 1607 a group of gentlemen adventurers, ultimately led by Captain John Smith, set up a colony in Jamestown, Virginia, which would come close to starvation several times before it began to flourish. Further up the eastern seaboard of America, a group of

puritans later known as the Pilgrim Fathers took the flight from religious persecution to great lengths and set up the first of the New England colonies. The strategically important island of Barbados was settled in 1624 along with St Kitts, the first of many British colonies in the West Indies. The public became aware of the growing empire when Shakespeare's *The Tempest* was first performed in 1610. In 1616 Princess Pocahontas, daughter of a powerful native American chief, visited London with her husband John Rolfe, to be presented to the King and attend various functions. She died at Gravesend on the Thames.

King James planned to marry his son Charles to the Spanish King's daughter, and the young prince travelled to Spain with James's favourite, the Duke of Buckingham. When they were rebuffed, the mood turned hostile and the king began to yield to popular pressure for war with Spain. Preparations continued after James died in March 1625 and his son became King Charles I. That autumn an expedition left for Spain, despite the lateness of the season and the slender financial resources of the crown.

ABOVE The English fleet at the Ile de Rhé in 1627, showing the high, narrow sterns that were characteristic of the ships of that time, with longboats towed astern.

OPPOSITE ABOVE 'A fight in boats with Barbary pirates', drawn by Willem Van de Velde the Younger in the 1680s, and showing how desperate these fights could become.

OPPOSITE BELOW A seventeenth-century German engraving of the slave market in Algiers. The image of European men and women suffering extreme humiliation and privation helped to whip up concern about pirates on the English coast.

It was disease, incompetence and bad provisions that ruined the expedition, rather than enemy action. The military side was badly handled, while sickness almost destroyed the crews of some ships. On the *Anne Royal* 130 died and 160 were sick out of a total crew of 800. One of the commanders wrote of 'the greatest part of the seamen being sick or dead, so that few of them have sufficient men to bring their ships about', and said there was 'a miserable infection among them, and they die very fast'.[15] The fleet returned, and a series of mutinies began. It was reported that,

Mannier Hoe de Gevange Kristen Slaven uit Algiers verkoft worden.

L. Luyken, inven. et f.

The mariners prest for Cadiz, and others retained in the king's ships, for that they never received their pay, came in troops to London at divers several times, and threatened the Duke of Buckingham, and once they made an attempt against his gate to pull it down, but at last they were pacified, and had their pay out of the loan of subsidy money, and discharged.

But this was early in 1627, more than a year after the expedition.[16] The political credibility of the government had sunk, and the seaman's reluctance to serve the King was greater than ever before.

There was another expedition in 1627, to support the Protestants of La Rochelle, who were in revolt against the French King. The ramshackle machinery was put in motion again, with equally depressing results. A total of 3,800 seamen were raised; many died, all were paid late or not at all, and hundreds faced starvation. After the return of the expedition one captain wrote of the 'miserable condition of the men, who have neither shoes, stockings nor rags to cover their nakedness ... all the seas are so infectious that I fear if we hold the sea one month we shall not bring men enough home to moor their ships.'[17]

In 1628 there was an attempt to set out another expedition, and it was said, 'the mariners being at Plymouth and almost ready to set to sea, being unpaid nine months, and seeing their best victuals sold away, they began to mutiny, in which mutiny there were three slain, and after the tumult was somewhat appeased many of them ran away.'[18] A disgruntled survivor of the expedition assassinated the Duke of Buckingham; with his death the aggressive policy ended.

The problem of piracy was already growing before the disastrous Spanish expeditions. There were Biscayers from northern Spain and Dunkirkers from just across the Channel, but at least they were Christians who only sought to plunder ships. Much more terrifying were the Barbary corsairs, mostly from the North African ports of Salé and Algiers. They were Muslims who had no moral constraints on inflicting cruelties on Christians, and they were frighteningly efficient. It was bad enough when they preyed on shipping in their local waters, and enslaved the crews in very harsh conditions. It got worse when they appeared off the English coast – 30 of their ships were seen off St Ives in 1625, while Plymouth, Poole and many other places feared for their safety. Naval patrols were unsuccessful, and a system of ransom broke down. Money was collected in churches for the relief of individuals, but put into a central fund run by the Crown, where it was used to release the favourites. Things became even worse in June 1631 when Algerian corsairs raided the Irish port of Baltimore, taking about 120 women and children into captivity. Tales were told of the horrors endured by captives ; in February 1632 the King received a petition 'of many poore women declaring yt mor than 500 of theyr husbands, sons and friends were lately taken and kept in bondage by the Turks and Moors of Algier and Tunis.'[19]

BELOW A drawing by Van de Velde the Younger showing sailors sitting astride guns to clean and load them. Clearly this picture was done in harbour but it is possible that guns were loaded from outboard in early seventeenth-century battles.

The most vociferous of the government's critics was Sir John Eliot, Member of Parliament and Vice-Admiral of Drake's old county of Devon. He was equally incensed by the debacle of the Cadiz expedition and the failure to deal with piracy. A conservative at heart, he did not attack the King in person but developed the doctrine of ministerial responsibility for their actions. He also used the tactic of refusing financial supply in an attempt to control the actions of the executive. In the 1629 parliament there was turmoil in the House when two of Eliot's associates held the Speaker down while Eliot read a paper calling for the people to refuse to pay illegitimate taxes.

King Charles decided to rule without parliament after that. In the absence of any large sums of money, he revived his feudal prerogatives in order to prepare a fleet. In 1634 he issued 'ship writs', which demanded that each of the larger ports should fit out and man a quantity of ships of specific sizes. London was to supply one of 900 tons, 'with 350 men at the least, as well expert masters as very able and skilful mariners', a ship of 800 tons and 260 men, four more of 500 tons and 200 men, and another of 300 tons with 150 men.[20] There was no serious doubt of the King's right to demand this; Queen Elizabeth had done the same as recently as 1591. Despite some grumbling the fleet was able to put to sea in 1636.

However, there were many difficulties with such an approach. The gap between men of war and merchantmen was continually widening, and Charles was already building a great ship, the *Sovereign of the Seas*, with more than 100 guns. Warships were growing in size faster than merchantmen, and it was not easy to find suitable ships among the resources of the port towns – only London actually supplied ships and men in 1635, the other places agreeing to a money payment instead.

In 1636 Charles extended the policy of issuing 'ship writs' to the inland counties and towns. Recognising that many towns were too small to provide a ship on their own, and that inland places could not easily find ships in any case, he allowed money payment in place of the actual provision of a ship. Buckinghamshire, for example, was to supply a ship of 450 tons and 180 men, or to raise the sum of £4,500. Smaller towns were not given the option of

ABOVE Peter Pett, the builder of the *Sovereign of the Seas*, and the highly decorated stern of his ship, with extensive carvings and gilding all intended to boost the royal image.

providing a ship: Derby was to pay £175, Hereford £220, Chesterfield £50, and Huntingdon £40.[21] The new policy was not supported by any constitutional precedent. John Hampden, a gentleman of Buckinghamshire, refused to pay the levy of Ship Money, and fought the issue through the courts. Eventually he lost his case by the narrowest of margins, but the issue became a cause célèbre, and stimulated opposition to the King as nothing had done for centuries.

Guns of the late sixteenth century were slow to load, and it was common for a ship to fire all of them, bringing them to bear by turning the ship. Captain John Smith describes an attack.

Edge in with him againe, begin with your bow pieces, proceed with your broad side, & let her fall off with the wind, to give her also your full chase pieces, your weather broad side, and bring her round that the sterne may also discharge, and your tackes close aboard againe![22]

After that, the ship would withdraw to load and come back for another attack, and finally board the enemy once his strength had been depleted.

By the early seventeenth century, the number of men allocated to the gun crews in action had increased, so reloading was faster. A simple piece of rope, the train tackle, was used to restrain the gun from rolling out again when it was reloading. The increasing size of ships made it more difficult to turn rapidly in action, so they would now have to fight it out broadside to broadside.

It was an age of insecure monarchy throughout Europe, and Charles, like other kings, reacted by building a great ship to demonstrate his power. In 1634 the King visited the dockyard at Woolwich where his favourite shipwright, Phineas Pett, was building a 'great ship' called the *Leopard*. '... and being in the ship's hold his Highness, calling me aside, privately acquainted me with his princely resolution for the building of a new great ship.'[23] This was to be far

bigger than the others, the *Sovereign of the Seas*, the first ship with 100 guns. It was an advanced design in many ways, and to cram in that many guns it was necessary to put the great majority of them on the broadside rather than firing fore and aft. This increased the move towards broadside action rather than old-fashioned turning and boarding. But what attracted most attention from the public was the elaborate decoration of the ship.

Not all the king's subjects could see the ship itself, but Thomas Lely did a painting of her stern with the builder, Phineas Pett's son Peter, alongside. For more general viewing John Payne, 'dwelling by the postern gate neere unto Tower Hill' produced a very detailed engraving with the help of Pett. And Thomas Heywood published a 'True Description of His Majesty's Royall Ship' in more than a thousand lines, including detailed description of the decorations from stem to stern. 'Upon the Beak-head sitteth King Edgar on horse-backe, trampling upon seven Kings ... I desire you to take notice, that upon the stemme-head there is a Cupid, or a child resembling him, bestriding and bridling a Lyon, which importeth, that sufferance may curb insolence, and Innocence restraineth violence; which alludeth to the great mercy of the King.' On the stern was the figure of Victory; '... on one Arme she weareth a Crowne, on the other a Laurell, which imply Riches and Honour.'[24]

But the King's political message was largely lost on his subjects, who were becoming increasingly rebellious. He tried to impose bishops on the Presbyterian Scots, but they rebelled. Charles launched an invasion up the east coast towards the Firth of Forth, with strong support from the seas, but the Scottish army was far superior to his half-trained levies and he was outmanoeuvred. In the meantime the Dutch and Spanish violated territorial waters by fighting a sea battle in the Downs off the coast of Kent. The king was forced to call parliament to mount a second campaign against the Scots in 1640, which was no more successful.

By spring 1641 parliament was the effective government of the country, and it wanted to cut the King

Gunnery (1620–1850)

ABOVE A gun crew in action around 1800. The position on the quarterdeck is very exposed, and one man has already fallen, while another is wounded.

A gun is simply a tube closed at one end. When an explosion occurs inside it, the force operates on one direction pushing a projectile out of its muzzle. Guns can be either muzzle or breech loading. In the former case the powder and shot is rammed in at the open end. Breech-loading guns need a means of opening up the closed end of the gun, and in Tudor times this was done by having a separate chamber, which was removed to be filled with powder then wedged into place. Such a gun had to be quite small so it was more useful against personnel than ships. Without precision engineering this mechanism could be dangerous to one's own side, and breech-loading guns tended to fall into disuse as powder improved.

Gunpowder is made from a combination of saltpetre, sulphur and charcoal. The early type, serpentine powder, was a simple mixture whose ingredients tended to separate in vibration and absorb damp, and air did not circulate freely within it. Corned powder was common by the early seventeenth century, made in grains of a suitable size, but guns had to be made stronger to cope with it. By 1800 it was common to prepare the charcoal in 'cylinders' or ovens, which made it burn more evenly and improved its efficiency.

Early guns, especially the breech-loading type, were often built up in sections and held together by hoops, hence the term barrel which is still used today. For larger guns it was more efficient to cast them in a mould, first in brass (actually an alloy that was more like bronze) and later in iron, which was far cheaper. Cast guns still retained the features of ancient guns, including reinforced rings and ogees which were reminiscent of barrel construction. Each had a ball or cascabel moulded at the breech end, to help in fitting a restraining rope. The English fleet began to use mostly iron guns soon after 1600, and bronze was reserved for special ships. In the following decades Thomas Blomefield, the Inspector of Artillery for the Ordnance Board, used the new technologies of the expanding iron industry to improve casting. He also simplified the design for greater efficiency, and added a ring above the cascabel to help retain the breech rope. These were the guns that fought the Napoleonic Wars and allowed Nelson to achieve his victories.

The design of the gun carriage was essential to the English victory against the Armada, for the Spanish tended to use land carriages barely adapted for the sea. The English adopted the truck carriage, named after its small wooden wheels, which took up minimum space on board ship. After about 1620 the gun was allowed to recoil, restrained by a strong breeching rope, to set it up in a position where it could be reloaded. The powder and shot were rammed in and held in the barrel with a wad of old rope while a rope to the rear of the gun, the train tackle, prevented it from running out again. When ready the gun was hauled out through the port by teams of men hauling on blocks and tackles on either side. Until about 1780 it was detonated by applying a lighted match to the touch hole. After about 1780 a flintlock, as used on muskets, allowed almost instantaneous fire, which gave the British a tactical advantage in aiming.

down to size. It abolished many of the old feudal pre-rogatives, partly out of a concern for civil liberties, but largely in an attempt to make him impotent. Ship Money was declared illegal, and any funds remaining from it were to be repaid. There is no doubt that the seamen of the king's navy supported parliament in 1642, as the country came close to civil war. In January, 2,000 of the men from Chatham marched to London, believing 'That great vessel, the parliament house, which is so richly fraught with no less value than the price of a Kingdom, is fearfully shaken, and in great danger.'[25] Later in the year parliament put the Earl of Warwick in charge of the fleet, and when he arrived at Chatham all the ships except five supported him. According to one leading Royalist, 'the devotion generally of the seamen' was 'so tainted and cor-rupted to the king's service, that, instead of carrying away the ships, the captains themselves were seized, taken and carried by their own men to the Earl; who committed them to custody, and sent them up prison-ers to the Parliament.' According to the same authority, this left the king 'without one ship of his own in his three kingdoms'. It was 'of unspeakable ill consequence to the king's affairs, and made his condi-tion much the less considered by his allies and neighbour princes; who saw the sovereignty of the sea now in other hands.'[26]

The civil war that followed was mainly fought on land, but parliament still needed a navy to deter any foreign intervention, to stop Royalist gun-runners, to intervene in sieges of coastal towns such as Lyme and Plymouth, and to protect their commerce and sup-plies against privateers and pirates. Parliament invariably used both the carrot and the stick to recruit its seamen. Early in 1643 wages were raised from 15 shillings to 19 shillings per month, but at the same time an act of 1642 allowing pressing was renewed for another year, and it was to continue being renewed until 1660. By a proclamation of April 1643, ale-house keepers and innkeepers were forbidden 'to harbour or entertain any mariners, seamen, watermen and co., prest into any of His Majesty's or merchant ships

employed in the service, after the beat of the drum and proclamation made to give them notice to repair on board the several ships to which they belong.'[27] This suggests a relatively mild form of impressment, remi-niscent of the time of Henry VIII. Presumably seamen were given the prest money in advance, to be called by the beat of a drum and the reading of a proclamation around the town.

During the civil war the fleet comprised about 6,000 men for the summer campaigns, and about 2,000 in winter. A few new ships were built, but these were mostly small, fast frigates, so the navy needed about the same number of seamen as in the days of the ship-money fleets. Parliament was generally better organised, and had far better financial resources than the king, so it could pay its seamen more, and feed them better. The first civil war ended in 1646, and Charles, who had surrendered to the Scots, was handed over to parliament and impris-oned by them. Up until this time parliament had maintained the fiction that it was really fighting to save the King from his pernicious advisors, but this became increasingly difficult, and the winning side became divided over what to do with him, and about the extent of the social revolution that would follow victory. This gave the Royalists an opportunity to launch a revolt in 1648. A considerable part of the fleet went over, not because they were underpaid and underfed as in 1642, but because they objected to parliament's attempt to rule without any allegiance to the King. Officers largely led this revolt, though they had some support from the seamen. Prince Rupert, the King's dashing young nephew, took command, and led his fleet away to Holland. The Par-liamentarian army, now a force of great political as well as military power, crushed the main revolt. Many of the seamen with the revolted ships returned to the parliament's service when it was clear the rising had failed. Early the following year Charles was executed.

Though it was victorious, parliament was far from secure. The Scottish Parliament was not entirely in support of the English one, while the Royalists held many outposts such as the Scilly Isles. Ireland was in revolt against English rule, and foreign opinion was outraged by the execution of the King. The new regime was never to be entirely at peace during its lifetime. Ships rather than armies were needed now, as most of the state's enemies were overseas. Very soon after the execution of the King, parliament began to build several new ships, the beginning of a programme that was to have significant consequences.

In a sense this was the true take-off point of the British navy. It had had its ups and downs over the previous two and a half centuries, reaching its peaks under Henry V, Henry VIII, Elizabeth, and Charles I. The navy had always maintained some kind of existence since the days of Henry VII, but there was no real tendency to increase in size. Charles I's fleet had been no bigger than that of Henry VIII, and probably not bigger than Henry V's.

This was to change in the mid-seventeenth century. In 1642, parliament had taken over a fleet of 35 effective ships, capable of employing about 7,300 men if fully manned. By 1652 it had doubled, to 102 ships and 12,500 men. In 1660, as Charles II was restored to the throne, the fleet comprised 157 ships employing 21,910 men. It had virtually trebled in size in 18 years. The fleet would continue to grow in every war fought over the next two centuries, but never again would it have such a large proportional increase in so short a period. A fleet of 6,000 men could be maintained without too much upheaval, provided finance was forthcoming, the government had popular support, and the war did not go on for too long. After 1649 none of these conditions would fully apply, and the fleet would need far more than 6,000 men.

Between 1649 and 1660 the English Republicans would fight wars with the exiled Royalists, with the Scots, the Irish, the French, the Dutch and the Spanish. It would emerge victorious from these wars, increasing Britain's overseas territory, and her rule over the seas. It would develop radical new tactics, for it used the fleet line of battle for the first time in 1653.

Warrant to Execute King Charles the First. AD 1648.

Besehl zur Hinrichtung König Karls I. von England vom 8. Februar 1649 (29. Januar 1648).

After that the difference between the warship and the merchant ship widened yet further, as only specially designed ships could stand in the line against enemies of approximately equal force; from this time, the naval force of the country would depend almost entirely on purpose-built warships, and it would be extremely rare to find a converted merchantman which could fight with the main fleet. The range of war would be greatly increased, with naval squadrons being sent to the Mediterranean and the West Indies (though the main strength still remained in home waters). England had already acquired colonies in Barbados, Virginia and New England, but these were products of private enterprise. In 1656 Jamaica was captured by a naval and military force, and for the first time the state was in the business of acquiring territory outside Europe. All this would put an enormous strain on the resources of the seafaring population.

ABOVE The execution warrant for King Charles. Oliver Cromwell's name appears third in the first column. After the restoration of the monarchy, all the surviving signatories were liable to be tried for regicide.

OPPOSITE The *Constant Reformation*, one of James I's great ships, later built up with higher sides and many more guns, drawn by Van de Velde the Elder. She was taken to the Netherlands after the Royalist revolt in 1648.

LEFT Robert Blake, General-at-Sea. The title reflects his early experience as a soldier, and he brought much-needed military discipline to the navy. A later painting by Henry Perronet Briggs in Romantic style in 1829, as commissioned for the Naval Gallery of Greenwich Hospital.

Chapter 3
DUTCH WARS

In October 1651 the English Parliament passed the Navigation Acts, 'For the increase of shipping and the encouragement of the navigation of this nation, which under the good providence and protection of God is so great a means of the welfare and safety of this Commonwealth'. Foreign goods were only to be imported to England and her colonies by English ships with English crews, or by ships belonging to the country where the goods originated. This was a blow to the Dutch, who made a living by shipping goods around the world without regard to their origin. The English and Dutch governments were both Protestant republics in a Europe dominated by Catholic monarchies, but even so this issue was enough to divide them and led to open war in 1652. It was perhaps the most maritime war ever fought – neither side even contemplated the land invasion of the other. And this Anglo-Dutch war, like the others that followed it, was hard-fought on both sides. Neither fleet retreated even when it was at a disadvantage. It was mostly fought in the narrow waters and sandbanks of the southern end of the North Sea, so there was little chance of fleets evading one another. Totally dependent on maritime trade, the Dutch could only win by challenging the English blockade of their ports, not by sitting in harbour as the French and Germans would do in later generations.

As General-at-Sea, Robert Blake had some success in two battles during the summer, defeating the Dutch off Dover and in the Thames estuary. Early in December he encountered a Dutch fleet of around 80 warships off Dungeness, led by the great admiral Marten Tromp and escorting a large convoy. Blake only had 42 ships himself, but they were larger, so the fleets were almost equal in gun power. Many of Blake's ships were short of men and some of them hung back because of this. Blake's own ship, the *Triumph*, was damaged while the *Vanguard* and *Victory* only just avoided capture and two others were taken. All the faults in the English navy had been exposed. One of the greatest was the lack of discipline among captains – out of 42 ships, 'not 20 came not to the engagement, pretending want of men'. Blake wrote that there was 'much baseness of spirit, not among the merchantmen only, but many of the State's ships'.[28]

In reaction to this chaos, parliament passed an act enforcing discipline on the fleet. The Articles of War were drafted in three days and enacted by parliament on Christmas Day 1652 (for the Puritans did not believe in such holidays). It was a fearsome document,

in which 13 articles out of 39 demanded that an offender 'shall suffer death' without any alternative. In a further 12, a court martial could sentence a man to death, or lesser punishment as it saw fit. In later years it would become associated with the oppression of common seamen, but its initial intention was to keep the officers, and especially captains, under control. It was particularly severe on indiscipline, treason and cowardice, offences which captains of the day were liable to commit.

There were other reforms during December 1652. The care of the wounded was greatly improved, and seamen were given a substantial pay rise to boost recruitment. As a result it was reported from Dover, '... since the Parliament resolves for paying and encouragement of seamen, a great number are come in for the service of this Commonwealth'.[29]

BELOW The development of the line of battle. This illustration shows part of the enormous line of battle during the St James's Day Fight in 1666. Both the English and the Dutch had about a hundred ships of the line each.

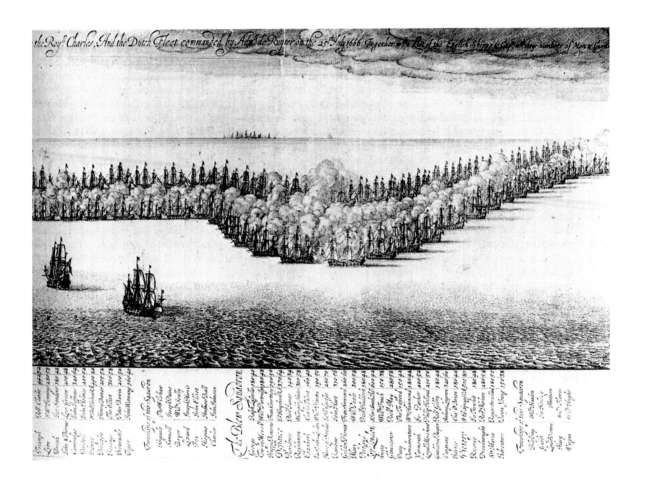

In December two soldiers, George Monck and Richard Deane, joined Blake and shared the command with him. But still there was no success at sea: a battle off Portland in February proved indecisive because the Dutch exploited the separation of the English squadrons. The soldiers were horrified with the disorder in which ships fought. Deane was an artilleryman who could see the value of ships as gun platforms; Monck had fought in many land battles and saw the advantages of forming his forces in line; while Blake provided the seafaring experience. Between them they drew up new Fighting Instructions for the fleet by the end of March 1653. A key clause demanded that 'all the ships of every squadron shall endeavour to keep in line with their chief'. The fleet was to fight in a single line ahead, the 'line of battle'. The new tactics were tested off the Gabbard sandbank in the mouth of the Thames at the beginning of June.

> ... the English found the Dutch fleet in at the height of Dunkirk, and when they approached them, they stayed upon a tack, having the wind, within twice cannon shot about half an hour, to put themselves in their order they intended to fight in, which was in file at half cannon shot, from whence they battered the Hollanders furiously all that day, the success whereof was the sinking of two Holland ships. Towards night Tromp got the wind, but soon lost it, and never recovered it the two following days during which the fight continued, the Dutch steering with a slow sail towards their own coast. The second day the English still battered them in file, and refusing to board them upon equal terms, kept them at bay but half cannon distance, until they found some disordered and foul one against another, whom they presently boarded with their frigates ...[30]

This was the turning point of the war. The Dutch fought another battle, off their own coast at Scheveningen in July, but lost their great leader Tromp. They began peace negotiations in October.

The development of the line of battle was also a turning point in tactics and shipbuilding. Every major warship had to be strong enough to stand in the line against the most powerful opponent, which led to the 'ship of the line' of at least two decks, with a strong structure and a heavy gun armament and far bigger than most merchant ships. Soon navies would begin to measure their strength in the number of ships of the line they had available. Boarding was no longer fashionable, and ships were now fully committed to using their broadside guns rather than those on the chase, pointing forward or aft. As a result, chase guns began to fall into disuse. By chance, most of the English ships were already suitable for the line of battle. The 'great ships' of Charles I, including the *Sovereign of the Seas*, were heavily gunned and Samuel Pepys would later claim, 'Twas the old great ships that did the service against the Dutch, built by our royal master's father, Charles I'.[31] Meanwhile the frigates had been built up into more effective fighting machines, and new ones were ordered. The *Speaker*, completed in 1649, carried 50 guns and was the prototype of the two-decker ship of the line.

Victory against the Dutch brought no peace to the Commonwealth. Colonel Pride had already purged parliament and Oliver Cromwell took on greater power as Lord Protector in 1653. The Royalist privateers were still active, there was a revolt in Scotland, and war with Spain led to the capture of Jamaica, though not the much richer Hispaniola that Cromwell had hoped for. Because of this constant war, relations between the government and the seamen began to decline again. Despite wage rises it became increasingly difficult to recruit enough men without rather crude impressment. At Ipswich this practice encountered serious local opposition. The prestmaster, Captain Edmund Curtis, was told by the local bailiffs that there were few seamen in the port, only masters and mates who were exempt from pressing. He did not believe this, as he saw that there were

King Charles. II.

ABOVE Charles II, painted by Sir Peter Lely – a king 'who best understands the business of the sea of any prince the world ever had', according to Samuel Pepys.

over 100 ships in the river. Next day, without giving advance notice to the bailiffs, he came at the head of an armed press gang to seek out the seamen: 'but when our people began to press, and had taken a man or two, the town's people fell upon our men, and rescued them, by which means there was likely to have been blood spilt had not our men been civil'. Events like this were repeated in other ports and it was clear that the government was losing the support of the seamen.

When Cromwell died and his son proved inadequate as a ruler, Monck went back to his natural element and secured the army in support of a restored monarchy. Edward Montagu, a neighbour of Cromwell in Huntingdonshire, had been brought into the navy in 1656 partly as a counterweight to the more extreme Republicans. He was suspected of plotting with the Royalists during a failed plot in the spring of

1659, and in the following year he was appointed to command to help bring the navy on side. He dismissed Republican officers, or sent them away on distant convoys.

Finally the navy was at the centre of politics again in May 1660 when a fleet commanded by Edward Montagu in the great flagship *Naseby* sailed to Holland to pick up the prince who would be restored to the throne as Charles II. Montague took with him his young secretary, his impoverished cousin Samuel Pepys. Edward Barlow was on board the *Naseby* to witness the King's reception.

> At his first coming to the ship's side all the men in the ship gave a great and loud shout, many of them hurling their caps or hats into the sea as a token of their joy to see His Majesty. That done, and he coming on board, we fired above 70 pieces of cannon, three times, one after another ... and all the admirals having fired then began all the rest of the fleet to fire, they all firing together, which made a great rattling in the sky as though it had been a great storm or tempest of thunder and rain.[32]

It was strangely appropriate, as fire of one kind or another would come to dominate Charles's reign. The ship, named after Cromwell's great battle, was quickly re-named *Royal Charles*. Pepys watched as the symbols of the Commonwealth were removed or covered in canvas. The figurehead, showing Cromwell trampling on his enemies, was later hung from a gibbet and burned. Montagu was made Earl of Sandwich while Pepys became Clerk of the Acts, a senior naval official.

Charles took over a navy three times the size of the one his father had lost, with many more modern ships and far clearer discipline and tactical doctrine. The Fighting Instructions of 1652 were kept on, but acts of the Commonwealth Parliament were no longer valid. To remedy this, the Restoration Parliament passed new Articles of War remarkably similar to

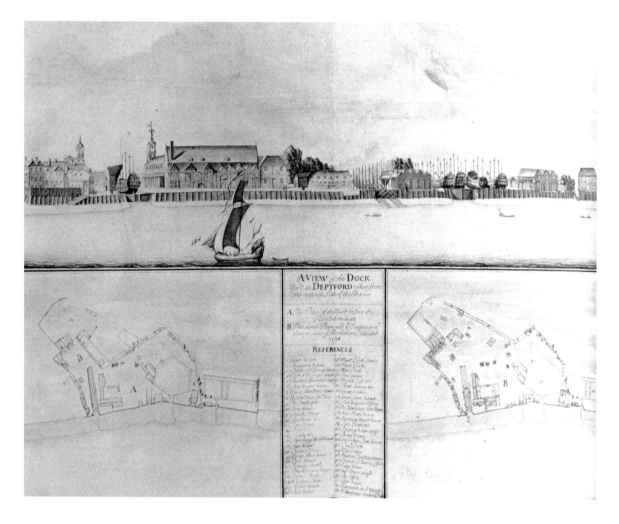

ABOVE The Royal Dockyard at Deptford, showing its development between 1689 and 1697. Despite some investment, it remained the most old-fashioned of yards, with mostly vernacular buildings.

those drawn up in 1652, and a new Navigation Act which was even stronger than the old one, applying to exports from Britain as well as imports. It would be at the centre of British commercial policy for nearly two hundred years, and one of its main aims was to foster merchant shipping as a 'nursery for seamen' for the king's navy.

Pepys was a member of the Navy Board, which looked after the material interests of the fleet, under the Lord High Admiral or Board of Admiralty, which decided on strategic questions. He soon came to admire King Charles in many ways, and later he told the House of Commons, 'By the King's personal application to building ships, skill has been advanced, beyond any memory of man, and perhaps beyond any improvement. More docks have been built. No age at any time had so many encouragements for navigation.'[33] But Pepys would also see something of the King's feckless side. By October 1662 he was hearing reports that the King spent far more time with his current mistress, Lady Castelmaine, than with his queen; a few months later he heard that 'the King do mind nothing but pleasure, and hates the very sight or thoughts of business' – though presumably he made an exception for naval affairs. Nevertheless, during England's greatest naval crisis in 1667, it was said that

Samuel Pepys (1633–1703)

On the face of it Samuel Pepys was born to a very humble background in London in 1633, to a tailor and a butcher's daughter, but his aunt married well and his cousin Edward Montagu rose high as a sea officer in the service of the Commonwealth. Pepys won a scholarship to Magdalene College, Cambridge, and began to work for Montagu in 1654. He married Elizabeth St Michel, the daughter of an impoverished Catholic French émigré, and he began his famous diary on 1 January 1660. It was to prove an eventful year. In May he accompanied Montagu to bring Charles II back from exile, and was appointed Clerk of the Acts to the Navy Board.

Pepys achieved what his diaries show to be a very satisfactory work-life balance, as well as indulging in office politics of the most vicious kind. He soon came to despise his colleagues at the Navy Office in Seething Lane. They were mostly sailors ignorant of land affairs, or courtiers. He took great pains to learn every aspect of the business, and his friend, the shipbuilder Anthony Deane, produced a manuscript on naval architecture for him, with an intention 'to leave nothing unfolded which may advance anything to the meanest capacity'. Pepys managed to avoid blame for the disasters of the Second Anglo–Dutch War and emerged with his position strengthened.

Pepys found corruption all around him and was not immune to it himself, but he could see some invisible line beyond which it damaged the navy, and did not step over it.

As well as a supreme degree of efficiency and an eye for detail, Pepys also began to develop a vision for the navy – of professional officers, ships built to the best available technology, dockyards to service them and sound financial method behind them. He went some way towards achieving that in his lifetime, allowing for an imperfect world and his own imperfect character.

He gave up his diary in 1669, fearing he was going blind, and Elizabeth died the following year. He became involved with Mary Skinner, whose brother had worked for the puritan John Milton – thus the two key women in his life represented the opposite poles of the day, Catholic and puritan. But they were not his only women; he had numerous affairs, including one with his maid. In addition he loved the theatre, music and good food and found time away from his work to enjoy them to the full.

When the Duke of York fell from office in 1673, the King took much of the running of the Admiralty into his own hands with Pepys as the Secretary. Pepys increased his power through election to the House of Commons. He supported the Royal Society, Trinity House and the Royal Mathematical School, but his main achievements were to set up a regular career structure for officers in 1677, and to steer an act through parliament for building thirty new ships.

In 1679, during the scare known as the 'Popish plot', he and Deane were accused of leaking naval secrets to the French, and imprisoned in the Tower of London for a year until they could clear their names.

Pepys returned to government work in 1683 when he helped to wind up business in the evacuated colony of Tangier. In 1684 he was reappointed as Secretary to the Admiralty and set up a special commission to restore the navy's ships after years of neglect – though as usual he greatly exaggerated the scale of his achievement. He remained in office when the Duke of York succeeded to the throne as James II and became increasingly powerful under the new regime, though he held back from James's pro-Catholic policies.

Nevertheless, he was driven from office after William and Mary came to the throne, and lived in retirement for the next 14 years. His projected history of the navy was never written. His diaries were first published in 1825 and are perhaps the best-written and most intimate works of that genre. They give a picture of a hedonistic, lecherous and frivolous man, very different from the highly competent administrator who set the navy on its course for the following century.

OPPOSITE Samuel Pepys by Sir Godfrey Kneller. It was painted in 1689, the year that Pepys was forced to retire from the Admiralty.

THESE PAGES Greenwich looking towards Deptford late in the seventeenth century, by Jan Griffier the Elder. From left to right: the Royal Observatory, St Alphege's Church, the Queen's House and the first block of the Naval Hospital.

ABOVE Some of Charles's yachts at sea in a strong wind, escorting a warship flying the Royal Standard and presumably carrying the King or his brother, by Willem Van de Velde the Younger.

the King spent the evening with his mistress, 'mad in hunting of a poor moth'.[34]

The King's brother, James, Duke of York, was appointed Lord High Admiral in charge of the navy, and Pepys would see far more of him over the next few years. He lacked his brother's charm and intelligence, but Pepys had no complaints about his hard work and dedication to the navy. And the brothers shared a common interest. On his restoration Charles was given a small ship called the *Mary* by the Dutch and it introduced a new word, yacht, to the English language. More Royal yachts were built (often named after the King's mistresses), and Pepys's fellow diarist John Evelyn wrote in October 1661,

> *I sailed this morning with his Majesty on one of his yachts (or pleasure boats), vessels not known among us till the Dutch East India Company presented that curious piece to the King; being very excellent sailing vessels. It was on a wager between his other new pleasure boat, built frigate-like, and one of the Duke of York's; the wager £100; the race from Greenwich to Gravesend and back. The King lost it going, the wind being contrary, but saved stakes in returning.*[35]

The idea was taken up by other wealthy men; Lord Mordaunt, for example, built a yacht of more than 500 tons in 1681.

Despite the constant lack of money, the Duke of York's naval administration set new standards for office procedure. Standing instructions, the forerunner of modern job specifications, were issued for the members of the Navy Board and other officials. The board members became more expert, with a shipbuilder as Surveyor of the Navy and an accountant as Treasurer. The notable exception was Pepys, who was not a sailor or a shipbuilder – he might be seen as an early example of the civil service tradition, of an intelligent outsider brought in to give a dispassionate judgement on the issues. Pepys learned shorthand to

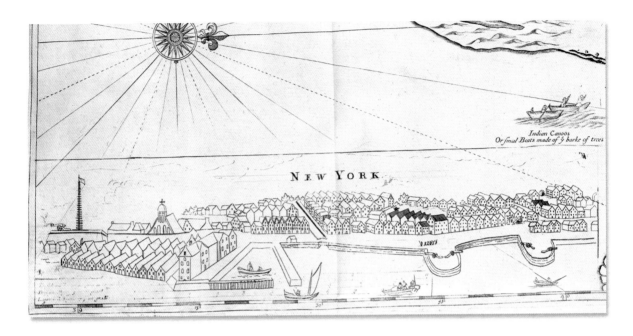

NEW YORK

Indian Canoos
Or small Boats made of ÿ barke of trees

ABOVE New York in 1677, not long after the English took it over, showing the south end of Manhattan. From a portfolio of charts belonging to Pepys.

take notes; his minutes, unlike most, give a good idea of the spirit of the meeting and the ebb and flow of debate. He devised ledgers and filing systems to keep track of the complex business of the navy.

The reign was not to remain peaceful at sea. Charles was reluctant to go to war with the Dutch in 1664, but a strong war party in parliament could see great profits to be made from their empire and trade. In the colonies Captain Robert Holmes anticipated matters by seizing Goree on the west coast of Africa. In North America, Captain Richard Nichols arrived at a small and rather dissolute Dutch colony. It had a population of around 1,500 and it was claimed that one house in four was a tavern, but it overlooked one of the finest natural harbours in the world and had good communications with the interior of the continent.

According to the Reverend Samuel Drisus,

On the 26th August there arrived in the Bay of the North River, near Staten Island, four great men-of-war, or frigates, well-manned with

sailors and soldiers. They were provided with a patent or commission from the King of Great Britain to demand and take possession of this province, in the name of His Majesty ... They intended, if any resistance was shown, to give a full broadside on this open place, and then take it by assault, and make it a scene of pillage and bloodshed.[36]

The Dutch made no efforts to defend New Amsterdam and it was re-named New York in honour of the Lord High Admiral. It was retaken by the Dutch during a later war in 1673, but restored in exchange for Surinam. By this time it was at the centre of the English empire in North America rather than on the fringes of the Dutch one. New docks were constructed and trade boomed. This city had trebled in population by the end of the century, which was only the beginning of its rise to become perhaps the greatest city in the world.

At home, parliament voted £2½ million to conduct the war against the Dutch, which began formally in February 1665. There were some doubts about the legality of the press gang, but once the war had started the government applied it to its limits and beyond. In July 1666 Pepys watched men being shipped off at the Tower of London.

> *But Lord, how some poor women did cry, and in my life never did see such natural expression of passion as I did here – in some women's bewailing themselves, and running to every parcel of men that were brought, one after another, to look for their husbands, and wept over every vessel that went off, thinking they might be there, and looking after the ship as far as ever they could by moonlight, that it grieved me to the heart to hear them.*

He was concerned about the legality as much as the sadness of the situation: 'to see poor patient labouring men and housekeepers, having poor wives and families, taken up on a sudden by strangers was very hard; and that without prest money, but forced against all law to be gone. It is a great tyranny.'[37]

The first battle of the war was fought off Lowestoft in June 1665. The Dutch had learned much from their defeat last time; they had built bigger ships and learned to fight in line. Both sides now had huge fleets. On 3 June, 109 English ships, commanded by the Duke of York and the King's uncle, Prince Rupert, met 103 Dutch men-of-war 40 miles off Lowestoft. The result was a stunning victory for the English, with the Dutch flagship blown up, seven more of their ships burnt and nine captured. The English pursued, but during the night one of the Duke's courtiers came on deck and ordered the fleet to shorten sail. The reasons for this have never been established but it raised suspicions about the loyalty of the Duke, who was married to a Roman Catholic.

In the following year Monck, ennobled as Lord Albemarle, took charge of the fleet at sea along with Prince Rupert. France declared war on England at the beginning of the year, much to the distress of the King, whose beloved sister Henrietta Anne was married to Louis XIV's brother. Unwisely it was decided to divide the fleet and Albemarle took command of two-thirds of the ships to meet the Dutch, while Rupert took the rest to the west to look out for the French. The Dutch came out and on 1 June 1666 began what Captain Jeremy Roch called 'the most terrible, obstinate and bloodiest battle that was ever fought on the seas ... The day was very hot, more ways than one, for between the flames of burning ships, the fiery flashes from the guns, with the beams of the sun, we seemed to be in the fiery Region'.[38] In the *Monck*, Edward Barlow was wounded:

> *... we had not engaged above an hour but that an unlucky shot that came from the Hollands came through the ship's side, hit me on the hollow of my ham on the right leg, it striking me lame for the present, but I praise the Lord it was spent before it hit me, or else it would have carried my leg away, but it did me no great harm; ... but my leg swelling so that I could not go on, I was forced to go down amongst the wounded men, where one lay without a leg and another without an arm, one wounded to death and another groaning with pain and dying, ... which is a sad sight to see ...*[39]

After three days of battle Prince Rupert joined Monck but both sides were now exhausted. It became known as the Four Days Fight, perhaps because there were not enough geographical names in such a small area of sea off the Thames estuary.

On 25 July, St James's Day, the fleets met again in the same area and this time the English were united and Captain Roch was excited in anticipation of a glorious battle. 'Here was a glorious naval prospect of 2 fleets, drawn up in such order as perhaps was never observed on the sea before, for here every ship fought single so that valour was not oppressed, nor could cowards well avoid fighting.'[40] The English had 89 ships, the Dutch 88, though mostly smaller. The English claimed a great victory with the taking of 40 ships. In fact the Dutch lost far less, though they did lose many of their leaders.

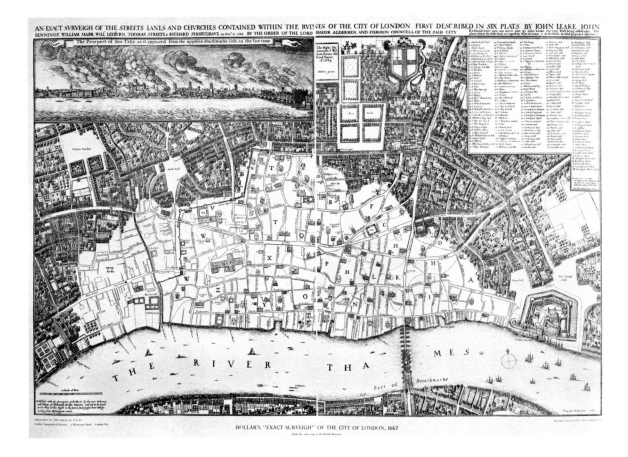

HOLLAR'S "EXACT SURVEIGH" OF THE CITY OF LONDON, 1667

ABOVE The area devastated by the Great Fire of London in 1666, including St Paul's Cathedral, but not the Tower of London or old London Bridge, by Wenceslas Hollar.

OPPOSITE The Dutch advance up the Medway. It shows several events taking place simultaneously: the attack on Sheerness, the breaking of the chain and the burning of the ships at Chatham.

FOLLOWING PAGES The Dutch fleet sailing away with the *Royal Charles* in triumph after the Medway raid.

In any case the English were greatly buoyed up by the battle, which they believed showed their natural supremacy at sea.

Sir Robert Holmes raided the Dutch shipping sheltering within the Frisian Islands and burned the town of Terschelling. Less than a month later London itself was ravaged by its Great Fire and the Dutch were happy to view it as divine revenge, however disproportionate. Following the plague the year before, this meant that Charles's government had now been tested in two great crises, but the third was to involve the navy more directly. Most of the ships were laid up during the winter of 1666–7, which was quite normal; but parliament's £2½ million was not enough and it was reluctant to find any more. In the spring the cash-strapped government made the great mistake of not putting the fleet to sea again, while demanding stiff peace terms from the Dutch. The enemy responded by attacking the half-built fort at Sheerness and entering the Medway. They passed through the chain across the river and destroyed several ships off the dockyard at Chatham. Their greatest coup was to capture the *Royal Charles*, which had brought the King back in 1660. Her huge royal coat of arms, fitted to her stern as a symbol of the Restoration, remains on display in the Rijksmuseum in Amsterdam to this day. Pepys visited the site two weeks later.

Thence by barge, it raining hard, down to the chain; and in our way did see the sad wracles of the poor Royall Oake, James and London, and several other ships by us sunk; and several of the enemy's whereof three men of war that they could not get off and so burned. We did also see several dead bodies lie by the sides of the water. So to the chain, and there saw it fast on the Upner side of the river; very fast, and borne up upon the several stages across the river – where it is broke, nobody can tell me.[41]

Peter Pett, the Commissioner of Chatham Dockyard, was blamed, largely because he had failed to move ships further up river out of reach. Pepys was scornful when he appeared before the Privy Council.

'He is in his old clothes, and looked most sillily.' He was accused of using dockyard boats to rescue his own possessions, to which he replied, again 'very sillily', that they were mainly his ship models, which would have revealed the secrets of his designs – 'he did believe the Dutch would have made more advantage of the models than the ships' – which caused laughter in the council.

The whole affair led the poet Andrew Marvell to ask a series of questions.

Whose counsel did this mad war first beget? ...
Who would not follow when the Dutch were
beat? ... Who did advise no navy out to set?
And who left the forts unprepared? ... Who all
our ships exposed in Chattham nett?[42]

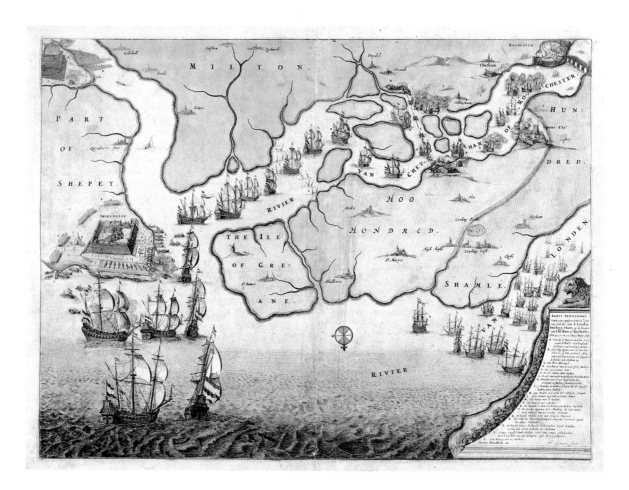

In each case in Marvell's satire, the answer was 'none but the fanatick Pett'. But it did not need much insight to see what Marvell was getting at, that the faults were much wider and deeper than a single scapegoat, in the roots of British political society. Treason was feared in the very highest ranks.

In 1670 Charles agreed to the secret Treaty of Dover, parts of which were even concealed from his own ministers. He was to receive subsidies from Louis XIV of France, and at some stage he was to announce his conversion to Catholicism – in that case, Louis would provide the means to quell any revolt by the people. He was also committed to join Louis in crushing the Dutch republic.

The Third Anglo-Dutch War began in 1672 with a botched pre-emptive strike on the richly laden Dutch merchant fleet returning up the English Channel from Smyrna in Turkey. Although the Dutch had been national enemies in past decades, the power of France was rising after a period of disunity, and she now seemed far more threatening to the English.

Charles went to war without public support, in aid of the arrogant superpower of the day. Louis XIV's France was everything that England was not and,

indeed, what the navy had stopped it from becoming. In comparison with Elizabeth's moderate Protestantism, it was repressively Catholic. There were strong communities of Huguenot refugees in London and elsewhere, always ready to remind the English about the St Bartholomew's Day massacre of a century ago, when up to 30,000 Protestants had been killed and many more had fled to England. France had an absolute monarchy and Louis ruled without a parliament. He was able to raise taxes at will, or so it seemed to the English, and a move towards the French system would be to revisit all the battles over ship money and other taxes of forty years ago. Louis had a huge army even in peacetime, whereas Charles's regular forces were restricted to a few household troops. As well as echoes of the repressive rule of Cromwell's Major-Generals, this raised the spectre of a body that would collect taxes by force without the need for parliament. France had an efficient bureaucracy, while England relied on the genius of a few individuals such as Pepys. Louis was exploiting every means to consolidate his power over French territory, including using lawyers, genealogists and historians to discredit the rights of local landlords and minor princes. France was now trying to build up a strong navy, but that did not give them any more in common with the English. It was clearly not needed for national defence, for there was no prospect that the English or anyone else would invade France by sea. It could only be used to build an empire at the expense of others and dominate the rest of Europe, especially England and the Netherlands.

Charles hoped opinion would soon swing in his favour after a quick victory, but that did not materialise. At a battle off Southwold on the Suffolk coast in May 1672, Pepys's patron Lord Sandwich was killed and the French failed to come to the support of the English. Three more battles were fought among the sandbanks off the Dutch coast but none was decisive,

OPPOSITE The burning of the English flagship at the Battle of Solebay, off Southwold in 1672. The ship is shown in flames to the right, with Dutch and English ships locked in combat in the centre.

BELOW The Battle of the Texel in 1673, by Willem Van de Velde the Younger. A Dutch flagship, possibly the *Gouden Leeuw*, is on the left with the disabled English flagship *Royal Prince* in the centre.

while the Dutch flooded their lands to prevent a French advance. There was trouble at home as the Test Act imposed more restrictions on Roman Catholics. It included an oath that no Catholic would be able to accept, and the Duke of York was obliged to resign as Lord High Admiral. The King took the business into his own hands, and one positive result was that Samuel Pepys became Secretary to the Admiralty, and virtual Navy Minister. Eventually Charles was forced to withdraw from the war, with his regime irreparably damaged. Alongside religion it was mostly naval activity and finance, or the lack of them, which had brought King Charles onto a collision course with parliament and public opinion; things would get worse before they would get better. The Dutch Wars had been a mixed period for the navy, and early successes were soon overcome by political failures. But they did establish a new and far more cohesive navy, far more disciplined and effective than the semi-piratical forces led by Francis Drake during England's last great foreign war.

Chapter 4
REFORM AND REVOLUTION

Pepys was promoted to Secretary to the Admiralty during the crisis of 1673, directly under the King as Lord High Admiral. After peace in 1674 he took the opportunity to carry out a much-needed reform of the navy. The officers in any age need a suitable combination of technical skill and leadership, but the Restoration navy was a long way from striking a good balance. Officers were either 'tarpaulins', men of humble origins who had served in merchant ships and risen to prominence under the Commonwealth; or 'gentlemen', courtiers who had been appointed by Charles after his restoration, often as a reward for services rather than any skill in seamanship. In 1666 Pepys noted in his diary that,

> ... the fleet was in such a condition as to discipline, as if the Devil had commanded it; so much wickedness of all sorts ... the pilots do say, that they dare not do nor go but as the Captains will have them; and, if they offer to do otherwise, the Captains swear they will run them through. ... Captain Digby, my Lord of Bristol's son, a young fellow that never was but one year, if that, in the fleet, say he did hope he should not see a tarpaulin have the command of a ship within these twelve months.[43]

Pepys agreed that '... gentlemen ought to be brought into the navy, as being men that are more sensible of honour than a man of meaner birth...' but that they should be 'brought up by times at sea'.[44] The answer was to train them as midshipmen then subject them to a stiff examination before they were commissioned as lieutenants. According to the king's orders of

ABOVE The *Britannia*, the largest ship of the 1677 programme, drawn by Van de Velde the Younger. She has the characteristic equestrian figurehead used by first rates.

1677, as drafted by Pepys, each candidate had to pro that he was at least 20 years old and,

> *To have spent so much time actually at sea in one or more voyages in our service as ... shall together amount to 3 entire years at least, and to have served in the quality of an ordinary midshipman in some one of our ships for the space of one year of the three ...*

He would be examined by a board of captains who had to be satisfied 'in his ability to judge of and perform the duty of an able seaman and midshipman, and his having attained a sufficient degree of knowledge in the theory of Navigation capacitating him thereto.'[45] The rules were bent many times during the next century and a half, and were changed to demand six rather than three years' service, but they provided the basis on which a professional officer corps could be built. In an age when birth counted for a great deal, and many appointments were made in return for political favours, it was a radical if not a revolutionary step, the first towards what became known as meritocracy. It is significant that it came from the navy, where incompetence was not easy to conceal. It was no longer possible for the aristocratic fighting captain to issue orders to the sailing master as he had done in the Middle Ages, for the gun-armed ship was now a weapon in itself and not just a carrier of weapons. Separately neither the gentleman nor the tarpaulin made the ideal officer, but a combination of the two, in this case a gentleman trained in seamanship, could be a world-beater.

The war between the Netherlands and France continued, and both sides were building up large navies, so there was the real threat that Charles's fleet might be left behind. It was Pepys, now Member of Parliament for Harwich, who had to persuade the House of Commons to supply the money to remedy the situation. When the Members proposed twenty ships, Pepys was scornful: 'To have it said abroad, "You will build twenty ships", twill be laughed at!'

Eventually parliament agreed to provide £600,000 for one 100-gun ship, nine of 90 guns and twenty of 70 guns each. Parliament still mistrusted the sovereign and the final bill included clauses on 'penalties to the king', which Charles must have found insolent and infuriating. In the developing history of the conflict between the executive and parliament, this was an attempt by the latter to assert more control, but it was a clumsy one and a blind alley. Instead of setting the general lines of policy for the executive, parliament had interfered in matters it did not understand, such as the tonnage of ships.

When the matter came before the Admiralty Board, it was the King himself who ordered that the tonnages be increased from those demanded by parliament, whatever the expense: 'His Majesty was pleased graciously to add that if such increase of charge should nevertheless be excepted against by Parliament ... he would rather choose to make it good out of his own purse than hazard the wronging of the ships for want of it.' This would set alarm bells ringing with anyone who had anything to do with his cash-strapped administration, but the building went ahead anyway.

It was the largest programme so far and it offered much opportunity to standardise design, fitting and armament, for as Pepys said, 'the many inconveniences every day met with in time of action from the disproportions and unsizeableness of the old fleet' would be avoided. The dimensions were to be standardised for each type, so that a common set of masts and fittings could be used. Each ship was to be armed according to 'a solemn universal adjustment for the gunning and manning of the whole fleet'. It was sensible enough at the time, and in fact the rules of 1677 were never applied very strictly; but in the next century this would lead to excessive rigidity.

But before the ships were finished the regime came under serious pressure, when Titus Oates claimed to have discovered a 'Popish plot' which aimed to overthrow it, and he implicated many officials who were dismissed and others who were unjustly and brutally executed. Pepys himself was

forced to leave office and was locked up in the Tower of London for a time. The navy was left in far less efficient hands. Charles was forced to appoint members of the opposition as his ministers, which Pepys deplored.

> *No king ever did so unaccountable a thing to oblige his people by, as to dissolve a Commission of the Admiralty then in his own hand, who best understands the business of the sea of any prince the world ever had, ... and put it into hands which he knew were wholly ignorant thereof, sporting himself with their ignorance ...*[46]

With hindsight it might be seen as a bold constitutional experiment. The general election of 1679 was the first ever to be fought on party political lines, and the resulting parliament was not sympathetic to Charles. By taking government ministers from the former opposition he did what most future kings would have to do, agreeing to the will of the political nation as expressed through parliament. But that did not make the King happy to accept the situation on a permanent basis, and it did not make the new Board of Admiralty any more competent. To work it would have needed a permanent civil service behind it to stop the administration descending into chaos. Samuel Pepys was the nearest thing to that in this age, but he was out of office and suspected of treason.

Charles had re-gained his political initiative by 1684, and Pepys was appointed to a special commission to look into the condition of the navy. He was shocked when he saw his beloved ships, mostly laid up at Chatham.

> *The greatest part ... of these thirty ships (without having ever yet looked out of harbour) were let to sink into such distress, through decays contracted in their buttocks, quarters, bows, thick stuff without board, and spirkettings upon their gundecks within; their*

buttock planks some of them started from their transoms, tree-nails burnt and rotted, and planks thereby become ready to drop in the water ... and their whole sides more disguised by shot-boards nailed, and plasters of canvas pitched thereon (for hiding their defects) than has usually been seen upon the coming in of a fleet after a battle; that several of them had been newly reported by the Navy Board itself, to line in danger of sinking at their very moorings.[47]

Charles died in 1685 and James acceded to the throne, taking the title of Lord High Admiral back for himself. Pepys returned as Secretary to the Admiralty, and the new king took as much interest in the navy as any sovereign has ever done, including his brother. But it was not his greatest interest. Like that other great master of detail, Phillip II of Spain, James II was determined to restore the Roman Catholic religion in England. Unlike Phillip he was both a native and a convert, with all the enthusiasm that brought. As a result his reign was a series of crises as James's actions offended the Protestant majority in the country. It began with revolts in Scotland and England and even a relatively strong navy could not prevent individual rebels from landing and seeking support. The Earl of Argyll came over from Holland but found little backing even among his own Campbell clan. The Duke of Monmouth, an illegitimate son of Charles II, landed at Lyme but was soon defeated at Sedgemoor. His supporters were tried by the brutal Judge Jeffreys and sentenced to severe punishments – 800 were transported to slavery in the West Indies.

To a certain extent King James could claim that his policies were of religious tolerance rather than in favour of any particular branch of Christianity, and indeed he released Quakers from prison and allowed William Penn, the Quaker son of one of his admirals, to set up the colony of Pennsylvania, the first to allow

de Charles   le Duches   de Windsor Castle   de Breda.   de Albemarle.   de Royal Prin

ABOVE A royal visit to Chatham in the 1680s, showing some of the thirty ships laid up and in need of attention, including the *Duchess*, *Windsor Castle*, *Breda* and *Albemarle* to the right.

RIGHT The opening page of Pepys' diary, 1660. It was written in shorthand with an occasional word spelled out. After giving thanks to God for his health, he describes the political situation of the country.

freedom of worship. But his Declaration of Indulgence of 1687 went too far for his subjects, and in 1688 seven of the bishops were tried for refusing to read it out. James's control of the courts was far from complete, and they were acquitted.

Neither the nobles nor the commoners had any taste for a republic after the Cromwellian experiment, but there was an alternative monarchy across the water in the Netherlands. William, Prince of Orange, was already in the line of succession as a grandson of Charles I, while his wife Mary was James's eldest daughter and the direct heiress to the throne, so the crown would eventually return to

Naval Administration

A strong naval administration was essential, especially for a fleet that ranged over all the seas of the world.

The first full-time naval administrator was the Clerk of the King's Ships appointed by the late medieval kings. In Henry VIII's time the Clerk was replaced by a body that became known as the Navy Board. Its four principal officers – Comptroller, Treasurer, Surveyor of the Navy and Clerk of the Acts – had separate but overlapping functions and were added to over the years. Between them they administered the money, ran the Royal Dockyards and built and supplied the ships.

Above them was the Lord High Admiral, a nobleman of the highest rank who controlled strategy and appointed officers to ships. From Charles II's time onwards it became increasingly common to place the Admiralty 'in commission', with a board of politicians and naval officers instead of a single official. Its head was the First Sea Lord, who might be either a politician or an admiral. By the 1800s the other naval officers on the board, the Sea Lords, were beginning to take on specialised functions. Most of the detailed work, however, was done by separate committees, which included the Victualling Board, the Transport Board and the Sick and Hurt Board. In 1832 the Navy Board was merged into the Admiralty, which tended to increase its obsession with detail. By about 1900 the First Lord of the Admiralty was invariably a politician and the First Sea Lord was his naval adviser. Other Sea Lords were responsible for personnel, material including shipbuilding, and naval bases.

The Admiralty has had its share of corruption, maladministration, incompetence and failure to adapt to change, but over the centuries it has run the most successful armed force in the world, as well as handling large budgets and managing huge industrial enterprises in the Royal Dockyards. Its office procedures have often been adopted by other departments and organisations.

BELOW The Board of Admiralty in 1808. Pugin drew the building and Thomas Rowlandson the figures, which explains why they are out of proportion. Charts of the world hang on the wall above the fireplace.

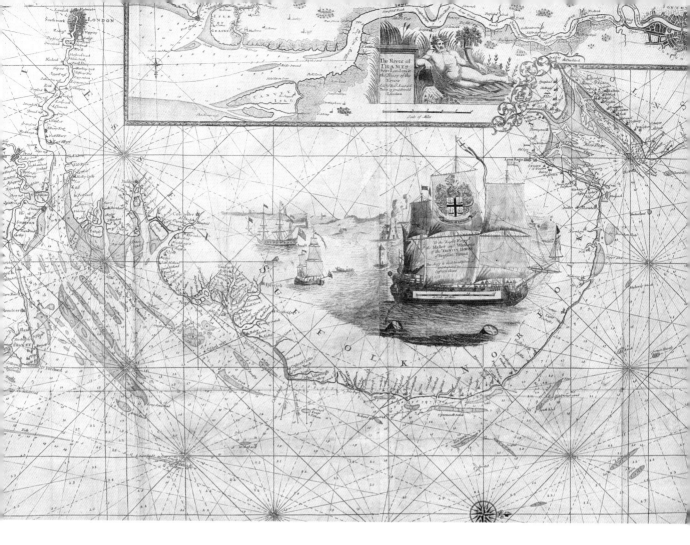

Protestant hands. The only thing that would disrupt this was if James's second wife Mary of Modena gave birth to a son, who would be brought up as a Catholic and take precedence over Mary and her sister Anne. This indeed happened on 10 June 1688, though the King's opponents claimed that a baby had actually been smuggled into the palace in a warming pan.

Across the water, William and Mary heard the complaints of their potential subjects, and worried about their possible inheritance. William fitted out a fleet of about 50 warships and 200 transports carrying 12,000 troops. In response, James ordered the Earl of Dartmouth to take charge of the English fleet. He was a gentleman captain who had taken command of a ship in 1667 after one year at sea, and had served James in many capacities over the years, but his captains and officers were less loyal.

... there was a meeting of such captains as were inclined to the Prince [of Orange], to consult what measures they should take upon coming up with the enemy. Some of them were of opinion that if my Lord attacked them, that in honour they should do their duty against them. But the general opinion, to which they agreed, was that on such an occasion to leave him (and to range themselves on the other side).[48]

Not knowing where William intended to land, Dartmouth anchored his fleet behind the Gunfleet sandbank off Harwich, where he hoped he could go either north or south as needed. But a north-east wind

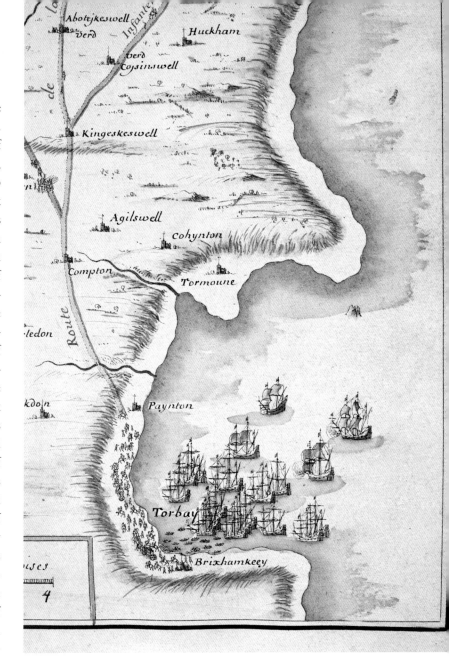

confined him to the anchorage while William was able to sail. As with Elizabeth's defeat of the Armada a century earlier, William's supporters were able to claim that it was a 'Protestant wind' which had wafted his ships across the North Sea and down the English Channel. The Dutch ships sailed through the Strait of Dover watched by hordes of spectators on both sides, and with the English in pursuit. On 5 November Dartmouth held a council of war off Beachy Head and his captains, largely influenced by the Protestant captains, urged him not to proceed. William landed his army at Brixham in the sheltered waters of Torbay. The desertion of the King's immediate supporters led to panic within the regime and James fled. His boat anchored off Faversham in the Thames estuary to await a favourable tide, and was boarded by local fishermen who searched and robbed him – the most humiliating experience of a very difficult life. William assumed the throne with Mary – the only joint reign in British history. Well aware of the dangers of executing or imprisoning a former monarch, William allowed James to escape from imprisonment in Rochester and seek refuge in France. This began a long series of wars with England's neighbour over the channel, which would last for the greater part of a century and a quarter. It also meant that James's supporters, the Jacobites, would conspire and rebel to have him or his son put on the throne for the next half century.

William's accession sparked off the 'Glorious Revolution', which formed the centre of British gov-

ernment for more than a century. Apart from the overthrow of James it was rather a conservative affair, with no executions, no dispossession of property and a strengthening of the power of parliament. Largely facilitated by the navy, it in turn facilitated the growth and importance of the fleet over the next era of British history. For the second time in almost exactly a century the Royal Navy had saved Protestantism in Britain, this time largely by its inaction. That would be of great importance in the century to come. As a modern historian has put it,

OPPOSITE William of Orange's landing at Brixham in the sheltered anchorage off Torbay. Later it became an important anchorage for the Channel Fleet taking shelter in winter storms.

LEFT William of Orange after the landing, with his fleet at Torbay shown in the background, and the population apparently welcoming his men ashore, by the Dutch painter Jan Wyck.

Protestantism meant much more in this society than just bombast, intolerance and chauvinism. It gave the majority of men and women a sense of their place in history and a sense of worth. It allowed them to feel pride in such advantages as they genuinely did enjoy, and helped them endure when hardship and danger threatened. It gave them identity.[49]

In the fleet of 1688 were 173 ships totalling nearly 102,000 tons, including exactly a hundred of the line. It was battle-hardened in three major wars and several campaigns, with a coherent tactical doctrine and well-established shipbuilding policies. It had a principal national enemy in France, whose absolute monarchy, religion and expansionist policies were anathema to most of the British. Most important of all, the navy was now a force for national unity rather than division. Eighteenth-century kings did not give up all their power, but in general they were aware of the need to work in partnership with parliament rather than against it, and both were united in seeing the need for a strong navy. There was never again a danger that it would fall into disrepair or extinction.

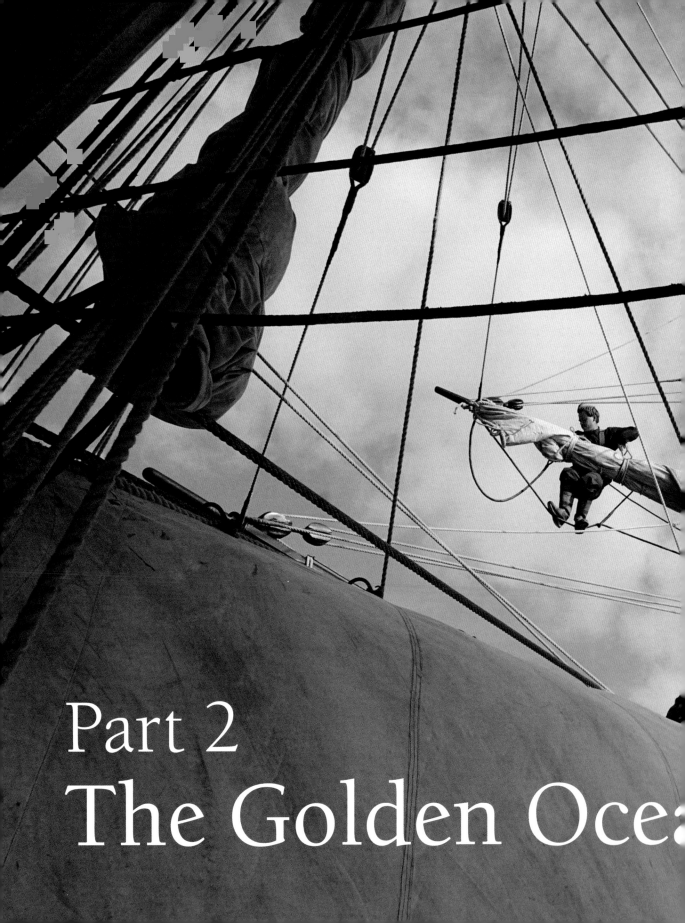

Part 2
The Golden Ocea

n

BELOW The *Soleil Royal*, flagship of Louis XIV, the 'Sun King'. The ship was built at Brest in 1669 and highly decorated, with the figurehead of a seahorse flanked by winged maidens. She served as flagship at Beachy Head in 1690 and was destroyed by fireships after Barfleur in 1692.

LE SOLEIL ROYAL

Chapter 5
EUROPEAN WAR

War with France began formally in July 1689, for Louis XIV could not tolerate the overthrow of his protégé James, and planned to restore him to the throne. Britain was not a united country; there were many Jacobites who were unhappy about the overthrow even in the highest levels of government and the navy, who would willingly help James to return. France, like the Netherlands, was a major naval power and one of Britain's closest continental neighbours, but war with her was different in many ways. France was far less dependent on maritime trade and could not be defeated by sea power alone. She had an autocratic and efficient state, with fewer internal political conflicts and contradictions than the Dutch or the British. She was able to raise a huge and efficient army, which Britain could never hope to match, so it was always necessary to have continental allies to defeat France.

France was also a tougher nut to crack from the sea. England could blockade the Netherlands almost by her very existence, sitting astride her routes to the wider world, but France had ports on the Atlantic coast and in the Mediterranean, which could only be closed with great effort and difficulty. Like the Dutch, the French had built up a great overseas empire, and it was essential to prevent communication between the mainland and the distant territories. Since the French had a separate coastline in the Mediterranean, the British would have to develop strategy and bases to deal with that if French sea power was to be contained.

The problem was especially difficult in 1689, because France had as large a fleet as the English and the Dutch, also built up by a great navy minister. Like Pepys, Jean Baptiste Colbert had risen from a relatively humble background. Unlike Pepys he was a workaholic who had no embarrassment about becoming rich through his offices, which included finance and culture as well as the navy. Starting from almost nothing, he

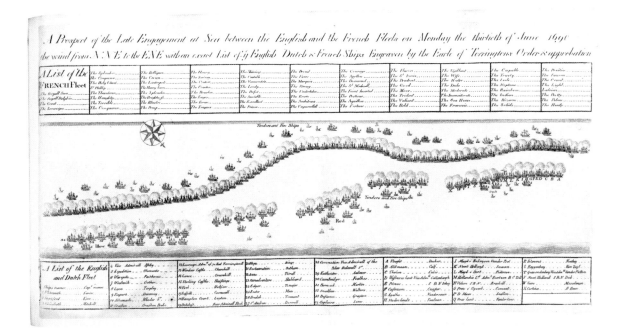

ABOVE The Battle of Beachy Head in June 1690, with the Anglo-Dutch squadron nearest the viewer. The Dutch to the right are fully engaged; the English centre squadrons are not.

OPPOSITE The BBC film crew on Rye Beach, where the wreck of the 70-gun ship *Anne* lies buried. Sometimes, when the sands shift, she re-emerges like a ghostly reminder of a forgotten moment in history.

had ships built in the Netherlands and brought in shipwrights from abroad (including Pepys's friend Anthony Deane) until the French builders were ready. He founded the Inscription Maritime, a far fairer and more efficient system of conscription than the English press gang, on paper at least. He too set out a regular career structure for officers, starting as cadets or Gardes de la Marine. Though he died in 1683, he left behind a strong fleet with a certain amount of battle experience against the English and Dutch. When war began in 1689, the French had 93 ships of the line, almost equal to the English despite the addition of Pepys's thirty new ships, and almost half as big again as the Dutch fleet.

As well as fighting between the main armies in Flanders, much of the early conflict took place in Ireland where James landed in 1689 to get the support of the Catholic population. On 1 May a French force was escorting a convoy out of Bantry Bay in the south-west of the island when it was caught by a smaller English force under Admiral Herbert. There was a brief skirmish in which neither side showed much competence or suffered much damage. There was a much more serious battle when the French fleet sailed up the English Channel in 1690, hoping to blockade the River Thames and prevent the English and Dutch joining forces. This failed, and the Anglo-Dutch fleet entered the Channel. Though the French were superior in numbers, the Queen ordered the Earl of Torrington to fight them: 'should you avoid a battle, we must lose more than we can possibly [lose] by one.' The two fleets met off Beachy Head on 30 June 1690 – the French had 73 ships of the line, the Anglo-Dutch force had 56. The Dutch squadron in the van was fully engaged, the two English squadrons held back. Only one Dutch ship was lost during the battle with three further Dutchmen lost afterwards, but Torrington decided to retreat to the Gunfleet in the Thames estuary. The only English ship to suffer damage was the 70-gun *Anne*, one of Pepys's thirty ships and now commanded by John Tyrrell. Torrington ordered her

to be towed out of danger, but on the morning after the battle her captain reported,

> *... having a hundred odd men killed and wounded. Our main mast, mizzen mast and boltsprit all shattered to pieces, and foremast shot away. We received above sixty shot betwixt wind and water. I have got up a topmast for a jury foremast, but the foresail is too small, she will not work with it. The French are still to leeward with the wind ENE and NE. Our ship being so much battered God Almighty send us clear of our enemys.*[1]

The weather got worse on 3 July and the *Anne* was run aground at high water near Hastings. Tyrrell wrote, 'I lie within pistol shot, at high water, of the shore, and at low water one may walk round the ship. If the French fireships do not come in and burn me I hope to save her.' But the French did attack on the 5th, causing a certain amount of panic in Rye 12 miles along the coast where the merchant Samuel Leake recorded, '... their intention were to fire and plunder the towne ...'.[2] Captain Tyrrell ordered the ship to be

burnt, and until very recently the remains of her hull could be seen at low tide.

News of Torrington's defeat arrived in London at the same time as that of King William's victory against the Jacobites at the Boyne near Dublin. There was consternation in the city. The French, unlike the Dutch in previous wars, had the capacity to invade England and now they were in control of the Channel. Fortunately they lacked the will to do so. Torrington defended his conduct, claiming that it was necessary to keep his 'fleet in being' and that the French would not dare to invade while it was still intact – the opposite of the Queen's idea to fight a battle at all costs, and the one that naval strategists and historians have tended to support over the years. He was proved right; the French attack never materialised.

The English and Dutch spent 1691 building more ships, while the French built very few because resources were strained to the limit. During the winter of 1691–2 both sides made plans to invade the other. The English built barges and trained gunners for a landing at St-Malo or Brest. Meanwhile King Louis and ex-King James assembled an invasion force at La Hogue in the Cotentin peninsula to sail to Torbay, where William had landed. But an Anglo-Dutch fleet of nearly a hundred ships was put together and on 19 May 1692 they encountered a French force of less than half their size off Barfleur. The battle was fought in the variable weather of the English Channel and was described by an officer in the 90-gun *Ossory*, another of Pepys's thirty ships.

> *May 19 at two P.M. we gained the weather gage of the enemy. The Dutch intended to tack upon them, but fell to leeward; but our red and the rear-admiral of the blue surrounded them. It proving calm we got our oats out ahead, towed towards the enemy, and renewed the action. About three the wind chopped to the eastward and presently proved calm with a great fog, insomuch that we could not see the enemy to fire at them. At four the weather cleared up and we got sight of them to the northward of us. At seven the French vice-admiral of the blue was set on fire by one of our fire-ships and blew up. Three third-rates were also burnt, and two more three-decked ships sunk. The night approaching, and the wind veering to the north-east, gave the enemy the weather gage, and about nine we lost sight of them.[3]*

The French escaped into La Hogue, where the allies attacked them with boats and fireships on the 23rd. It became a truly amphibious affair when French cavalry was sent into the shallow waters to

OPPOSITE A French view of the attack on the Smyrna convoy in Lagos Bay in June 1691.

BELOW A rather romantic view of the Battle of Barfleur in 1690, painted by George Chambers more than a century later for the Greenwich Hospital Collection.

*Combat naval de Lagos ou de Vedra 17 Juin 1693 /
Sur les lagunes et tuile la flotte anglaise et hollandaise d'Anvers en tête de la Portugal*

attack the boats, and the seamen fought them off with boathooks. Ex-King James was camped nearby with a division of the army and watched with mixed feelings. 'Ah, none but my brave English could do so brave an action', he exclaimed. In all the French lost a dozen major ships. There was jubilation in London, as the threat of invasion had been removed.

With their main fleet heavily defeated, the French gave up any hope of building a new one in competition with the English and the Dutch, and they did not revive as a major naval power for many years. Instead they turned to another type of naval warfare, which they called the *guerre de course*. Privately owned men of war, or privateers, were fitted out in ports such as St-Malo and Dunkirk. Each was supplied with a letter of marque signed by government officials to protect its

crew against a charge of piracy (which carried the death penalty). They hoped to make a substantial profit by capturing and selling English and Dutch shipping, and many did. During 1692, 59 privateers fitted out at St-Malo alone took 200 ships. The English navy was forced to set up a system of convoys and cruisers in an attempt to protect the merchantmen, but resources were spread thinly and there was much criticism from the merchant interest in parliament.

During 1693 the need to protect trade coincided with a developing interest in the Mediterranean. The merchants trading with Turkey had waited nearly two years for a convoy to escort their ships past the dangerous waters off France, and finally in May Sir George Rooke was put in command of a squadron to escort the 400 ships. He was supported by the main English fleet for the first part of the journey, but they turned back eventually to protect the coasts of the homeland, leaving Rooke with 21 warships. They did not know that the French had got wind of their plans and 90 ships from the Brest and Toulon fleets were lying in wait in Lagos Bay on the south coast of Portugal. Rooke had to decide what to do when the ambush was sprung.

I concluded it was the enemy's whole fleet, but did at the same time believe it was too late to retreat with any manner of security to the merchant ships. I therefore resolved to make it my endeavour to secure them, though I might myself fall a sacrifice to their safety; but upon second consideration, I thought the Vice-Admiral's message would have rendered me inexcusable to the world, and left an internal infamy on me.

I had no time to advise and very little to consider, for if we had not brought to, as we did, we must have been engaged in less than a quarter of an hour; and as the ships we had fought with had disabled us, fresh ones would have wrought up to have completed our ruin; and the five ships that stood off would have weathered us, fallen in among the merchantmen and made what havoc they had pleased with them; so that I verily do believe if we had engaged, the whole fleet had been taken and destroyed that night.[4]

Rooke made a fighting retreat but 92 merchantmen were taken, a disaster equivalent to the Great Fire of London. The prizes were sold for three million livres, equalling the whole French naval budget for a year. At home, there were numerous bankruptcies and uproar in parliament.

The defeat at Beachy Head had already produced a good deal of panic in government, and in 1691 it inspired parliament to pass another act, based on

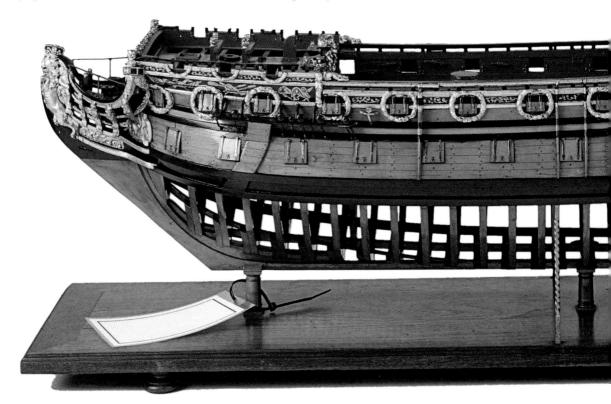

BELOW A model of the 80-gun third rate *Boyne*, named after William's recent victory in Ireland, and one of the 80-gun ships of the 1691 programme. She was completed as a two-decker.

Pepys's one of 1677, to add more ships to the navy. Unfortunately there was no Pepys to guide it through, and King William was too preoccupied with the war to modify it as Charles had done. It was generally agreed that English ships of the line were too small compared with the French but parliament, still not fully aware of the boundaries between legislative and administrative competence, simply scaled up the dimensions of the twenty 70-gun ships of 1677 and made them two-decker 80s. The resulting ships were not successful, and the *Sussex* was lost off Gibraltar in 1694. After that the remaining ships were completed as three-deckers, and the existing ones were rebuilt in due course. This only made them worse, as their high centres of gravity made them unstable and their tall sides caught the wind.

The other type adopted by the act of was the 50-gun ship, which appeared to have some advantages, especially after the main threat came from the priva-

teer rather than the battle fleet. In theory the 50 was just large enough to serve in the line of battle, but nimble and cheap enough to be spread round the seas in patrol and escort duties. In practice it was an unhappy compromise, which did neither job very well. Parliament would eventually learn to leave the details of matters such as ship design to the executive, but it took some time.

The war cost a huge amount of money, large parts of which were spent on William's war in Flanders. In order to make payments there, and also to finance the naval war, the Bank of England was founded in 1694. Its main projector was William Paterson, who would later lead his fellow Scots on a disastrous attempt to set up the colony of Darien in Panama. The first Director of the Bank was John Houblon, a London merchant and financial expert who had recently become one of the Lords of the Admiralty, and who would also serve as a commissioner for navy

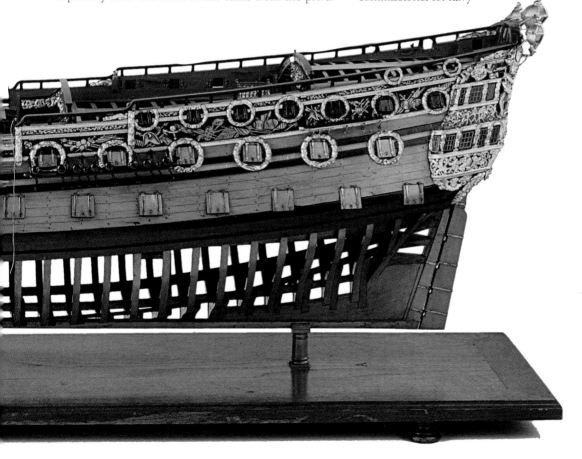

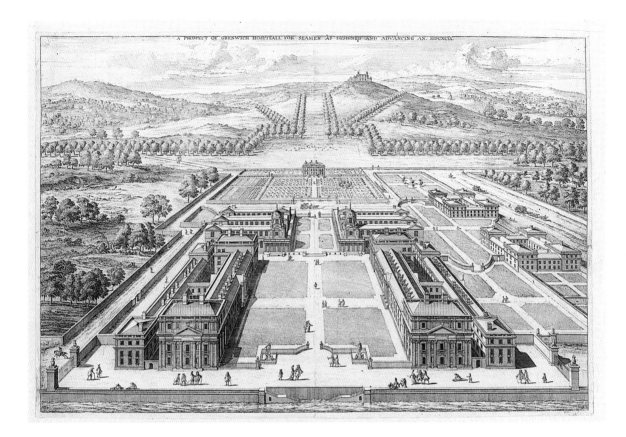

victualling. This created the concept of the national debt, and providing ways of deferring the cost of the war by issuing bills, so that it was not necessary to go to parliament for every new requirement. Among the initial investors was Samuel Jeake, who had feared the French invasion of Rye. He put in the substantial sum of £500. He was joined by people of all classes, starting with the King and Queen with £10,000, down to bricklayers and domestic servants.

Whole industries expanded to support the navy, which grew from 109 to 176 major ships during the war, despite many losses. Apart from shipbuilding itself they included timber supply, iron working, cannon casting and the supply of food. A typical warship required five tons of iron nails, and Ambrose Crowley set up a business on Tyneside to supply many of them, using an early form of mass production.

Food was just as important. By orders of 1701, each seaman was entitled daily to 'One pound of good sound, clean, well bolted with a horse-cloth, well baked and well conditioned wheaten biscuit'. On two days a week he was allowed 'Two pounds of beef, killed and made up with salt in England, of a well fed ox', and on two others he had 'one pound of bacon or salted English pork, of a well fed hog weighing not less than ¾cwt., and a pint of peas, Winchester measure'. On other days he was entitled to 'an eight part of a full-sized North Sea cod 24 inches long' as well as 'two ounces of butter and four ounces of Suffolk cheese (or two-thirds of that quantity of Cheshire cheese)'. There were various substitutions for foreign service; for example rusk instead of biscuit, rice instead of fish, and olive oil in place of butter or cheese. He was given a full gallon of beer per day, or half a pint of brandy if it was not available.[5]

No Man can have greater Contempt for Death, for every Day he constantly shits upon his own

*Grave, and dreads a Storm no more, than he
does a broken Head, when drunk. He has met so
many Escapes, that his Mind is grown as callous
as his Palms, and dreams no more that he shall
be drown'd, than be damn'd; and yet he may
meet with both, when he least thinks on't.*

*He looks then most formidable, when others
would appear most drooping; for see him in
bad Weather, in his Fur-cap and whapping
large Watch-coat, and you'd swear the Czar
was returned once more from Muscovy; yet he's
never in his true Figure, but within pitch'd
Jacket, and then he's invulnerable to a Cudgel,
as a hog in Armour.*[6]

In 1697 a peace treaty was agreed with France,
accepting William III as King of England and Scotland.
Since then the war of 1688–97 has attracted little attention from artists and writers. There were few memoirs
written from the sea, the characters are unattractive
and the ships were ungainly, being less beautiful than
those of Charles II and less nimble than those that

came after them. Even historians cannot agree about
what the war should be called – King William's War,
the Nine Years War, the War of the League of Augsburg
and the War of English Succession are among the alternatives. Yet the war set the pattern for a century of
conflict against France. It produced two of the most
famous phrases in naval strategy – fleet in being and
guerre de course – though both of these were to be
used mainly by Britain's enemies.

The war also produced perhaps the most notable
and lasting monument to British maritime aspira-
tions, in Sir Christopher Wren's Naval Hospital at
Greenwich. The story began in 1692 when Queen
Mary became distressed about the condition of
seamen discharged from the fleet. She gave over a
large tract of royal land at Greenwich where King
Charles had already built one block, and she commissioned Sir Christopher Wren to build a 'hospital' (or
hostel in modern terms) for them. It took half a

THESE PAGES Thomas Kip's aerial view of Greenwich Hospital of
1699 based on Sir Christopher Wren's plans, and the buildings
today, with a view towards the Queen's House.

Navigation

Early sailors carried knowledge of coastlines, landmarks, shoals and rocks in their heads, like Chaucer's shipman from around 1400.

> He knew all the havens, as they were,
> From Gotland to the Cape of Finisterre,
> And every creek in Britanny and in Spain

This is pilotage, still used in local situations today.

From about 1400 the navigator had the compass to give direction, though it did not point directly at the North Pole but at a variable point known as magnetic north. A navigator found the speed of his ship by throwing over the stern a wooden log attached to a line of knots, and measuring the number of knots that passed in a given time. Several factors – tide, leeway, direction and distance travelled – were used to calculate the ship's position. Each practice was subject to errors that might put the ship many miles off track, so the navigator always had a tense moment as land was sighted on the other side.

Since ancient times navigators have used the stars and governments heavily funded astronomy. Charles II set up the Royal Observatory at Greenwich in 1675 under John Flamsteed, who had instructions to 'apply himself with the most exact care and diligence to rectifying the tables of the motions of the heavens, and the places of the fixed stars, so as to find out the so much desired longitude of places for the perfecting of the art of navigation'.

Any sailor in the northern hemisphere can use the Pole Star to find North. Apart from that, he relies on a clear view of both the body in question and the horizon. Any measurement from a single star will put the ship on a particular circle on the earth's surface. The navigator needs at least two to show where they cross, and preferably three to check the readings.

The ancient cross-staff was simply a piece of wood that moved along a rod, graduated in degrees. The navigator pointed the rod at the horizon and moved the wood until its upper end was in line with the star or planet, giving a reading on the rod. The quadrant was a sector of a circle made in brass, with a weighted line hung from its apex. The operator pointed one edge at the star, looking through pin holes, and took a reading where the line fell in the scale. It was impossible to look directly at the sun for more than a second or two so the astrolabe was developed, a heavy brass dial marked with a scale and hung from the hand. Two holes on a swivel were lined up on the sun and could be checked by the shadow falling on the deck. The angle was then read off on the scale. With the backstaff or English quadrant the observer had his back to the sun and used the fall of shadow on the instrument to measure the angle.

The breakthrough came with the invention of the octant by John Hadley in 1731. It used mirrors to increase the angle it could cover and coloured glass to protect the eye. The sextant improved on the octant. It was made of brass and incorporated a Vernier scale for more accurate measurements – an almost perfect design, which has changed little to the present day.

Latitude was quite easy to find by measuring the angle of the sun above the horizon at noon but longitude is related to the movement of the earth and therefore the time. After the loss of Sir Cloudesley Shovell's fleet on the Scilly Isles in 1707, the Board of Longitude offered a prize of £20,000 for discovering a means of measuring it. Proposals included lightships across the oceans, and even barking dogs.

John Harrison, a Yorkshire carpenter, designed a clock that was accurate to seconds over a period of months, which could stand the stresses of the sea and could compensate for changes in temperature around the world. His first chronometer, known as H1, was ready by

1735 but he was only paid £500 to continue development. After various tribulations H4 was successfully tested on a journey across the Atlantic in 1764, but the board imposed further conditions and it took a special Act of Parliament for him to get his final payment, three years before his death in 1776.

OPPOSITE Navigational instruments on the *Matthew* replica include the log and line and sandglass.

ABOVE AND BELOW The sextant is an important instrument still used today.

The GREENWICH PENSIONER.
By Mr.DIBDIN

'Twas in the good ship Rover, | That time-bound strut to Portugal, | Neat in a Frigate sailing | Yet still I am enabled
I sail'd the World around, | Right fore and aft we bore; | Upon a squally night, | To bring up in life's rear,
And for three years and over, | But, when we made Cape Ortugal, | Thunder and lightening hailing | Altho' I'm quite disabled,
I ne'er touch'd British ground | A gale blew off the shore, | The horrors of the fight. | And lie in Greenwich tier.
At last in England landed. | She lay, as it did shock her, | My precious limb was lopped off. | The King, God bless his royalty,
I left the roaring main; | A log upon the main, | I when they'd eased my pain, | Who saved me from the main.
Found all relations stranded, | Till saved from Davy's locker. | Thank'd God I was not peppo'd off. | I'll praise with love and loyalty,
And went to Sea again. | We put to Sea again. | And went to Sea again. | But ne'er to Sea again.

Published by N. Carpenter & Spencer &c. Soho

century to build, continuing long after Mary's death in 1694, but ended up as 'the most stately procession of buildings we possess.'[7] The great Painted Hall, not normally open to the naval pensioners, took its name from the triumphalist pieces by Sir James Thornhill. King William is shown in the centre, having defeated Louis XIV and brought peace and prosperity to Europe. That was a little premature in the 1690s, though the hall was not to be finished until 1726 when the claim made more sense. The hall was reminiscent of the Sistine Chapel, and in a sense it proclaimed Britain's new cult of sea power.

Of course great architecture alone could not solve all the seamen's problems, and Thornhill's paintings were above their heads both literally and figuratively. They were still subject to the press gang and oppressed in many other ways, and the situation would only get worse over the next century or so. They were prone to mutiny and desertion, but remained highly dedicated and professional at sea and in battle – perhaps the greatest asset that the British empire possessed.

During the peace William Dampier, an unusual combination of pirate and scientist, was put in command of the *Roebuck* and sent to the South Pacific on the first truly scientific voyage of exploration. He lost his ship but arrived back in an East Indiaman with many plant specimens, and the news of several important discoveries.

King William died in 1702 and was succeeded by his sister-in-law Anne, just as another war with France was in prospect. The feeble-minded King Charles II of Spain had died after a surprisingly long life for one in his condition in those days, and the French wanted to enforce the claim of the Bourbon candidate for the throne. The war opened with an echo of the gentleman and tarpaulins controversy – between upper-class officers and those of humble origins – in a notorious action in the Caribbean, when Admiral Benbow pursued a small French squadron over six days. At least four of his six captains let him down, possibly because of class resentment over the admiral's humble origins. Captain Richard Kirkby was well known as a bully and a coward and his own boatswain testified of him,

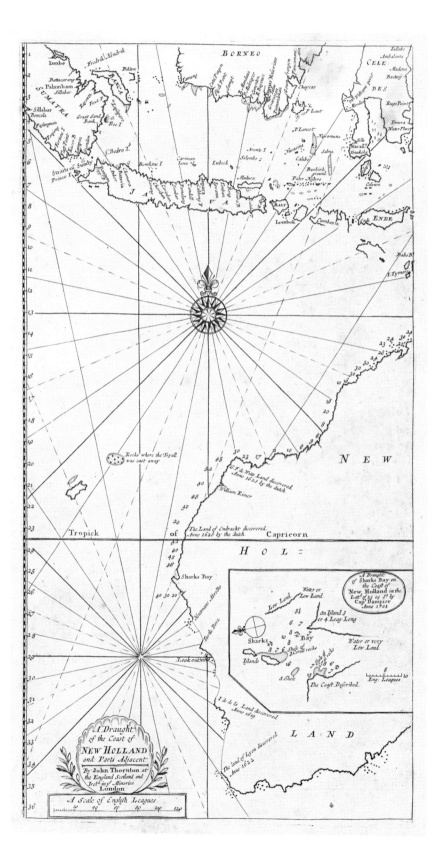

OPPOSITE A Greenwich pensioner in the late eighteenth century, to illustrate Charles Dibdin's popular song, with a rather crude view of the hospital across the river.

LEFT William Dampier had already made a name for himself with a published account of an earlier circumnavigation. During his voyage in the *Roebuck* he reached the north west coast of Australia and created this chart, including Borneo, Java and Sumatra, and (inset) Sharks Bay, which he named.

... during the whole time of the engagement, he did not know of any encouragement his Captain gave to any of his men, but the contrary rather from his own pusillanimity by walking and dodging behind the mizzen mast and falling down upon deck ...

Of Captain Cooper Wade it was said that,

... during the six days' engagement he never kept the line of battle, fired all his shot in vain and not reaching half way to the enemy, that he was often told the same by his Lieutenant and other officers, that notwithstanding he commanded them to fire saying they must do so or the Admiral would not believe they fought if they did not continue their fire, that during the fight they were engaged in, the said Captain Wade received but one shot from the enemy, that he was in [drink] the greatest part of the time of action ...[8]

Kirkby and Wade were tried and executed for their cowardice; Benbow died of his wounds and became a folk-hero in story and song.

But the war was less maritime than its predecessors. For once Britain had developed an efficient army under the Duke of Marlborough and he won four great battles against the French and their allies, beginning with Blenheim in 1704. At sea, Admiral Rooke set out to take Cadiz, but found it too risky. At a council of war off Morocco in July 1704, it was decided to attack Gibraltar, where the garrison was known to be very weak. There was a fearsome bombardment: '... our fifteen Sail poured in their Shot in such a degree as made the Houses shake, and I believe our Hearts quaked as much as the Houses shaked.'[9] Marines were landed, there was confusion when a magazine was detonated by accident, but the garrison surrendered.

The French fleet came out to contest the capture, and the two forces met on 13 August off Malaga. The French employed galleys in battle, mainly for towing

ships disabled for lack of wind. Edward Bishop describes the action as seen from the decks.

We were closely engaged, and for my part I loaded twelve times the eleventh gun, in steering [steerage?] on the starboard quarter. And would have loaded more, had I not been prevented, by a cannon ball which cut the powder boy almost in two, and I thought had taken my arm off ... I went down to the doctor and he put a red plaister to it, and would have had me to have staid below; but I said I would go up and see how my comrades sped, and do all I could as long as I had hand or leg to support myself. When I came up I found four of those I had left killed, and another wounded.[10]

By nightfall, both fleets had suffered considerable damage, but no ships were sunk or captured. Rooke had used up nearly all his ammunition and was desperately distributing what remained among his ships. The French gained the advantage when the wind shifted, but used it to slip away leaving the British in control. The French navy did not leave Toulon in force again.

Naval power was a major factor in the Union of Scotland and England, to create the United Kingdom in 1707. Scotland had maintained a tiny navy of three 20-gun ships to protect her commerce against French privateers, but it was clearly inadequate. The country had become well aware of the vast profits the English were making from their empire, and had tried to set up its own colony in Central America. Without naval support Darien soon foundered disastrously and the Scots had to find other ways. In 1707, with the promise of a share in England's empire, the Scots reluctantly agreed to the union of their parliament with England's – 'The end of an auld sang'. It has been described as 'a political necessity for England, a commercial necessity for Scotland.'[11] One opponent of the union had predicted, 'I think I see our Mariners delivering up their Ships to their Dutch Partners; and what through presses and necessity, earning their Bread as Underlings in the Royal English Navy.'[12] But in fact the Scots were to do very well in the Royal Navy, as they did in the empire.

In the spring of 1707 the allies attempted unsuccessfully to take the French base at Toulon. Admiral Sir Cloudesley Shovell was returning home from this with a fleet of 19 ships when in the haze he misjudged the longitude. It was too late when St Agnes Light on the Scilly Isles was sighted, and three ships, including Shovell's flagship the *Association*, were wrecked with the loss of more than 1,300 men. Shovell himself struggled ashore but was clubbed to death by a woman who stole his ring. The disaster had a positive effect, in that it showed the need for a reliable means of determining longitude. The Board of Longitude was set up by an act of 1714, inspired by the Cambridge mathematician William Whitson.

Gibraltar was useful as a post for guarding the entrance to the Mediterranean, but it had a poor harbour, open to southerly winds, and could provide no supplies for a fleet. Admiral Sir John Leake and General Stanhope paid attention in 1708 when they heard that the troops on Minorca were prepared to support Charles III. The island was much closer to the French base at Toulon, and it had one of the best natural harbours in the world. It was clear that possession of Minorca would allow a British fleet to operate full time in the Mediterranean, instead of going home every winter. Troops were duly landed but a thousand French and Spanish held Fort San Felipe, guarding the entrance to the main harbour at Mahon. The island had virtually no roads at the time, so sailors landed more than 50 heavy guns on a cove near the fort and they were dragged into position. The enemy surrendered after a heavy bombardment.

By the end of the war in 1714, the Royal Navy had begun to take on some of the trappings of a permanent force, for its officers at least. Commissioned officers were allowed half pay when they were not employed afloat, which was to become quite common during the next 25 years of relative peace.

ABOVE The chronometer K1, produced by Larcum Kendall, was a copy of Harrison's H4 and went on James Cook's second expedition in 1772–5.

The conflict became known as the War of Spanish Succession and if that is an accurate title, then the British had failed, for by the Treaty of Utrecht which ended the war, the Bourbon candidate took over the throne of Spain. But in fact the British had gained much, and Spain was gravely weakened from the great power of a century ago. Outlying parts of the Spanish empire in Europe were detached and her king had to renounce any claim to the French throne. Britain's ally Portugal was confirmed in her possession of Brazil. The British had gained in many other ways, in North America and in taking and holding Gibraltar and Minorca, which were their first overseas bases in Europe. They gained a foothold in the Spanish empire, which they believed to be immensely rich, by means of the *Asiento* or contract to supply slaves. They had fought no conclusive fleet battles, but had gained enormous confidence in their naval superiority. The next 50 years would show how justified that was.

A Sailor's Rations

In Episode 2, Dan Snow went on board the square-rigger *Phoenix*. He got a taste of the sailor's rations and, while working on the vessel, appreciated how much physical effort was required to sail a ship effectively.

The navy seaman's diet gave him about 5,000 calories a day. One of the staples was salted meat, typically beef, which would generally be eaten in some kind of stew with suet. 'If you think salty boot leather, that's about right.' The other staple was ship's biscuit, a bread substitute, that was rock hard. 'An added complication was that this became a home for little weevils … some people liked to bang them until the weevils fell out … others used to go into a dark corner and simply eat the biscuit, weevils and all.'

The most dangerous disease at sea was scurvy, caused by a lack of vitamin C, which became ever more common as ships sailed further across the ocean. The worst was on Anson's voyage of 1740–44 when 1,051 men, more than half of those who set out, died from it. Those who survived would spend the rest of their lives without teeth or hair. It was obvious that lack of contact with the shore was a factor, but apart from that doctors of the age did not know what caused it.

Dr James Lind was the first to get on the right track. Though it was a matter of centuries before vitamins were fully understood, Lind discovered, by observing cases at Haslar Hospital near Portsmouth, that fresh fruit would cure it. The difficulty was to ensure that supplies were available at sea. On his first voyage in 1768–71, James Cook carried 'portable' or condensed soup and sauerkraut, which had remarkably positive results. As Physician to the fleet in the West Indies in the American War of Independence, Dr Gilbert Blane issued fruit juice to crews. Lemon juice became common during the wars against revolutionary France and lime juice was later subsituted for cheapness.

S^r HEN MORGAN

Part. 2 Page. 60

Chapter 6
STABILITY AND STAGNATION

Several things happened to change the world at the same time as the Treaty of Utrecht came into effect in 1714. Louis XIV, the most ambitious of all France's kings, died. So did Queen Anne of England. The Elector of Hanover was invited to take the British throne as George I. He was not an attractive man and his accession inspired a Jacobite revolt. It started in Scotland, partly because the navy was weakest there. The Jacobites captured a ship loaded with guns in the Firth of Forth, then crossed the estuary in fishing boats. Meanwhile James Stuart, son of James II, was blockaded in St-Malo so he and his party, improbably dressed as seamen, had to travel by road to Dunkirk from where they sailed to Peterhead. Thus James, according to *1066 and All That*, was 'late for his own rebellion' and cut a sorry figure among the rebels, who became isolated and mostly went into exile.

After a century of turmoil and civil war, British political leaders craved stability. The constitution, as established in the 'Glorious Revolution' of 1688, was seen as sacrosanct and decisions were usually based on precedent dating from that period. There was one extremely radical innovation: Sir Robert Walpole took on much of the work of the King, who had little interest in British affairs. But the effect of this was concealed, and the title of 'prime minister' was never used except by his opponents.

After the peace of 1714 the conditions were ripe for piracy, which enjoyed its 'golden age'. There was great wealth travelling across the seas in the form of gold, silver, slaves, spices, sugar, furs and tobacco. Navies had been paid off and the post-war trade boom was very short, so there were thousands of seamen, mostly skilled in fighting, who could not find

ABOVE A medal commemorating Robert Louis Stevenson's *Treasure Island*, and its most famous character, Long John Silver. The book was first published in 1883, and contributed greatly to the piracy myth, which survives to this day.

regular work. Many pirates were ex-privateers who had their livelihood suddenly removed. Captain Benjamin Hornigold announced that he had not been consulted about the peace treaty and continued as if the war was still on, refusing to attack British and Dutch ships until he was overthrown by his multi-national crew. There were competing sovereignties on the seas as the Spanish, Portuguese, French, Dutch and British controlled different parts of the Caribbean and the West African coast where piracy was rife, and none of these nations had the resources to patrol its empire adequately. It is estimated that about 2,000 pirates were operating at any given moment in the years after 1715, while the Royal Navy had a total strength of 13,000 men, with many other commitments.

The navy itself had been much closer to piracy in the past. Hawkins and Drake were numbered among its founders and heroes but had never shaken off their buccaneering past. Henry Morgan had captured Portobello in Panama as a pirate in 1671 but was later knighted and became deputy governor of Jamaica.

But now the British were the masters of the seas, and had most to lose from piracy. The Royal Navy had finally developed into an organisation with a formal career structure and a good deal of social status among its officers, and it needed to leave this past behind. The slave trade had always been close to piracy, as in the days of Drake and Hawkins, but the *Asiento* with the Spanish turned it into big business. Humphrey Morice, a governor of the Bank of England and Member of Parliament, was the principal merchant in the trade and led the campaign for the navy to do something about pirates – at that point the public did not know that he was defrauding the Bank out of £29,000. The colonies on the eastern seaboard of North America were highly vulnerable. In 1717 Captain Edward Teach, the infamous Blackbeard, blockaded Charleston and placed the port 'in great terror', and later the trade of Philadelphia was halted for a week. The colonists complained, 'except effectual measures are taken the whole trade of America must soon be ruined'. It is estimated that around two thousand vessels were attacked in the ten years or so after the Treaty of Utrecht, as much as in a major war.

Pirate ships are unusual in that they exist to serve the interests of the crew, rather than ship owners, merchants or a government ashore. They share that feature with modern yachts, and in a sense they have a similar kind of organisation. In a well-run yacht the crew might set the aims of the voyage but accept the skipper's authority at sea. In a pirate ship the crew was represented by the quartermaster, and major decisions were taken by a vote. But the captain's word was law 'in fighting, chased or being chased'. The pirates gained a certain amount of romance as an alternative idea of authority to the conventional Georgian one, but in no sense were they a Marxist proletariat. For one thing, they did not produce anything, and indeed they often destroyed wantonly. And there were never likely to be nearly enough of them to take over society as a whole. Some of them were capable of savage cruelty. Bartholomew Roberts' men once burned a

ABOVE Alexander Selkirk was marooned at his own request on the Pacific island of Juan Fernandez by William Dampier, and spent more than four years alone there before being rescued, as this contemporary illustration shows. His story was taken up by Daniel Defoe and made into a novel, *Robinson Crusoe*.

slave ship with the captives still on board, because the owners refused to pay a ransom.

The decline of the pirates began in 1718 when the privateer Woodes Rogers was appointed Governor of the Bahamas with orders to put down piracy by any means necessary. He was welcomed by the inhabitants, many of them ex-pirates who wanted a more stable lifestyle. He issued pardons to those who would reform, and all except Blackbeard and Edward Vane agreed to this. When some of them reverted to piracy, they were tried and hanged. The pirates had lost a base and many of them transferred to the other side of the Atlantic, where the slave trade offered possibilities of ransom, and slave ships could easily be converted into pirate ships. Captain Chalenor Ogle took His Majesty's ships *Swallow* and *Weasel* to the West African coast in 1721 and came up against the pirate captain Bartholomew Roberts, who had recently added 10 more prizes to his total of 400. Posing as merchantmen, Ogle's ships were attacked in turn by the *Ranger* and the *Royal Fortune*. Naval gunnery prevailed in both cases and the pirate ships were captured. Out of 262 prisoners, the Africans were sold into slavery and most of the rest were tried in the confines of Cape Coast Castle. Fifty-two were hanged including Roberts, whose motto was 'a merry life and a short one'. Ogle went home and was knighted. It was not the end of piracy but it was no longer a major threat to commerce and colonisation. According to a modern historian, 'The defeat of Roberts and the subsequent eradication of piracy off the coast of Africa represented a turning point in the slave trade and even in the larger history of capitalism.'[13] Rather like their contemporaries the Jacobites, the pirates were more successful in capturing the popular imagination of later generations than they had been in their own time.

The sea contributed to literature, for shipwreck was a main theme of both *Gulliver's Travels* and *Robinson Crusoe*, while the novelist Tobias Smollett (1721–71) served as a naval surgeon. Marine art was born in this period. In the 1670s the Van de Veldes, father and son, had come over from the Netherlands to work for Charles II, but at first native followers, such as Isaac Sailmaker and his school, had little understanding of perspective. Peter Monamy from Jersey started by copying the Van de Veldes, while Samuel Scott was best known for his views of the Thames, inspired by Canaletto. John Cleveley painted scenes in the dockyards and shipyards of the same river, and founded a dynasty of marine painters. Charles Brooking learned the technical part of his trade from his father who was a painter and decorator in Greenwich Hospital. He produced some precocious work by the age of 17 in 1740. These artists were best known for peaceful scenes, filled with a lively wind in Brookings' case.

As the main pillar of Georgian society, the navy reflected it as well as making it possible. It protected the trade and defended the colonies which fuelled economic growth. The profits funded an age of great architecture, and the navy put up many fine buildings for itself during the eighteenth century, including the screen to the Admiralty Building in Whitehall, designed by John Nash to keep out rioting seamen, and the Commissioner's House in Chatham Dockyard, decorated with a painting that had originally dominated the cabin of the 100-gun *Royal Sovereign*. The grand architecture of the Royal Dockyards was largely unknown to the public until at least the 1970s.

The Royal Navy regarded itself as all-conquering even though it had not been seriously challenged since Beachy Head in 1690, and 'Rule Britannia' was first sung in 1740. In the 1720s and '30s there seemed to be no reason to alter any of the navy's practices,

which became frozen. This was especially true of ship design. By now there were three-decker ships of the line of 100, 90 and 80 guns, two-deckers of 70, 60 and 50, and single-deckers of 20 guns, though the 30-gun ship was phased out to disturb the symmetry slightly. Within each group, the smallest ships were the problem. The 80s were notoriously unstable, the 50s were too weak to stand in the line of battle, and the 20s were too small to carry a serious armament. But the Admiralty had no new ideas on ship design. If a ship was lost, another of the same type was ordered in its place. If it was old and decayed it was 'rebuilt'. Originally this meant that a substantial part of the old structure was re-used, but by 1720 it was quite common for a ship to be rebuilt using little or none of the old timber. Shipbuilding was controlled by the 'establishment of dimensions', descended from the rules Pepys had laid down for building the thirty ships of 1677. By 1706 there were detailed rules in place for each class of ship, down to the dimensions of the hatchways and even the coamings that surrounded them to prevent seamen stumbling down. What had begun as a sensible means of standardisation had become obsessive and restrictive. Small amendments were made to the establishments in 1719 and 1733 and that, along with gradual replacement of the 50-gun ship with the 60, was the only perceptible change in ship design.

Across the Channel the French navy began to revive, and it was able to do so with a clean sheet. The 22-year-old Comte de Maurepas took charge. He had a reputation as a playboy who 'did not know the colour of the sea or how a ship was built' but began a new shipbuilding programme that made the best use of limited budgets. He knew that the French would never again challenge the Royal Navy in terms of numbers, so he developed the doctrine of 'the mission'. Instead of seeking to control the seas or destroy the enemy fleet as the British tended to do, the French ships would set out with a particular task: to take a distant colony, bring in a vital convoy, support a rebellion in Scotland or Ireland or even

ABOVE 'An English Squadron Going to Windward', by Charles Brooking. During a short life of 36 years, he produced some of the finest of all seascapes.

attempt an invasion of England if local superiority could be gained. Even the threat of these things could cause the British to divert resources from elsewhere.

Like the weaker navy throughout the ages, the French were able to concentrate on the quality of individual ships rather than the overall numbers. Compared with the restrictive establishments that tied the hands of the British builders, French shipwrights like Blaise Ollivier and Pierre Morineau were given free rein. It was an age of relatively static technology and they produced no radically new ideas,

but they evolved the ideal sizes of ships for the line of battle and for cruising. They built no three-deckers, but developed the single-decker frigate and a vessel that would come to dominate the world's battle-fleets, the 74-gun ship of the line.

The strength of a naval tradition can be measured by how well it survives in peacetime, when there is no immediate enemy or threat. In that sense,

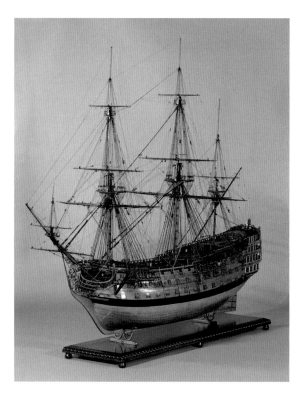

ABOVE A model of the 100-gun *Victory* of 1737, the largest ship of the day, possibly made for the Admiralty boardroom. The ship was lost with all hands in 1744.

BELOW A Navy Board-style model of the *Lowestoft*, a 20-gun ship of 1723. Ships of this type could be rowed on occasion, hence the row of small ports along the centre.

the early Georgian navy was quite successful. King George I and his son George II, who ruled from 1727 to 1760, had comparatively little interest in the sea apart from the route to their other kingdom of Hanover, while Sir Robert Walpole stood for economy and peace. But the public had come to love its navy and relish its traditions. The active fleet was reduced from 40,000 men to around 10,000 during the long peace, and ships were laid up 'in ordinary', in care and maintenance and more or less ready for any future action. Naval officers were retained on half pay, ready to be recalled if needed. There was no permanent reserve of men, except the whole of the merchant fleet, which was carefully fostered as a 'nursery of seamen'. The early Georgian navy was complacent and blinkered, but it was never likely to fall into decay as Charles II's fleet had done during the political crisis of his reign.

The years between 1714 and 1739 were not completely peaceful and there were two brief wars with Spain in 1718–19 and in 1726–7. Both were settled very quickly due to the poor state of the Spanish navy. On 11 August 1718 Admiral Sir George Byng met a Spanish fleet off Cape Passero in Sicily and captured or burned most of them. Captain George Walton was responsible for some of the captures. In

Wooden Shipbuilding

In the traditional method of shipbuilding, almost the whole hull was made from wood: elm for the keel and oak preferred for the remainder. Large ships were built in dry docks, others on building slips where they were angled slightly so they could slide into the water when launched.

The first stage was to lay the keel, which was long and straight and usually made out of several sections joined by scarphs. The curved stem post, rising ahead of it, would support the knee of the head, the decorative head rails and the figurehead. At the after end of the keel was the sternpost, straight and slightly angled to the vertical so that it could support the rudder.

The frames or ribs that made up the basic shape of the ship were each made in several sections known as floor timbers, futtocks and toptimbers. After about 1815 they were usually fitted together in pairs, with the joins of one arranged so that it overlapped with the adjacent one. Each gunport had a wooden sill at its top and bottom, and further frame timbers were added between them to make a structure that was about two-thirds solid before it was planked. Most of the structure was held together with wooden pegs known as trenails, except for key areas where metal was used. Towards the bow the timbers were canted increasingly forward, until those furthest forward which ran parallel to the keel and were known as hawse pieces. At the stern the main part of the lower structure was made up of horizontal timbers known as transoms;

above that, the structure was very light and was a noted weak point in battle.

Strong deck beams were placed between the frames, to support the guns and help brace the structure. The beams were held in place by L-shaped knees where they met the sides, and were supplemented by lighter pieces known as carlines and ledges, so that a gun could operate anywhere on the deck. The outside hull had heavier planks known as wales just under the levels of the gunports, while the underwater planking was trimmed as smooth as possible using an adze. Inside, there

were thick planks over the joins of the futtocks and under the deck beams. There was a strong internal structure over that, formed of riders and breast hooks. When the woodwork of the hull was finished the gaps between the planks were caulked by filling them with oakum and tar.

By the early 1800s, as ships saw much greater service in the open sea, Robert Seppings of Chatham Dockyard became aware that all the pieces in the

structure were at right angles to one another, ignoring the principle 'known to the meanest mechanic' that a triangle is much more rigid than a square. He developed a new method of construction based on diagonal bracing in place of the old riders, but with many other features that made the ship stronger, which allowed the building of larger ships.

BELOW The stern of a model of a 64-gun of about 1770, which was made to show the principles of shipbuilding to George III. Many of the timbers are marked with their names.

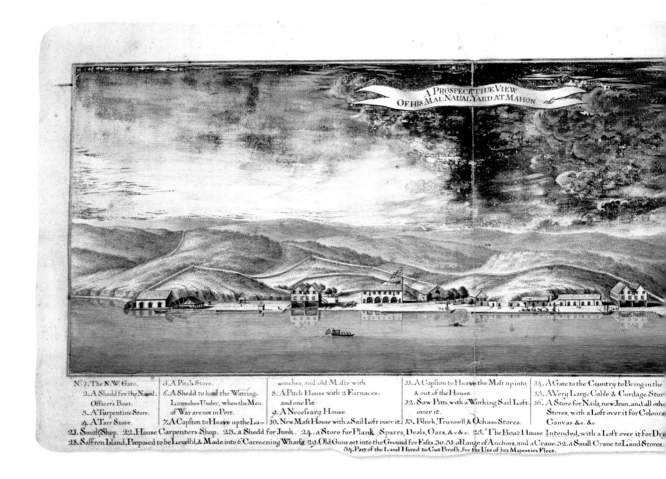

A PROSPECT TIUE VIEW OF HIS MAI. NAUAL YARD AT MAHON.

N° 1. The N.W. Gate.	5. A Pitch Store.	...unches, and old Masts with	11. A Capston to Heave the Mast up into,	34. A Gate to the Country to Bring in the
2. A Shedd for the Naual.	6. A Shedd to hauſ the Watring.	8. A Pitch House with 2 Furnaces.	& out of the House.	35. A Very Large Cable & Cordage Stor
Officer's Boat.	Launches Under, when the Men.	and one Pot.	12. Saw Pitts, with a Working Sail Loft.	36. A Store for Nails, new Iron, and all othe
5. A Turpentine Store.	of War are not in Port.	9. A Necessary House.	over it.	Stores, with a Loft over it for Colours
4. A Tarr Store.	7. A Capston to Heave up the La=	10. New Mast House with a Sail Loft over it	13. Block, Trunnell & Ocham Stores.	Canvas &c. &c.

21. Smith Shop. 22. House Carpenters Shop. 23. a Shedd for Junk. 24. a Store for Plank, Sparrs, Deals, Oars, & c&c. 25. The Boat House Intended, with a Loft over it for Dry
28. Saffron Island, Proposed to be Leuell'd, & Made into 6 Carreening Wharfs. 29. Old Guns set into the Ground for Fasts. 50.51. a Range of Anchors, and a Crane. 52. a Small Crane to Land Stores.
54. Part of the Land Hired to Cut Brush, for the Use of his Majesties Fleet.

ABOVE The naval dockyard in Minorca around 1730, as seen from the town of Mahon across the harbour. The rock to the right was eventually levelled to produce Saffron Island.

an age of long-winded letters and convoluted sentences, he gained fame by his dispatch, 'We have taken and destroyed all the enemy's ships upon this coast, the number as per margin.'

As the threat of war in Europe lessened, the importance of trade with the empire increased. The navy devoted a good deal of its resources to its overseas bases so that it could operate permanent fleets in the Mediterranean and Caribbean without having to send ships home for repair or withdraw during the winter or the hurricane season. In the Mediterranean, Minorca had an excellent natural harbour at Mahon and was less than 250 miles from the great French base at Toulon. Fort St Philip at the harbour mouth was greatly strengthened, though in an elementary mistake the local population was allowed to build its houses too close. A naval hospital was built and Saffron Island, opposite the town of Mahon, was flattened and developed as a place for careening – hauling ships down on one side or the other so that their bottoms could be cleaned. The beautiful harbour of Mahon still bears many of the marks of British occupation today. English Harbour in Antigua in the West Indies offered all-round protection against hurricanes, while other anchorages such as Carlisle Bay in Barbados and Prince Rupert's Bay in Dominica were only protected against the prevailing trade winds. Careening was also made possible there, along with anchor shops, boat stores, rigging houses and all the necessities of naval maintenance.

37. A Shedd for old Rope, Paper Stuff, Hammocks,
    & Rotten Raggs of Sails.
38. A Gate into a yard, that Contains Bricks, Tyles, Lime
    and all Necessary Utensils of the Masons.
39. A Watch & Guard House. 20: Braziers Shop.
26: a Necessary House. 27: The S.E. Gate of the Yard.
Wall 6' Feet High, Round the yard from the NW to y.e S.E. Gates.

RIGHT Richard Glover's poem of 1739 is
illustrated by the ghosts of Hosier and his
men rising to haunt a new British
expedition to the Caribbean.

Scurvy was becoming an increasing problem as voyages became longer, but for the moment the most dramatic loss of men was through fever, especially in the West Indies. In 1726 Rear-Admiral Francis Hosier sailed to Portobello with a squadron of five ships manned by nearly two thousand sailors. They were already weakened by scurvy when yellow fever came on board, and more men died than the original complements of the ships, as replacements were found in Jamaica. Hosier himself died and the affair was commemorated in a melancholy ditty, still popular with seamen in the following century.

See these mournful spectres sweeping
Ghastly o'er this hated wave
Whose wan cheeks are stained with weeping;
These were English captains brave.
Mark those members pale and horrid
Who were once my sailors bold;
See, each hangs his drooping forehead,
While his dismal fate is told.[14]

Chapter 7
BROADENING HORIZONS

In 1738 Captain Robert Jenkins, formerly of the merchant brig *Rebecca*, was ordered to appear before a House of Commons committee investigating Spanish depredations in the Caribbean. In the event he never appeared, but his claim that he had been beaten and half-strangled by a Guard Costa officer who had cut off part of his ear captured the popular imagination. It fuelled a popular desire for war after a quarter century of near-peace. The public was convinced that there were rich pickings in the decaying Spanish empire and its legendary gold and silver mines. The Walpole government was reluctant to commit to an expensive operation it did not really believe in, and parliament was happy to fight it but less keen to pay for it – a situation reminiscent of 1664 and the disastrous Second Anglo-Dutch War. Parliament had its way and the 'War of Jenkins' Ear' was declared in October 1739. Walpole commented, 'They now ring the bells, but soon they will wring their hands.'

Among the most vocal advocates of war was Edward Vernon, a vice-admiral and Member of Parliament. He claimed that he could take the Spanish staging post of Portobello (in modern Venezuela) with ease, and indeed he took it in November, partly because the Spanish had allowed their powder to go damp. Vernon became a national hero, with towns and streets named after his victory. His next expedition was against Cartagena in Colombia and it turned into disaster as disease took hold among the sailors. The most lasting effect of the expedition was on the drinking habits of the navy and in a sense the nation. It had long been common to issue the local beverage to the crew, and rum was standard in the West Indies. Vernon insisted on diluting it, two parts water to one part rum, to reduce drunkenness, and it became known as 'grog' after the Admiral's

Edward Vernon (1684–1757)

Vernon was the son of an early newspaper editor and future secretary of state under William III. He entered the navy in 1700 as a volunteer in the flagship of Sir George Rooke and was rarely far from the leading admirals in his early career. He was with Cloudesley Shovell at the indecisive Battle of Malaga in 1704, and got his first command in 1706, serving under Shovell and Sir George Byng. In 1708 he was with the squadron under Byng that prevented a Jacobite expedition landing in Scotland, and had a share in the only ship captured. Later in the year he was based at Port Royal in Jamaica and

began to see how ineffective the Spanish were at sea, a conviction that would come to dominate his career. A very political officer, his Whig connections possibly counted against him during the latter years of Queen Anne's reign, but after the accession of George I he took part in a diplomatic mission to Turkey. During the war with Spain in 1718–20 he took command at Jamaica and fought three Spanish ships of superior force, but he was never to take part in a major fleet battle.

Vernon entered parliament in 1722 for the borough of Penryn in Cornwall, one of several controlled by Viscount Falmouth. He was a strong Whig and when the King died in 1727, he was sent home from the Baltic with a loyal address to the new king, George II, from the fleet. He became an increasingly outspoken critic of the government's sterile naval policy.

When most of Admiral Hosier's men died of fever in the West Indies, Vernon claimed that it was not necessary to blockade Spanish ports; it was far simpler to attack them direct. He claimed that he could take the Spanish trading post of Portobello with three hundred men. He spent most of the 1730s on his estate at Nacton in Suffolk, but when war threatened with Spain again in 1738 he was prominent among its advocates. He had already served several times in the West Indies and knew the region well, and was a dynamic commander. He was promoted to Vice Admiral and in November 1739 he took Portobello with six ships (rather than 300 hundred men) to become a national hero.

He remained in the West Indies but was far less successful in joint army–navy operations with General Thomas Wentworth. At first Wentworth deferred too much to Vernon's experience; then the Admiral went ahead in planning an attack on Cuba without reference to his general. Men began to die through disease in an echo of the Hosier affair, though he often refused to allow his seamen ashore.

Vernon came home late in 1742 and his popularity was still high, as no other naval hero had yet arisen to take his place. He took command of a force to prevent Jacobite supporters getting out of Flanders during the 1745 Rebellion, but his relations with the Admiralty deteriorated. He criticised many aspects of their policy, including inadequate ship design, especially the notorious 80-gun ships. Several pamphlets were published and he refused to say whether he had written them or not. As a result, he was unceremoniously struck off the list of flag officers. He remained active in parliamentary politics until his death in 1757, but the navy had no further use for him. He had been right about many things and assessed both the capabilities and weaknesses of the navy quite accurately, but as a naval hero he was eclipsed by others and his flamboyant style was often counter-productive.

ABOVE Edward Vernon, by the fashionable portrait painter Charles Phillips.

LEFT As well as the famous Portobello Road in London, Vernon's exploit also led to the naming of a resort near Edinburgh.

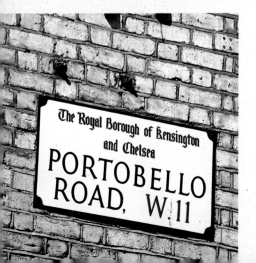

The Royal Borough of Kensington and Chelsea
PORTOBELLO ROAD, W.11

nickname: a notoriously scruffy admiral in the days before uniforms were established, he wore a cloak of grogram or grosgrain. Vernon went home to become an even more vocal and rather unstable critic of the naval administration.

On 19 September 1740 Commodore George Anson set off with five warships and two transports on a voyage that would highlight many of the navy's weaknesses. In the first place the concept was outdated: a raiding voyage against Spain on the model of Drake a century and a half ago. Secondly, the manning of the ships was very badly handled, despite the promise of great prize money. It was the task of the army to provide marines for the fleet, and they reasoned that they were simply soldiers who did not have to march, so they sent Chelsea pensioners. Most of them deserted as soon as possible, and none was to survive the voyage. The departure was delayed by administrative problems and the squadron was very late in rounding Cape Horn, a process that was filled with great hardship and disappointment. As the crew looked forward to 'the celebrated tranquility of the Pacifick Ocean',

> ... the next morning, between one and two, as we were standing to the northwards, and the weather, which until then had been hazy, accidentally cleared up, the Pink made a signal for seeing land right ahead; and it being but two miles distant, we were all under the most dreadful apprehensions of running on shore.[15]

In fact they had not succeeded in rounding the Horn, but had been driven back by contrary winds. After several more weeks they reached Juan Fernandez, where Alexander Selkirk had been marooned to give Defoe the idea for *Robinson Crusoe*. The other ships turned back, sank or were abandoned leaving only the flagship, the 60-gun *Centurion*. Even worse, the crews suffered terribly from scurvy. Nearly a thousand men had set off on the voyage, only 351 were left when Juan Fernandez was reached and after a second

outbreak only 71 men were fit for work.[16] Anson persevered, crossed the Pacific and captured a Spanish treasure galleon off Manila. He returned home after a four-year circumnavigation.

It took 32 wagons to carry the treasure from Portsmouth to the Tower of London. The chaplain of the *Centurion*, Richard Walter, published an account of the voyage which remained a bestseller for many years. Anson became a rich man, the son-in-law of the powerful Lord Chancellor, a Baron and a reforming member of the Board of Admiralty, where his effects were to be felt for decades to come.

In fleet battle, naval tactics relied far too heavily on the Fighting Instructions drawn up by the Generals-at-Sea 90 years earlier. A few additional instructions were added over the years, but there was a great lack of tactical flexibility. In February 1744, while Britain was at war with Spain but not France, Admiral Thomas Mathews was patrolling off Toulon when he encountered a Franco-Spanish fleet. He decided to engage but the squadron led by his second-in-command, Admiral Lestock, did not support him and only one Spanish ship was captured. A series of courts martial ensued, in which Lestock defended himself by claiming that Mathews had not formed a proper line of battle as demanded by the Fighting Instructions. As a result, Mathews was dismissed from the service and caution was established as the main naval principle.

The faults of British ships became clear as early as April 1740, when three 70-gun ships engaged the Spanish *Princessa* of nominally equal force but much greater dimensions, and took six hours to defeat her. The 70s were simply too small for the work they had to do, for they now had to fight across the oceans rather than just the North Sea and the Mediterranean. The problem with the three-decker 80s was far more serious; they were fundamentally unstable. Admiral Mathews pointed out that most of them could not open their lower gunports to deploy their heaviest armament. 'I have now but two ships of 90 and three of 80 guns that can make use of their lower

tier of guns if it blow a cap full of wind. ... as for the
rest of them, they can scarce haul up a port.'[17] A few
amendments were made to the establishments of
dimensions in 1741, but four years later Anson was
determined to force them into even greater changes.
The master shipwrights of the dockyards met
together in the mould loft in Deptford and discussed
various plans, but a committee of sea officers
rejected Anson's idea of getting rid of the old 80s.
They were 'sorry to differ with your Lordships
therein, but we having observed on many occasions
the advantage which 80-gun ships with three decks
had over those with two and a half, judged it for the
benefit of the service that so useful a class of ship
should be continued.'[18]

When Prince Charles Edward Stuart wanted to
lead a rebellion in Scotland in favour of his father (the
son of the displaced James II), his advisers were scep-
tical partly because the navy was already blockading
the French coast. Nevertheless he set off with two
ships in July 1745, but the larger one was quickly disabled by the Royal Navy and had to go back, so he
landed in Scotland with a very small party, the legendary 'seven men of Moidart'. As the rising gathered
momentum, the navy moved General Cope's army
from Aberdeen to the east of Edinburgh, only to have
it defeated by the rebels at Prestonpans. There was
another disaster for the government at Montrose
when the sloop *Hazard* was taken by the Jacobites,
but on the whole the naval blockade was effective and
forced the rebels to move inland for their march
south, where they lost heart due to their isolation and
turned back at Derby. They were pursued into Scotland and in April 1746 the *Shark*, off the coast of
Inverness, watched a battle on shore. 'About noon
saw the engagement begin betwixt His Royal Highness and the rebels on Clydon Moor about three
miles south-east from Inverness. ... Saw a party of

THESE PAGES The capture of the Spanish treasure galleon *Nuestra
Senōra de Covadonga* by Anson's *Centurion*. Samuel Scott's painting
tends to exaggerate the difference in size between the two ships.

ABOVE The taking of the Spanish 70-gun ship *Princessa* by the British 70-gun ships *Kent*, *Lenox* and *Orford* in April 1740, painted by Peter Monamy.

horse coming alongshore: sent the boat to enquire what news: at 3 spoke with the aforesaid party, who told us they had got a compleat victory over the rebels.'[19] The Jacobites were defeated at Culloden and the rebellion was over.

'Bonnie Prince Charlie' escaped and the navy hunted him throughout the highlands and islands. His most implacable pursuer was Captain John Fergusson, a Scot himself and a fierce anti-Jacobite. To Hugh MacDonald of North Uist he was 'most bent of any I had heard to take the Prince'. To Nanie Mac-Donald of Skye he was 'a very cruel, hard-hearted man' and 'a man remarkably rigid and severe in his way'.[20] His tactics were oppressive to say the least. He 'ordered one Lieutenant Dalrymple ashore to execute his vengeance against the island, who burnt Rasay's good house to ashes, and also the whole houses upon the island excepting two small villages that escaped their sight, with all the poor people's furniture. The number of houses burnt, according to a strict account taken of them, exceeded three hundred.'[21] But he never found the prince, and only left a legacy of bitterness in the Highlands.

This time the navy had only played a secondary role in defending Protestantism, compared with its part in 1588 and 1688, but it was to be the last. There were no more Jacobite rebellions and many Scottish families became reconciled to the Hanoverian regime,

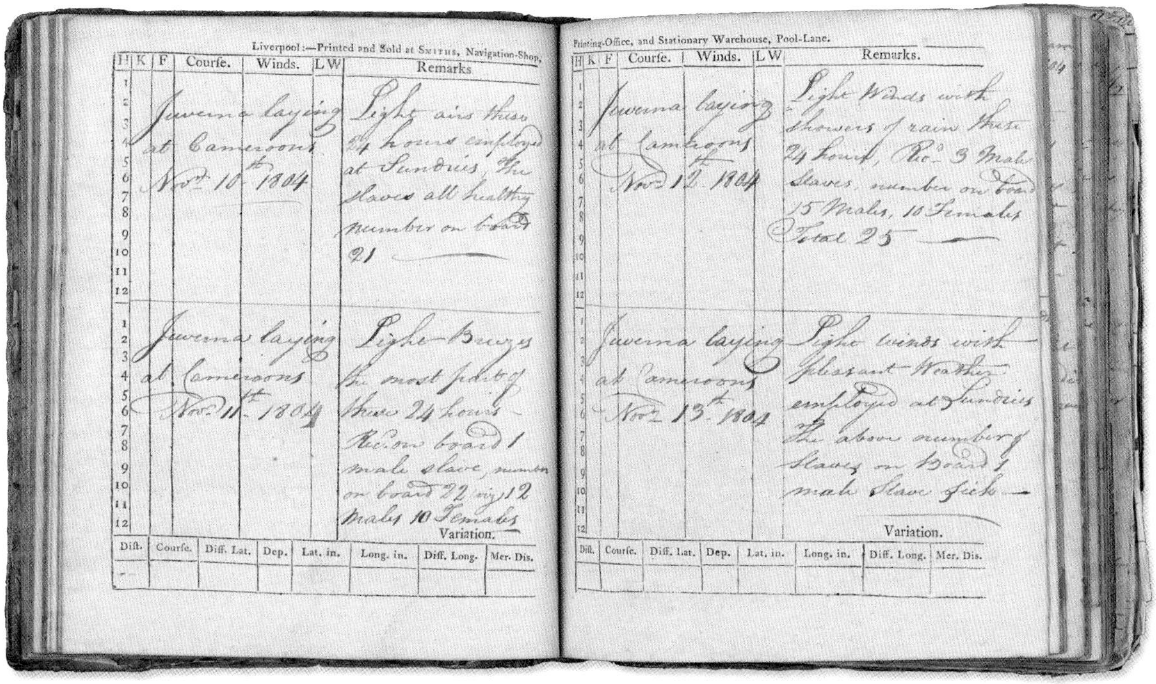

The logbook image showing handwritten entries:

H K F	Courfe.	Winds.	L W	Remarks.
	Juverna laying at Camroons Nov: 10 1804	*Light airs these 24 hours employd at Sundries, the slaves all healthy number on board 21*		
	Juverna laying at Camroons Nov: 11th 1804	*Light Breezy the most jolly these 24 hours Recon board 1 male slave, number on board 22 viz 12 Males 10 Females*		

H K F	Courfe.	Winds.	L W	Remarks.
	Juverna laying at Camroons Nov: 12 1804	*Light Winds with showers of rain these 24 foot, Rec: 3 Male Slaves number on board 15 Male, 10 Females Total 25*		
	Juverna laying at Camroons Nov: 13th 1804	*Light winds with pleasant Weather employd at Sundries the above number Slaves on Board 1 male Slave fick*		

ABOVE The logbook of the slave schooner *Juverna* in 1804, recording the bringing on board of small numbers of male and female slaves, and the numbers on board.

RIGHT A slave collar dating from around 1790. Men were usually shackled in pairs with iron rings rivetted to their ankles, and below decks they had no room to sit up.

Longboat returned with 11 slaves; viz 3 men, 1 woman, 2 men boys, 1 boy (4 foot), 1 boy and 3 girls undersized, which makes our number 26 ...

Bought 2 small girls, 1 of 3 foot and the other of 3 foot 4 inches. Sent the steward ashore again in the yawl to purchase a woman slave and he brought her off again in the evening, No 46, she cost 65 Bars, though she has a very bad mouth.

including the Elphinstones whose son George eventually became Admiral Lord Keith. And in any case that kind of religious sectarianism would play a lesser part in future wars, which were more about colonial expansion and revolution than dynasties.

In the following century the Royal Navy would take great pride in putting down the slave trade, but for the moment it was fighting to defend the British share in it, in the form of the *Asiento*. More generally the slave trade was flourishing despite the war. Thirty-eight ships were operating during 1743 and they brought nearly 9,000 slaves, twice the peacetime figure in 1734. John Newton, a young seaman from Wapping, was initially quite happy to take part in the trade with naval support as he recorded coldly in the log of the slave ship Duke of Argyle.

Newton eventually began to see the horrors and became one of the leaders of the abolition movement.

Olaudah Equiano, a native of West Africa, was sold at the age of 10.

The first object which saluted my eyes when I arrived on the coast was the sea, and a slave-ship ... waiting for its cargo. ... When I was carried on board I was immediately handled, and tossed up, to see if I were sound ... and I was now persuaded that I had gotten into a world of bad spirits ... Their complexions too differing so much from ours, their long hair, and the language they spoke, ... united to confirm me in this belief.[22]

Though the new emphasis was on colonial war, Anson perceived that the blockade of Brest was the key to naval strategy. Since France had no large natural harbour on her north coast, it was the only place where a large fleet could be based with easy access to the English Channel. A squadron off Brest could also control the entrance to the Channel. As Vernon wrote in 1744, 'a Western Squadron formed as strong as we can make it' could 'speedily get into soundings, might face their united forces, cover both Great Britain and Ireland, and be in condition to pursue them wherever they went, and be at hand to secure the safe return of our homeward bound trade from the East and West Indies.'[23]

Anson went back to sea with the rank of Vice Admiral and on 3 May 1747 he came across a force of warships and East Indiamen carrying troops, which were intended to change the balance of power in India. The French commander, De la Jonquière, formed a line of battle including the larger East Indiamen. Anson formed his own line then signalled for his ships to sail more directly to the enemy. At this point the East India captains lost their nerve and fell out of the line, which soon descended into disorder. Anson saw a loophole in

ABOVE The 74-gun *Invincible* after her capture in 1748. She has been refitted with British masts and rigging, but her stern decorations are still in the French style.

OPPOSITE French masts come crashing down during Anson's victory off Cape Finisterre in May 1747. Though it was achieved quite easily against inferior numbers, it was a turning point in the war against France and in the development of naval tactics.

the Fighting Instructions, which allowed him to pursue a retreating enemy without too much regard to the line. He did, and his ships soon captured eight warships and three Indiamen. Though it had been won against inferior forces, it was a stunning victory, the first of the war. It demonstrated what was possible without the line of battle, and at last the Royal Navy was beginning to live up to what the public expected of it.

Among the prizes was the 74-gun ship *Invincible*, built at Rochefort in 1744 by Pierre Morineau. At 1,793 tons, she was almost as large as a British 100-gun ship but carried all her guns on two decks, which made her more stable and able to sail better in contrary winds. She had only four more guns than a British 70, but they were far heavier and her broadside was almost 70 per cent greater. She had been designed for the new kind of warfare, which might range all over the oceans, rather than the old style that was confined to the English Channel and the Mediterranean. British admirals had already learned that she represented the future, but

shipwrights needed some convincing. British design was at its lowest point of the century.

In October that year Sir Edward Hawke repeated Anson's achievement by defeating another French force in almost the same waters. The Second Battle of Finisterre removed any French hope of getting round British dominance at sea. The French and their allies were victorious on land, the British on the water, a pattern that would repeat itself over the years. Peace negotiations conducted by the Earl of Sandwich ended the war in 1748. The British had gained very little in nine years, except the knowledge that their navy had no room for complacency, and much reform was still needed.

PLAN SUBTERRANEOUS of the

ENTRANCE or

Chapter 8
DEFEAT INTO VICTORY

By the middle of the eighteenth century the British public had come to expect its navy to be invincible, a conclusion based on patriotic history rather than reality. By 1756 Captain Augustus Hervey could write of 'these Dutch wars where so many of our valiant commanders' praises are sung down to us'.[24] It was Hervey's friend Admiral John Byng who demonstrated just how fallible the naval system was.

By 1756 it was becoming clear that the peace of 1748 was not going to last, as armed conflicts broke out in India and North America, where a Colonel George Washington led an undersized expedition against the French base at Fort Duquesne and was forced to surrender. Knowing that the French had sent out reinforcements in 13 ships of the line equipped as troopships, the government in London ordered Admiral Edward Boscawen to intercept them. He found three of the enemy who had become separated in the fogs of the Grand Banks off Newfoundland and took them; it was enough to annoy the French but not to damage them seriously.

Intelligence showed that the French were fitting out a strong fleet in Toulon, with Minorca as a clear target. Admiral John Byng, son of the victor of Cape Passero, was appointed to command the British response and left Portsmouth on 6 April 1756 after many delays. In the meantime Admiral la Galissonère landed troops on the island and besieged the British in Fort St Philip. It was defended by the 82-year-old General William Blakeney, who had held Stirling Castle against the Jacobites in 1745–6. Byng stopped at Gibraltar, where he had a dispute with the governor about the use of troops attached to his command. Arriving off Minorca, he found a French fleet roughly equal to his own. He gained the weather gage – the favourable wind position – which should have given him an advantage, and the two fleets passed one another in opposite directions. Byng tacked his ships so that they would remain engaged with

THE ENGLISH LION DISMEMBER'D
the Voice of the Public for an enquiry into the loss of Minorca - with Ad:ᴸ B__g's plea before his Examiners.

ABOVE Cartoon 'The English Lion dismember'd'. On the left, Admiral Byng makes excuses for his failure; in the centre the British lion has lost a paw; while behind peasants threaten to revolt. On the right, the Gallic cock pecks the Union flag.

the enemy, but then things began to go wrong. A number of ships were out of position, and the fleet as a whole was too far away from the enemy. He used a procedure known as 'lasking' to bring his ships closer, but the crude signalling system of the day did not allow him to correct the line as it approached, and there was further disorder. Byng, a member of the Mathews court martial, knew the penalties for going into battle without a proper line, and withdrew. His orders also demanded that he protect Gibraltar, and he abandoned Minorca to guard the rock.

News of the battle passed quickly through France while Byng's dispatch took a long time to reach Britain by sea. Smugglers brought the French newspapers across the Channel and they were not free of exaggeration. The public was told of a great French victory and of a British admiral who had withdrawn from the battle without seriously engaging. Dozens of popular prints were published against Byng, showing him haunted by the ghost of his father or more interested in protecting his valuable porcelain collection; others showed the British lion being humiliated. Byng was recalled to face a public outcry and a court martial. Initially it was suggested that he had been guilty of cowardice, but it soon became clear that was not a factor. However, he was tried under the savage provisions of the twelfth Article of War:

> *Every person in the fleet, who through*
> *Cowardice, Negligence, or Disaffection, shall in*
> *time of Action withdraw or keep back, or not*

*come into the fight or Engagement, or shall not
do his utmost to take or destroy every Ship
which it shall be his duty to engage ... and
being convicted thereof be the Sentence of a
Court-Martial, shall suffer Death.*[25]

Though he was clearly not guilty of cowardice,
the court martial felt obliged to convict him of failing

to 'do his utmost' in the presence of the enemy. It had
to sentence him to death, fully expecting that either
the Admiralty or the King would commute it. But this
ignored the role of the London mob, perhaps the
most democratic force in the country in the days
when the franchise was confined to a narrow minor-
ity. They suspected a ruling-class cover-up in favour of
one of their own and the ominous slogan 'Save Byng
and lose your King' appeared on a wall. No politician
had the courage to stand up against this, while at the
Admiralty, Lord Anson perhaps felt it might be useful
to send out a message to any dilettante officers
remaining in the service, that failure would not be tolerated. Byng was brought to Portsmouth to be shot on
the quarterdeck of his flagship; the only concession to
his dignity being that he was allowed to drop a handkerchief to order his own execution. Voltaire's
character Candide witnessed it and was told by a
passer-by, 'In this country it is good to kill an admiral

LEFT AND BELOW Dan Snow re-enacts the moment captured in the painting below; as Admiral Byng releases a handkerchief on the quarterdeck of his former flagship to order his death by firing squad.

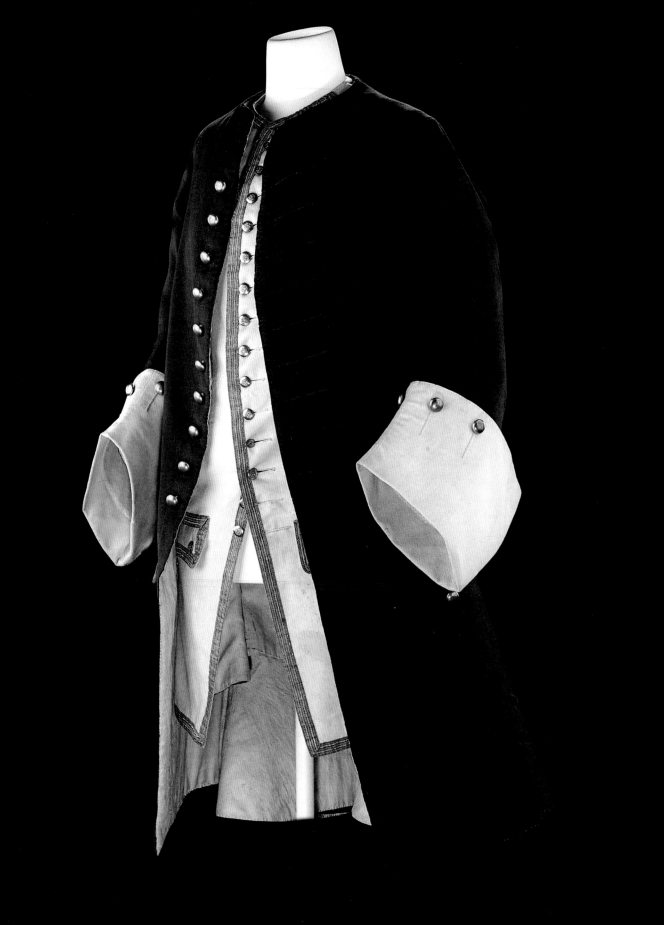

from time to time, to encourage the others (*pour encourager les autres*)'.

Though Anson came out of the Byng affair with little credit, his reforms were essential to the development of the Royal Navy. Often he just ignored established practices. Until 1744 the navy only had nine admirals, three each of the red, white and blue squadrons, but the Admiralty Board continued to appoint more and more until there were 188 in 1812. Another innovation was to promote inefficient or aged captains to the rank of Rear Admiral without a specific squadron, so that they would receive half-pay but never be employed again – the nearest thing to a retirement policy that the times allowed.

The steps from lieutenant to commander and captain were the vital stages in an officer's career – below that he was appointed partly by examination, above that it was entirely by seniority. The step was largely dominated by 'influence', by friends and family in high places. Anson could not change this completely, and it is doubtful that he would have wanted to. However, he introduced a new and more meritocratic system of promotion. The first lieutenant of a ship that was successful in a battle, whether that of a fleet or one between two ships, would be promoted. At the same time officers were given a regular rank structure in which a naval captain was equated with a colonel in the army and a lieutenant with an army captain – a system that largely survives to this day. Moreover, Anson brought a new spirit into the officer corps; the execution of Byng, however barbaric, did send the message that failure would not be tolerated, in that sense it really did '*encourager les autres*'.

It was the officers themselves who asked for a regular uniform; it was not long since Admiral Vernon had gained the nickname of 'Old Grog' because of his scruffy coat of grogram. But in 1747 a group of officers petitioned the Admiralty 'that a uniform military

clothing be appointed, thereby to distinguish the rank of each officer from the other'. A blue coat was chosen, according to legend based on one worn for riding by the Duchess of Bedford, and thus began a style that would influence both naval and civilian fashion to the present day. Armies have worn all sorts of colours over the years, whether for show or concealment; it is very rare to find a navy that does not dress in dark blue.

Anson's most lasting success was in ship design. He soon became disillusioned with the Establishment of 1745, which he himself had promoted but did not produce very successful ships. The Surveyor of the Navy, Sir Joseph Allin, remained as a barrier to progress on the eve of a new war with France just as more money was coming forward for shipbuilding. When Allin was suddenly taken ill in 1755, Anson hastened his retirement and brought in his own man, Thomas Slade. He was immediately ordered to build a class of 74-gun ships, influenced by French practices though not a direct copy of them. By 1757 he had designed the *Bellona* class, the model for 74s over the next half century. At the same time he built the first true frigates, again modelled on the French, starting with the *Southampton,* which was launched in 1757.

Slade's most lasting memorial is the 100-gun *Victory,* now preserved at Portsmouth Historic Dockyard, but not launched until 1765 when the war was over. Slade was as taciturn as Anson, and like the Frenchmen of the previous generation he brought no new principles to ship design, but merely refined existing practices to produce the ideal warships for Britain's needs. According to one of his followers, Slade was 'a truly great man in the line he trod, such a one I believe never went before him, and if I am not too partial, I may venture to say will hardly follow him.'[26]

Anson's circumnavigation had already given him reason to question the way in which the army appointed marines to ships. In 1755 it was agreed that their recruitment, training and appointment would be under the direct control of the navy, an arrangement that has continued to the present day. But aside from

LEFT The pattern suit for the first naval uniform, as approved by the King in 1748. This is a lieutenant's full dress coat and waistcoat, marked by the white cuffs.

George Anson (1697–1762)

Born the son of a minor Staffordshire landowner, Anson entered the navy at a relatively late age in 1712, but was a lieutenant four years later and served at the Battle of Cape Passero under Sir George Byng in 1718. By 1722 he was captain of the 20-gun *Scarborough*. He was sent to patrol the colony of South Carolina against piracy; he became popular and invested in land during six years there. In 1737 he was promoted to the 60-gun *Centurion*. Initially he was sent to the West Indies, but in 1739 he returned home to be caught up in the preparations for what became his round-the-world voyage against the Spanish.

During the four-year expedition, Anson showed enormous resolution and skill. He had cause to see many of the faults of the navy, in recruitment and ship design. By capturing a Spanish treasure galleon he became a very rich man and returned home a hero. Elected to parliament, he became a member of the Board of Admiralty, the most capable naval one and part of a strong partnership with the Duke of Bedford and the Earl of Sandwich.

One of Anson's first successes was to merge several smaller groups to form the Western Squadron off Brest, which became the cornerstone of British naval strategy throughout the age of sail. In 1747 he took command himself to win the Battle of Finisterre. As a result he became a baron and married Elizabeth Yorke, the daughter of the powerful Lord Chancellor Lord Hardwicke. She was much younger and more sociable but it was a happy marriage, though childless.

Anson took much of the lead at the Admiralty while Sandwich was negotiating the peace treaty in 1748, and became First Lord himself in 1751. He remained in office until his death, except for the political turmoil of 1757 when he was briefly replaced by Lord Temple. He formed an essential part of the William Pitt administration, which won the Seven Years War. During his time in office he reformed almost every aspect of the navy: ships, officer promotion, uniforms, victualling, manning, strategy and tactics. He was an excellent judge of character but he also gave the navy a new aggressive, unconquerable spirit. His biggest failures were in the loss of Minorca in 1756 and the subsequent scandal, and his unsuccessful efforts to replace the press gang as the main means of recruitment.

Anson was the essential link between the navies of Pepys and Nelson, and not just chronologically. Unlike the other two, he was successful both as a sea commander and an administrator in London; and it was Anson's reforms that created much of the navy that Nelson deployed so effectively.

ABOVE An anonymous portrait of Anson shows him looking typically taciturn and firm. The blue coat is not the proper naval uniform, which suggests it was painted before 1748.

LEFT Anson's camp on Juan Fernandez during his circumnavigation, 1740–44.

that, Anson's main failure was in personnel, largely because he needed to get his reforms through parliament. When a Navy Bill amended the Articles of War in 1749, Anson tried to add a clause subjecting half-pay officers to it, but had to withdraw it against opposition. He also tried to set up a system of half pay for seamen, who could be recalled in an emergency and perhaps make impressment less necessary. That too failed, and the press gang was left as the main means of recruitment in wartime.

The navy saw itself as a defender of liberty, but there was an exception in the press gang. According to the Scottish philosopher and historian David Hume, the people had a right to be protected from 'violence and usurpation', but there was a single exception in the pressing of seamen: 'The exercise of an irregular power is here tacitly admitted by the crown.' Unable to abolish or replace impressment, Anson concentrated on making the existing system more efficient. In the past, organised impressment had been concentrated on the south and east of England. Anson extended the area by appointing regulating captains to the major ports around Britain, and sending small ships known as pressing tenders to assist them. Seamen were offered the usual bounties, but they did not volunteer in greater numbers than before. Instead, more ways were found to recruit landmen and boys. The Marine Society, founded in 1756, recruited young male orphans and gave them a minimum of naval training. Foreigners were occasionally allowed to volunteer, and even prisoners of war could be taken on in certain circumstances. A number of towns were persuaded to offer extra inducements for men who volunteered, while debtors and smugglers were offered the navy instead of prison, if they were in reasonably good health.

The burden of impressment fell increasingly on the merchant seamen, as the navy began to take on an increasing share in the country's defence. At the same time its range of operations had expanded greatly during the War of Jenkins' Ear, when most of the early action was in the West Indies where fatal diseases like yellow fever were rife. Many merchant seamen hated and feared the navy because of the press gang, but not all. The young William Spavens was pressed at Hull in 1756 and confined in the 'floating prison' of a tender for a month until he joined the crew of the 70-gun *Gloucester*, where life was much improved. He later wrote, 'his Majesty's service is, in many respects, preferable to any other; first, as when a ship in the merchant service is cast away, the men and officers lose their pay ... And secondly, the provision is better in kind and more plentiful'.[27] Merchant service and Royal Navy wages were not very different in peace, but in wartime merchant wages increased three or four-fold, and an impressed seaman could not share in this bonanza. And naval seamen were not released at the end of a voyage but 'turned over' from one ship to another without any regard to their feelings, a practice that they hated. A chance to reform the system had been missed in the days of Anson, and things would only get worse as the navy expanded over the next few decades. The press gang has also had a profound effect on the English language. Originally the word 'gang' just meant a party of seamen sent on a particular task; today it has overtones of violence and criminality. 'Press' has many different meanings, but one of them is to force a person unwillingly into something, and to 'press gang' someone is to use even stronger pressure.

William Pitt the Elder, a turbulent politician in opposition, took office as Secretary of State at the end of 1756; he was out of office for a time during the following year, but restored due to popular pressure. As the nation began to put the Byng affair behind it, Pitt provided the vision and strategic leadership that was needed to win a world war. With Anson re-established as First Lord of the Admiralty after he too was out of office in 1756, the team was now in place to fight and win on the world stage. More aggressive policies were adopted, though results were mixed in the early stages. There was disaster as two attempts to take the Brittany privateer port of St-Malo failed; there were victories during 1757 and '58. In India, a British block-

A View of the Taking of QUEBEC September 13.th 1759.

Vue de la Prise de QUEBEC le 13 Septembre 1759.

ABOVE The taking of Quebec. General Wolfe's troops disembark at the foot of the cliff and confront the French on the Heights of Abraham, to take the city, the key to French North America.

OPPOSITE The plans of the *Victory* of 1765, as first built with highly decorated stern and figurehead. The red lines show interior detail such as decks, masts and capstan.

FOLLOWING PAGES The morning after the Battle of Quiberon Bay. French ships are burning on the far right; British ships are aground in the foreground, with the flagship *Royal George* in the centre and triumphant British ships on the left.

ade helped the East India Company to gain superiority over the French, and Admiral Sir Charles Watson was able to move Robert Clive's force of East India Company troops from Bombay to Calcutta, from where he was able to win his great victory at Plassey in June 1757. Dakar in West Africa was taken in 1758 to help secure the route to the east, while the capture of the fortress of Louisbourg cleared the entrance to the St Lawrence River in Canada.

The year 1759 began well with the capture of the sugar island of Guadeloupe in May. In August, Admiral Boscawen attacked a French squadron off Lagos in southern Portugal and took or destroyed five enemy ships out of twelve. In the meantime Vice-Admiral Sir Charles Saunders, one of Anson's protégés, was slowly working his way up the St Lawrence River. He had a fleet that included 22 ships of the line, carrying 8,000 troops under General James Wolfe, guided by James Cook as his pilot. He arrived off Quebec late in June and besieged the city. Wolfe was able to land at the Heights of Abraham and fight a successful battle, though he was to lose his own life. The capital of French Canada was now in British hands and the rest of the North American continent was there for the taking.

Saunders was able to sail back across the Atlantic and intended to join the main fleet under Admiral Hawke, until he received news of yet another victory. Admiral Conflans, commanding the French Brest fleet, had tried to escape while the British fleet under Hawke was scattered, but Hawke was able to rally his forces and Conflans retreated into the rocky waters of Quiberon Bay where he hoped he might be safe. A gale was blowing as Hawke's ships sailed in. When the master of his flagship, the *Royal George*, objected to the dangers, Hawke famously thanked him for doing his duty by the warning, but ordered, 'Where there is passage for the enemy there is a passage for me. You have done your duty in showing me the danger: now obey my orders and lay me alongside the Soleil Royal.' Captain Richard Howe led the way in the 74-gun *Magnanime* and fired a devastating broadside into the French *Formidable*. Hawke quickly sank the *Superbe* with two broadsides, for he had anticipated Nelson in his desire for close-range action, and ordered his captains 'on no account to fire until they shall be within pistol shot'. As a result, by the end of the day 11 French ships out of 21 were captured, destroyed or driven into the River Vilaine at spring tide, where it would take months to extricate them. It was a triumph for Anson's new navy. French sea power was crushed more comprehensively than ever before; there was no longer any threat that they might invade Britain, and the British conquests overseas were secure.

This was the great 'year of victories'. The naval anthem 'Heart of Oak' was written at that time and referred to the need to 'add more renown' to 'this wondrous year'. The writer Horace Walpole, son of the former prime minister who had once predicted that people would be wringing their hands, was moved out of his cynicism and wrote, 'Our bells are worn threadbare with ringing for victories'. Perhaps even the infant Horatio Nelson, just one year old at the time of Quiberon Bay, gained an impression of how naval victories might be celebrated in a remote corner of the countryside. It was the first war in which the United Kingdom was truly united – no risings in Scotland or Ireland, no rebellious colonists or radicals demanding reform, no great mutinies. It was also the first war for Anson's new navy, the first in which it had fought in any kind of uniform, in modern ships like the 74 and the frigate, and with the spirit which would eventually lead to the 'habit of victory'.

The victory at Quebec was the most significant in the long term. It ensured that English would become

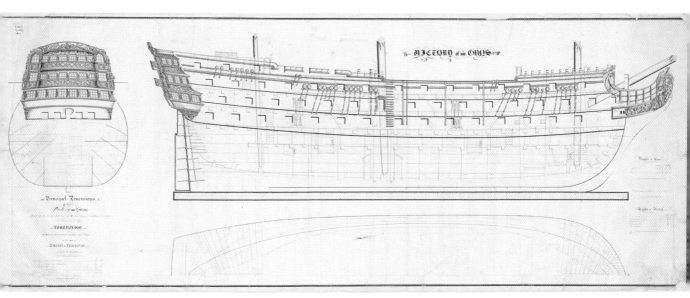

The Nations (not so blest as thee)
Must in their turns to Tyrants fall;
While thou shalt flourish great and free,
The dread and envy of them all. Rule &c.

Still more majestic shalt thou rise,
More dreadfull from each foreign stroke;
As the loud blast that tears the Skies
Serves but to root thy native Oak. Rule &c.

Thee, haughty Tyrants ne'er shall tame;
All their attempts to bend thee down,
Will but arouse thy gen'rous flame;
But work their woe and thy renown. Rule &c.

To thee belongs the rural reign,
Thy Cities shall with Commerce shine;
All thine shall be the subject Main,
And ev'ry shore it circles thine. Rule &c.

The Muses still with Freedom found,
Shall to thy happy Coasts repair;
Blest Isle! with matchless Beauty crown'd,
And manly hearts to guard the Fair. Rule &c.

RIGHT King George III in about 1800, forty years into a long reign. Painted by Sir William Beechey, he is wearing a general's full-dress uniform and stands in front of Windsor Castle.

the dominant language of North America, and eventually the lingua franca of the world. It was a vital stage in the process by which 'a few tribal and local German dialects spoken by a 150,000 people grew into the English language spoken and understood by about one and a half billion people'.[28]

King George II died in 1760 after what Captain Hervey described as 'the longest and mildest reign since the [Norman] conquest'– in spite of the Byng affair.[29] His 22-year-old grandson George III succeeded him. Unlike his predecessors George III was a native and told parliament, 'Born and educated in this country, I glory in the name of Briton'. But he was much less keen on continuing what he called a 'bloody and expensive war'. He dismissed Pitt, appointed Lord Bute in his place and began to take steps towards peace. Despite this, war with Spain began in 1762 and the navy was not slow to exploit a situation it had always longed for – the Spanish navy was weak and the French were already defeated at sea. Havana in Cuba and Manila in the Philippines were both taken, demonstrating the huge range of British sea power in its triumphant age.

Eventually a peace treaty was signed at Paris in 1763. Manila and Havana were given back and there was serious debate about whether the rich sugar island of Guadeloupe should be retained instead of Canada, but eventually it was decided to maintain the gains in North America, including Florida. Ultimately, the great military successes of what became known as the Seven Years War were followed by political failure. After fighting a global war, Britain was left with a global empire with effective control of India, North America and much of the highly profitable West Indies. But the American colonists no longer had to fear the French and their allies, there were divisions at home and within the empire, Britain had made peace by abandoning her continental ally Prussia, and the settlement of 1763 contained the seeds of its own destruction.

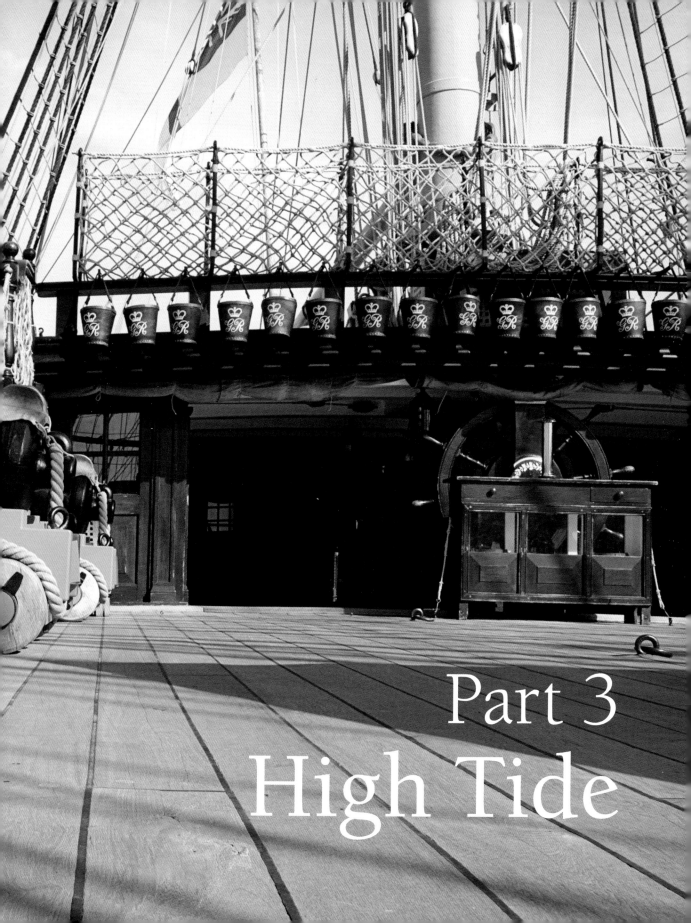

Part 3
High Tide

ABOVE Dominic Serres' painting of 1770 shows the gunwharf at Portsmouth, with guns and carriages. Naval ships including a two-decker are in the harbour, and across the water is Portsmouth Dockyard.

Chapter 9
THE LOSS OF AMERICA

Victory in the Seven Years War led to a wave of triumphalism, and one magazine claimed of Britain,

The trade of the whole world centred on this island; she was the mart of all nations: the merchants engrossed the riches of the universe, and lived like princes: and the manufacturers were enabled to live in credit and reputation, being supplied with many things necessary for their use from our conquests, at an easy rate for which they had been oblige to pay dear before.[1]

This euphoria had its effect on art as well as commerce, and many of the great marine artists began to flourish with the support of official and naval patrons. Dominic Serres was born in France but settled in Britain after arriving as a prisoner of war in the 1750s. He became a founder member of the Royal Academy in 1768 and eventually the first marine painter to King George III. One of his best works was The Battle of Quiberon Bay, in which the dramatic clouds and lighting dominated the scene. His son John Thomas was less successful as a painter but did more practical work, when in 1800 he sailed in the frigate *Clyde* to make drawings of harbours on the west coast of France and Spain. Nicholas Pocock was a ship's captain who started by making drawings in his ship's logbook and began to exhibit at the Royal Academy in 1782. He went to sea with the fleet in 1794 and produced drawings and sketches of the battle of the Glorious First of June, with many other battles, ship portraits and coastal views. Thomas Luny was another former sailor, probably a purser or supply officer, who first exhibited in 1777 but continued to go to sea until he set up his studio at Teignmouth on the

BOSTON, December 1, 1773.

At a Meeting of the PEOPLE *of* Boſton, *and the neighbouring Towns, at* Faneuil-Hall, *in ſaid* Boſton, *on Monday the 29th of* November 1773, *Nine o'Clock, A. M. and continued by Adjournment to the next Day; for the Purpoſe of conſulting, adviſing and determining upon the moſt proper and effectual Method to prevent the unloading, receiving or vending the deteſtable* TEA *ſent out by the Eaſt-India Company, Part of which being juſt arrived in this Harbour:*

IN Order to proceed with due Regularity, it was moved that a Moderator be choſen, and

JONATHAN WILLIAMS, Eſq;
Was then choſen Moderator of the Meeting.

A MOTION was made that as the Town of Boſton had determined at a late Meeting legally aſſembled, that they would to the utmoſt of their Power prevent the landing of the Tea, the Queſtion be put, Whether this Body are abſolutely determined that the Tea now arrived in Capt. Hall ſhall be returned to the Place from whence it came at all Events. And the Queſtion being accordingly put, it paſſed in the Affirmative. Nem. Con.

It appearing that the Hall could not contain the People aſſembled, it was Voted, that the Meeting be immediately Adjourned to the Old South Meeting-Houſe, Leave having been obtained for this Purpoſe.

The People met at the Old South according to Adjournment.

A Motion was made, and the Queſtion put, viz. Whether it is the firm Reſolution of this Body that the Tea ſhall not only be ſent back, but that no Duty ſhall be paid thereon; & paſs'd in the Affirmative. Nem. Con.

It was moved, that in order to give Time to the Conſignees to conſider and deliberate, before they ſent in their Propoſals to this Body, as they had given Reaſon to expect would have been done at the opening of the Meeting, there might be an Adjournment to Three o'Clock, P. M and the Meeting was accordingly for that Purpoſe adjourned.

THREE o'Clock, P. M. met according to Adjournment.

A Motion was made, Whether the Tea now arrived in Captain Hall's Ship ſhall be ſent back in the ſame Bottom—Paſs'd in the Affirmative, *Nem Con.*

Mr. Rotch the Owner of the Veſſel being preſent, informed the Body that he ſhould enter his Proteſt againſt their Proceedings.

It was then moved and voted, [illegible] That Mr. Rotch be directed not to enter this Tea; and that the Doing of it would be at his Peril.

Alſo Voted, That Captain Hall the Maſter of the Ship, be informed that at his Peril he is not to ſuffer any of the Tea brought by him, to be landed.

A Motion was made, That in Order for the Security of Captain Hall's Ship and Cargo, a Watch may be appointed——and it was Voted that a Watch be accordingly appointed to conſiſt of 25 Men.

Capt. Edward Procter was appointed by the Body to be the Capt. of the Watch for this Night, and the Names were given in to the Moderator, of the Townſmen who were Volunteers on the Occaſion.

It having been obſerved to the Body, that Governor Hutchinſon had required the Juſtices of the Peace in this Town to meet and uſe their Endeavours to ſuppreſs any Routs or Riots, &c. of the People that might happen.—It was Moved and the Queſtion put—Whether it be not the Senſe of this Meeting, that the Governor's Conduct herein carries a deſign'd Reflection upon the People here met; and is ſolely calculated to ſerve the Views of Adminiſtration—Paſſed in the Affirmative, nem. con.

The People being informed by Col. Hancock, that Mr. Copley, Son-in Law to Mr. Clarke, Sen. had acquainted him that the Tea Conſignees did not receive their Letters from London till laſt Evening, and were ſo diſperſed, that they could not have a joint Meeting early enough to make their Propoſals at the Time intended; and therefore were deſirous of a further Space for that Purpoſe,

The Meeting out of great Tenderneſs to theſe Perſons, and from a ſtrong Deſire to bring this Matter to a Concluſion, notwithſtanding the Time they had hitherto expended upon them to no Purpoſe, were prevailed upon to adjourn to the next Morning Nine o'Clock.

TUESDAY Morning Nine o'Clock,
Met according to Adjournment.

THE long expected Propoſals were at length brought into the Meeting, *not* directed to the Moderator, but to John Scollay, Eſq; one of the Selectmen—It was however voted that the ſame ſhould be read, and they are as follow, viz.

Monday, Nov. 29th, 1773.

SIR,

WE are ſorry that we could not return to the Town ſatisfactory Anſwers to their two late Meſſages to us reſpecting the Teas; we beg Leave to acquaint the Gentlemen Selectmen that we have ſince received our Orders from the Honorable Eaſt-India Company.

We ſtill retain a Diſpoſition to do all in our Power to give Satisfaction to the Town, but as we underſtood from you and the other Gentlemen Selectmen at Meſſ. Clarkes Interview with you laſt Saturday, that this can be effected by nothing leſs than our ſending back the Teas, we beg Leave to ſay, that this is utterly out of our Power to do, but we do now declare to you our Readineſs to Store the Teas until we ſhall have Opportunity of writing to our Conſtituents and ſhall receive their further Orders reſpecting them; and we do moſt ſincerely wiſh that the Town conſidering the unexpected Difficulties devolved upon us will be ſatisfied with what we now offer.

We are, SIR,
Your moſt humble Servants,
Tho. & Eliſha Hutchinſon,
Benja. Faneuil, jun. for Self and
Joſhua Winſlow, Eſq;
Rich'd Clarke & Sons.

John Scollay, Eſq;

Mr. Sheriff Greenleaf came into the Meeting, and begg'd Leave of the Moderator that a Letter he had received from the Governor, requiring him to read a Proclamation to the People here aſſembled might be read; and it was accordingly read.

Whereupon it was moved, and the Queſtion put, Whether the Sheriff ſhould be permitted to read the Proclamation—which paſſed in the Affirmative, nem. con.

The Proclamation is as follows, viz.

Maſſachuſets-Bay. } By the Governor.

TO JONATHAN WILLIAMS, Eſq; acting as Moderator of an Aſſembly of People in the Town of Boſton, and to the People ſo aſſembled:

WHEREAS printed Notifications were on Monday the 29th Inſtant poſted in divers Places in the Town of Boſton and publiſhed in the News-Papers of that Day calling upon the People to aſſemble together for certain unlawful Purpoſes in ſuch Notifications mentioned: And whereas great Numbers of People belonging to the Town of Boſton, and divers others belonging to ſeveral other Towns in the Province, did aſſemble in the ſaid Town of Boſton, on the ſaid Day, and did then and there proceed to chuſe a Moderator, and to conſult, debate and reſolve upon Ways and Means for carrying ſuch unlawful Purpoſes into Execution; openly violating, defying and ſetting at nought the good and wholſome Laws of the Province and the Conſtitution of Government under which they live: And whereas the People thus aſſembled did vote or agree to adjourn or continue their Meeting to this the 30th Inſtant, and great Numbers of them are again met or aſſembled together for the like Purpoſes in the ſaid Town of Boſton,

IN Faithfulneſs to my Truſt and as His Majeſty's Repreſentative within the Province I am bound to bear Teſtimony againſt this Violation of the Laws and I warn exhort and require you and each of you thus unlawfully aſſembled forthwith to diſperſe and to ſurceaſe all further unlawful Proceedings at your utmoſt Peril.

Given under my Hand at Milton in the Province aforeſaid the 30th Day of November 1773 and in the fourteenth Year of His Majeſty's Reign.

By His Excellency's Command, T. Hutchinſon.
THO'S FLUCKER, Secr'y.

And the ſame being read by the Sheriff, there was immediately after, a loud and very general Hiſs.

A Motion was then made, and the Queſtion put, Whether the Aſſembly would diſperſe and ſurceaſe all further Proceedings, according to the Governor's Requirement—— It paſs'd in the Negative, nem. con.

A Propoſal of Mr. Copley was made, that in Caſe he could prevail with the Meſſ. Clarkes to come into this Meeting, the Queſtion might now be put, Whether they ſhould be treated with Civility while in the Meeting, though they might be of different Sentiments with this Body; and their Perſons be ſafe until their Return to the Place from whence they ſhould come——And the Queſtion being accordingly put, paſſed in the Affirmative, Nem. Con.

Another Motion of Mr. Copley's was put, Whether two Hours ſhall be given him, which alſo paſſed in the Affirmative.

Adjourn'd to Two o'Clock, P. M.

TWO o'Clock P. M. met according to Adjournment.

A Motion was made and paſſed, that Mr. Rotch and Capt. Hall be deſired to give their Attendance.

Mr. Rotch appeared, and upon a Motion made the Queſtion was put, Whether it is the firm Reſolution of this Body, that the Tea brought by Capt. Hall ſhall be returned by Mr. Rotch to England in the Bottom in which it came; and whether they accordingly now require the ſame, which paſſed in the Affirmative, Nem. Con.

Mr. Rotch then informed the Meeting that he ſhould proteſt againſt the whole Proceedings as he had done againſt the Proceedings on Yeſterday, but that tho' the returning the Tea is an involuntary Act in him, he yet conſiders himſelf as under a Neceſſity to do it, and ſhall therefore comply with the Requirement of this Body.

Capt. Hall being preſent was forbid to aid or aſſiſt in unloading the Tea at his Peril, and ordered that if he continues Maſter of the Veſſel, he carry the ſame back to London; who reply'd he ſhould comply with theſe Requirements.

Upon a Motion, Reſolved, That John Rowe, Eſq; Owner of Part of Capt. Bruce's Ship expected with Tea, as alſo Mr. Timmins, Factor for Capt. Coffin's Brig, be deſired to attend.

Mr. Ezekiel Cheever was appointed Captain of the Watch for this Night, and a ſufficient Number of Volunteers gave in their Names for that Service.

VOTED, That the Captain of this Watch be deſired to make out a Liſt of the Watch for the next Night, and ſo each Captain of the Watch for the following Nights until the Veſſels leave the Harbour.

Upon a Motion made, Voted, that in Caſe it ſhould happen that the Watch ſhould be any Ways moleſted in the Night, while on Duty, they give the Alarm to the Inhabitants by the tolling of the Bells—and that if any Thing happens in the Day Time, the Alarm be by ringing of the Bells.

VOTED, That ſix Perſons be appointed to be in Readineſs to give due Notice to the Country Towns when they ſhall be required ſo to do, upon any important Occaſion. And ſix Perſons were accordingly choſen for that Purpoſe.

John Rowe, Eſq; attended, and was informed that Mr. Rotch had engaged that his Veſſel ſhould carry back the Tea ſhe bro't in the ſame Bottom, & that it was the Expectation of this Body that he does the ſame by the Tea expected in Capt. Bruce; whereupon he reply'd that the Ship was under the Care of the ſaid Maſter, but that he would uſe his utmoſt Endeavour, that it ſhould go back as required by this Body, and that he would give immediate Advice of the Arrival of ſaid Ship.

VOTED, That it is the Senſe of this Body that Capt. Bruce ſhall on his Arrival ſtrictly conform to the Votes paſſed reſpecting Capt. Hall's Veſſel, as tho' they had been all paſſed in Referrence to Capt. Bruce's Ship.

Mr Timmins appeared and informed that Capt. Coffin's Brig expected with Tea was owned in Nantucket, he gave his Word of Honor that no Tea ſhould be landed while ſhe was under his Care, nor touched by any one untill the Owner's Arrival.

It was then Voted, That what Mr. Rowe and Mr. Timmins had offered was ſatisfactory to the Body.

Mr. Copley returned and acquainted the Body, that as he had been obliged to go to *the Caſtle,* he hoped that if he had exceeded the Time allowed him they would conſider the Difficulty of a Paſſage by Water at this Seaſon as his Apology: He then further acquainted the Body, that he had ſeen all the Conſignees, and tho' he had convinced them that they might attend this Meeting with ſafety, and had uſed his utmoſt Endeavours to prevail upon them to give Satisfaction to the Body; they acquainted him, that believing nothing would be ſatisfactory ſhort of re-ſhipping the Tea, which was out of their Power, they thought it beſt not to appear, but would renew their Propoſal of ſtoring the Tea, and ſubmitting the ſame to the Inſpection of a Committee, and that they could go no further, without incurring their own Ruin; but as they had not been active in introducing the Tea, they ſhould do nothing to obſtruct the People in their Procedure with the ſame.

It was then moved, and the Queſtion put, Whether the return made by Mr. Copley from the Conſignees, be in the leaſt Degree ſatisfactory to this Body, & paſſed in the Negative. Nem. Con.

Whereas a Number of Merchants in this Province have inadvertently imported Tea from Great Britain, while it is ſubject to the Payment of a Duty impoſed upon it by an Act of the Britiſh Parliament for the Purpoſe of raiſing a Revenue in America, and appropriating the ſame without the Conſent of thoſe who are required to pay it:

RESOLVED, That in thus importing ſaid Tea, they have juſtly incurr'd the Diſpleaſure of our Brethren in the other Colonies.

And Reſolved further, That if any Perſon or Perſons ſhall hereafter import Tea from Great-Britain, or if any Maſter or Maſters of any Veſſel or Veſſels in Great-Britain ſhall take the ſame on Board to be imported to this Place, until the ſaid unrighteous Act ſhall be repeal'd, he or they ſhall be deem'd by this Body, an Enemy to his Country; and we will prevent the Landing and Sale of the ſame, and the Payment of any Duty thereon. And we will effect the Return thereof to the Place from whence it ſhall come.

RESOLVED, That the foregoing Vote be printed and ſent to England, and all the Sea-Ports in this Province.

Upon a Motion made, Voted, That fair Copies be taken of the whole Proceedings of this Meeting, and tranſmitted to New York & Philadelphia, And that Mr. SAMUEL ADAMS,
Hon. JOHN HANCOCK, Eſq;
WILLIAM PHILLIPS, Eſq;
JOHN ROWE, Eſq;
JONATHAN WILLIAMS, Eſq
Be a Committee to tranſmit the ſame.

Voted, That it is the Determination of this Body, to carry their Votes and Reſolutions into Execution, at the Riſque of their Lives and Property.

Voted, That the Committee of Correſpondence for this Town, be deſired to take Care that every other Veſſel with Tea that arrives in this Harbour, have a proper Watch appointed for her—— Alſo Voted, That thoſe Perſons who are deſirous of making a Part of theſe Nightly Watches, be deſired to give in their Names at Meſſieurs Edes and Gill's Printing-Office.

Voted, That our Brethren in the Country be deſired to afford their Aſſiſtance upon the firſt Notice given; eſpecially if ſuch Notice be given upon the Arrival of Captain Loring, in Meſſieurs Clarkes' Brigantine.

Voted, That thoſe of this Body who belong to the Town of Boſton do return their Thanks to their Brethren who have come from the neighbouring Towns, for their Countenance and Union with this Body in this Exigence of our Affairs.

VOTED, That the Thanks of this Meeting be given to JONATHAN WILLIAMS, Eſq; for his good ſervices as Moderator.

VOTED, That this Meeting be Diſſolved—— And it was accordingly Diſſolved.

Printed by EDES and GILL, 1773.

south-west coast of England. Philip de Loutherbourg was born in Strasbourg in 1740 but became the most dramatic of marine painters. Indeed he began by working at the Drury Lane Theatre with the actor David Garrick, and later produced moving panoramas showing shipwrecks and coastal views. Later he turned to battle scenes, covering both the First of June and Trafalgar. J M W Turner was perhaps the most original of all British artists and his first oil painting was a seascape, which he exhibited at the Royal Academy in 1796. He continued to produce many works with a maritime theme throughout his long and prolific life. John Constable, on the other hand, once wrote that pictures of boats were 'so little capable of the beautiful sentiment that belongs to landscape that they have done a good deal of harm'. Nevertheless in 1803 he sailed from London to Deal and produced a book of sketches including studies of HMS *Victory*, 'Some of the most delightful, and some as melancholy.'[2]

With North America and India largely under British control by 1763, the French began to look for new worlds to colonise and the British were obliged to follow them. One theory, supported to the point of fanaticism by the hydrographer Alexander Dalrymple, was that the South Pacific contained a great southern continent that would balance the land masses in the northern hemisphere, much larger and more fertile than Australia which had already been partly discovered by Europeans. The ocean also caught the imagination of philosophers who believed they might

OPPOSITE A local broadsheet newspaper of the time describes the events leading up to the 'tea party' in some detail, including motions passed by an assembly of citizens for action against 'the unloading, receiving or vending the detestable TEA sent out by the East India Company'.

BELOW A nineteenth-century American view of the 'Boston Tea Party' of 16 December 1773, with Boston citizens disguised as Native Americans throwing tea chests from a ship in the harbour while citizens look on from the quayside.

James Cook (1728-79)

As the son of a Yorkshire farm worker, James Cook had the humblest origin of any of the great naval heroes. In his late teens he was apprenticed to a Whitby ship owner, and in the coal trade to London he learned a great deal about navigation and seamanship in the difficult waters of the North Sea. He was the mate of a ship, and about to be promoted to master, when he volunteered for the Royal Navy in 1755.

Cook discovered a talent for hydrographical surveying and had his first chart, of the entrance to the St Lawrence River, published in 1758. The following year he was with the fleet sent up the river and was one of the masters who found a way past the Traverse, the main hazard on the way to Quebec, which Admiral Saunders and General Wolfe captured that summer. In 1762 his captain noted that he had 'Genius and Capacity' for hydrography and after returning home to marry the daughter of the landlord of the Bell Inn at Execution Dock on the Thames, he began a four-year survey of the coasts of Newfoundland in 1763.

In 1768 an expedition was being fitted out to go to the Pacific to observe the transit of Venus across the face of the sun, which would be of great use in astronomical measurement. Secretly, the expedition was also to look for the great southern continent and to claim any lands that were found for King George. It was decided to have a naval officer in command and Cook only just qualified, having passed his examination for lieutenant that year. He was appointed to command the *Endeavour*, converted from a collier of the type that he was familiar with from his early days. As well as an astronomer, he carried a staff of naturalists lead by Sir Joseph Banks, a wealthy and skilled amateur. Cook rounded Cape Horn and the transit of Venus was duly observed from Tahiti, though with less success than hoped. Then Cook began to execute the next part of his orders and searched for the southern continent. He reached New Zealand and carried out a detailed and accurate survey of its coasts over six months, and went west where he found a way round the Great Barrier Reef and onto the fertile eastern coast of Australia. Cook lost very few men during most of the voyage, but many died when they came into contact with disease in the Dutch colony of Batavia. He returned home in 1771 after three years. He was now a popular hero and was promoted Commander.

A second voyage was planned in 1772, using two ships, the *Resolution* and *Adventure*. This time Cook was ordered to circumnavigate the world in as high a latitude as possible, to make a last attempt to find the fertile southern continent. He did this three times, the first captain to cross the Antarctic Circle, and wintered in the islands to the north.

Cook was promoted to Post-Captain and brought out of retirement for a third voyage in 1776.

This time he was to look for a North-West Passage from the Pacific end, after many explorers had failed from the Atlantic side. He surveyed the whole coast of North America from Oregon to Alaska, but was stopped by ice from going any further north. He visited Hawaii where he was treated almost as a god, but when he was forced to return due to a damaged foremast, the natives turned against him. He went ashore with a party of marines to recover the ship's cutter and was killed in a scuffle along with four of his men. His body was

apparently scraped clean of flesh by the Hawaiians, according to their customs.

Cook was perhaps the greatest explorer of all time, responsible for removing many doubts about the Pacific as well as discovering new lands and a great variety of wildlife, and charting the coasts with amazing accuracy. His leadership on the long voyages should not be neglected, when compared with the problems encountered by others such as his former subordinate William Bligh.

OPPOSITE An anonymous painting of James Cook in the uniform of a captain.

THESE PAGES William Hodges, the official artist on Cook's second voyage, painted this view of Vaitepiha Bay, Tahiti, as a beautiful and peaceful place with sensual women, plus pagan symbols.

Fac similes of the Signatures to the Declaration of Independence July 4. 1776.
from Binns' Celebrated Engraving.

LEFT The Declaration of Independence, signed by 56 delegates in Philadelphia on 4 July 1776, on behalf of the 13 colonies along the North American seaboard. The most prominent signature is that of John Hancock of Massachusetts, who chaired the congress. This classic document transformed the war from a protest about taxation to a full-scale struggle for independence.

Carteret sailed further south than anyone else and at least proved that the continent did not exist in those areas. The most formidable French competition came from Louis-Antoine de Bougainville, who spread the myths about Tahiti and proved that Espiritu Santo in the New Hebrides was not part of the great continent. It was in this atmosphere that an obscure warrant officer, James Cook, was promoted and given command of a new British expedition.

But by the late 1760s in the well-established British colonies of North America trouble was brewing. Most American wars have been triggered by an incident at sea, including Pearl Harbor and the Gulf of Tonkin affair, which initiated the country's formal involvement in Vietnam in 1965. The initial American revolt against British rule in the 1770s also had a strong maritime dimension. This is not surprising as most Americans of the day, or their close ancestors, had recently crossed the seas to get there, whether willingly or not. Apart from the African slaves, some were convicts sentenced to a term of seven or fourteen years in which their labour could be sold, or indentured servants whose future labour would pay for their passage. Most Americans lived close to the sea or alongside the great rivers, as the interior of the continent remained little settled. The great towns were also

find the 'noble savage', the original of man before he was corrupted by civilisation, and early reports from Tahiti raised their hopes. Naturalists also hoped to find many new species of plant and animal, and they were not to be disappointed, while astronomers would discover new stars and planets and find out far more about the movement of known ones, to the great benefit of navigation.

The British were first off the mark after the war, when Captain John Byron carried out a rather desultory voyage in which he set a record for the fastest circumnavigation but achieved little else. He was followed by Captain Samuel Wallis and Lieutenant Phillip Carteret. The former turned back, while major ports and natural harbours, such as Boston, New York and Charlestown. Most prosperous Americans depended on seaborne trade to make a living, from the Boston merchant to the southern plantation owner who had to export his cotton or tobacco.

King George's government was determined that the Americans should pay for their own defence, but the colonials saw no need for it now that the French threat was removed, and they were not offered any say in the matter – hence their slogan 'No taxation without representation'. As the British Government attempted to impose stamp taxes and customs duties, there were several violent incidents. In 1768 the sloop *Liberty* belonging to the dissident leader John Hancock was seized by customs on the pretext of making a false entry, and the customs officers of Boston were assaulted by a mob. In 1772 the revenue cutter *Gaspee* ran aground off Rhode Island and was boarded by local inhabitants who fired at the captain and burned the ship. And in 1773, in the most celebrated incident, men dressed as Indians (as Native Americans were then known) boarded ships in Boston Harbour in protest about taxes on tea.

> *They, the Indians, immediately repaired on*
> *board Capt. Hall's ship, where they hoisted out*
> *the chests of tea, and when upon deck stove the*
> *chests and emptied the tea overboard; having*
> *cleared this ship, they proceeded to Capt.*
> *Bruce's and then to Capt. Coffin's brig. They*
> *applied themselves so dextrously to the*
> *destruction of this commodity that in the space*
> *of three hours they broke up 342 chests ... and*
> *discharged their contents into the dock. When*
> *the tide rose it floated the broken chests and tea*
> *insomuch that the surface of the water was*
> *filled therewith ...*[3]

The government imposed sanctions on the city of Boston, raising the stakes yet further. When open revolt finally broke out in the spring of 1775, it was the marines from the ships in Boston Harbour who fought the rebels successfully at Bunker Hill.

From that point, the British army was involved in a campaign across the Atlantic, and held only selected strong-points on the American seaboard. 'Every, biscuit, man and bullet required by the British forces in America had to be transported across 3000 miles of ocean.' By the end of 1779 the government was employing a fleet of more than 300 transports for this, totalling more than 100,000 tons. They mostly had to travel in convoys which stretched naval resources and caused delays, and it was complained in 1782, 'there are between 2000 and 3000 tons of shipping lying at this time, loaded with provisions, at Charleston; 5700 at New York, and in all probability 7000 at the Leeward Islands; so that we have 18,000 tons of shipping lying idle, at a time when we do not know where to get a single ship.'[4]

British commanders tended to believe that a single blow, perhaps the capture of the port and city of New York, would crush the American spirit. This had worked in 1759 when the taking of Quebec had ended French rule in North America, but it was never likely to succeed against a popular revolt. Relations between army and navy were usually one of the weakest points in the British command structure but that should have caused no problems in this case. Two brothers, Admiral Richard Howe and General Sir William Howe, were in command of the navy and army respectively. One of the navy's first tasks was to move the British headquarters from revolutionary Boston to the hopefully more compliant city of New York. In August 1776, just one month after the rebels had declared their independence from Britain, the brothers Howe landed forces at Gravesend Bay on Long Island to begin a campaign among the sounds and islands, opposed by General Washington. Loyalists from other parts of America fled to the city, swelling the population from 17,000 to 30,000. After a series of fires and other mishaps it was 'a most dirty, desolate and wretched place'.[5] After the British eventually evacuated the city on 25 November 1783, New Yorkers celebrated the date as Evacuation Day for many years afterwards.

ABOVE Augustus Keppel, painted by Sir Joshua Reynolds. Keppel was one of Anson's most important protégés, having sailed round the world with him, but he failed to defeat the French at Ushant in 1778, resulting in a series of courts martial which debilitated the naval effort.

Much of the navy's work was in routine patrols and harbour searches and Vice-Admiral Samuel Graves gave some idea of the difficulties in 1775 when he asked for old 50-gun ships, an unfashionable class for several decades.

> ... they are handy ships, and from their easy Draught of Water can go in and out of Harbours without that Risque and Delay which constantly attends the piloting those now with me. And as the principal part of the Duty here is done by Boats I shall be extremely obliged to their Lordships if they will be pleased to give directions that each Ship and Sloop coming out in future may have an additional Boat for her own use, and that Supply may be sent to the Ships now in America.[6]

Just as the navy was beginning to find its feet in a war of river voyages and transatlantic troop transports, it was drawn into a more traditional kind of conflict. The Bourbon kings of France had little in common with the American rebels, but they saw a chance for revenge for their defeat of 1763 and declared war on Britain in 1778. In peacetime French efforts at sea had not been confined to exploration. The Duc de Choiseul, a former diplomat and foreign minister, became navy minister in 1761. He was too late to reverse the defeats but he was determined to avenge them. Government money was short, but he asked for subscriptions from various towns and corporations who might have ships built in their honour – thus the Estates of Brittany paid for the 110-gun *Bretagne*, the capital for the 90-gun *Ville de Paris*, and the Farmers-General of taxes paid for the 54-gun *Utile* and *Ferme*. France was now building three-deckers as well as 74s and frigates, and also developed very powerful 80-gun ships which carried their armaments on two decks. Choiseul, and his cousin the Duc de Praslin who carried on his work, attempted to reform the officer corps with limited success, and built up the Royal Dockyards for war with Britain. France had a fleet of 52 ships of the line in 1778 compared with Britain's 66, but the French ships were more modern and better concentrated. British diplomacy had failed to find a strong ally on the continent, so the French were able to devote more resources to the navy rather than the army for once. They were boosted in the following year when their ally Spain joined the conflict, and the Dutch also declared war on Britain in 1780.

France began war with Britain in 1778, and a great battle took place at the end of July. After a four-day chase the British fleet under Admiral Augustus Keppel caught up with the French off Ushant just outside Brest. For once the British were in poor order and the French had the weather gage. There was a rather desultory battle in which neither side lost a ship. This was followed by recriminations that echoed the days of Mathews and Byng, as Keppel and his second-in-command endured long and debilitating courts martial.

After the Spanish joined the French in 1779, their Combined Fleet was able to muster 46 ships of the line. Invasion of England had been threatened in every major war since 1689, but this time it was far more real than at any time since Beachy Head, or even the Armada. Because of the fall-out from Ushant the British forces were headed by the incompetent and over-cautious Sir Charles Hardy. Fortunately the two enemy fleets were not well co-ordinated and there were many delays as well as indecision in Paris about whether to invade the Isle of Wight or Cornwall. The Combined Fleet stayed too long off the English coast where it found no shelter. Ships suffered damage and 8,000 men became sick. Bad weather forced them off station in the middle of September, after which the invasion season was over. They had caused a certain amount of panic in England but they had not encountered the Royal Navy, except to capture the 64-gun *Ardent* which had strayed among them in a fog.

Across the ocean the rebels initially had no navy of their own, but the various ports took up privateering very enthusiastically. John Paul Jones had been born in Scotland in 1747 and was apprenticed in a merchant ship from Whitehaven just across the border in England. He was in America in 1775 when the revolt broke out and became a lieutenant when the rebels founded their 'Continental Navy'. He took command of the 18-gun sloop *Ranger* based in France, and raided the east coast of Scotland, which had seen very little of foreign wars. He landed near his original home town and tried to capture the local landowner, the Earl of Selkirk. He allowed his men to plunder the house as 'in America no delicacy was shown by the English'. He captured a small warship in Belfast Lough and returned to Brest. In August 1779 he was given a bigger

ship, the 42-gun *Bonhomme Richard*, and sailed round the north of Scotland. With three ships he terrorised the inhabitants of the Firth of Forth, who were also largely undefended, until he was driven away by contrary winds. Eventually the *Bonhomme Richard* met the *Serapis* of 44 guns and forced her to surrender after a bloody battle; but the *Bonhomme Richard* was so badly damaged that she sank the next day. Jones's voyages created a legend on both sides of the Atlantic, using sea power just as effectively as Drake had once done. He was regarded as the founder of the United States Navy, by far the most powerful force of its kind in the world today but which began from small beginnings. In 1945 its midshipmen were told that Jones was 'Preeminent among tradition makers' and that Lord Sandwich had written, 'If you take John Paul Jones you will be as

BELOW A head and shoulders bust of John Paul Jones, born in Kirkcudbrightshire, Scotland in 1747 and revered as the founder of the United States Navy after his voyages in the *Ranger* and *Bonhomme Richard*, in which he took on the British *Serapis*.

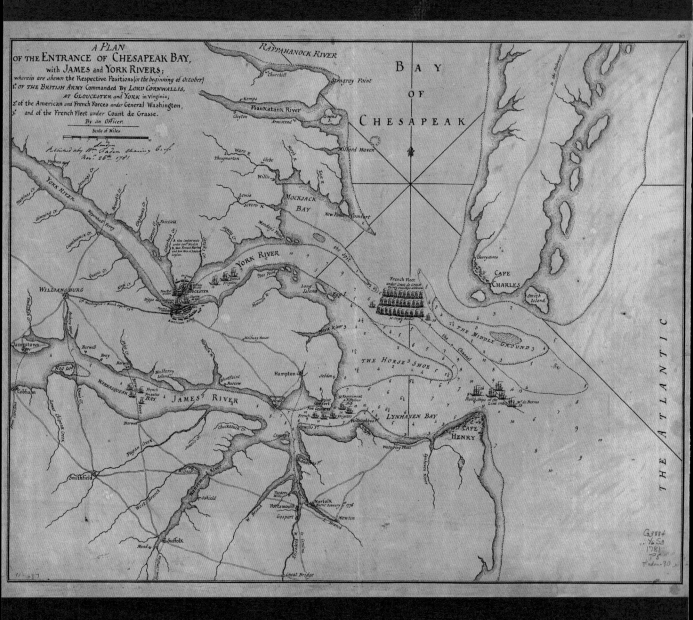

ABOVE The Siege of Yorktown, showing the British position on the south bank of the York River, the French fleet blocking the entrance to the river, and the difficult navigation. The Battle of Chesapeake Bay was fought off the mouth of the river, when Rear-Admiral Thomas Graves failed to dislodge the French.

high in the estimation of the public as if you had beat the Combined Fleets.'[7] The USN still uses Old English terms such as 'Aye, aye' and 'boatswain' and later Royal Navy terms such as 'show a leg' and 'wardroom'. And even in science fiction, the USS *Enterprise* kept up the naval custom of piping the captain on board, even when his molecules had been disassembled and reassembled for transport.

The crisis of the war in America came in 1781, when the main British army under General Cornwallis was besieged at Yorktown in Virginia. Admiral De Grasse arrived off Chesapeake Bay with 24 French ships of the line and a force of troops to assist the Americans and was met by Rear-Admiral Thomas Graves with 19 ships of the line. The two sides never really engaged; the battle was tactically indecisive but its strategic effects were much wider. Graves's failure to fight meant that the forces at Yorktown could not be relieved. Cornwallis was forced to surrender, the most humiliating moment for the British Empire for more than a century. The British war against the colonists was lost and it was only a matter of time until their independence was recognised. The other question was how much of the rest of the British Empire would survive as the French and their allies massed naval and land forces to grab parts of it. In India in 1782–3, a squadron under Admiral Sir Edward Hughes fought a series of five battles against Admiral Suffren; by and large the French had the advantage, though neither side lost a ship.

By the early 1780s the scientific approach fostered by the First Lord, Earl of Sandwich was beginning to bear fruit in two important areas, and he was seconded by Charles Middleton as Controller of the Navy. It is not clear why Sandwich picked out an undistinguished captain for the vital post; perhaps because of his political connections, or perhaps a shared interest in ancient music. In any case, Middleton soon proved a very efficient administrator and one of his clerks wrote, 'The load of business he goes through at the Board, at the Treasury, Admiralty and his own house, is astonishing, and I am confident no other man will be able to execute it.'[8]

Using a ship model, Sandwich and Middleton demonstrated to the King the principle of coppering ships' bottoms before embarking on an expensive but highly successful programme, which lasted until the end of the war. It allowed a major fleet to operate in the West Indies where there were no dry docks, and it also had tactical uses. One captain wrote to Middleton,

The advantages from the helm alone is immense, as they feel them instantly, and wear in one third of the distance they ever did; it keeps them tight, and covers the neglects from your dockyards from bad caulking; increases their speed in every situation, more particularly in light winds tending to a calm, which is no small advantage in this and every fair weather country. Its greatest effect is in sailing large.[9]

It also led to a boom in the copper industry. Production in Cornwall expanded quite moderately from around 30,000 tons a year in the 1770s to 50,000 in the '90s, but the great boom was in the Anglesey mines, for which no statistics were kept. An American scientist, Benjamin Silliman, visited Dolcoath, the largest Cornish mine, in 1805.

... we descended two hundred feet more, and were then at full six hundred feet from the surface. This was the principal scene of labour; at about this depth, there were great numbers of miners engaged in their respective employment. Some were boring the rock; others charging with gun-powder, the holes already made; others knocking off the ore with hammers, or prying it with pick-axes; others loading the buckets with ore to be drawn to the surface; others working the windlasses, to raise the rubbish from one level to another, and ultimately to the top; in short, all were busy; and, although to us their employment seems

ABOVE The surface workings of Dolcoath Mine, the largest copper mine in Cornwall, as seen around 1830. The industry was greatly boosted by the decision to copper the bottoms of all the Royal Navy's ships, and it employed many highly skilled workers in Cornwall and Wales.

BELOW Timber seasoning sheds at Chatham Dockyard, built as part of Sandwich's policy of having a ready supply of timber in all the yards, which was frustrated by the beginning of the American war and the end of supplies from that region.

only another name for wretchedness, they appeared quite a contented and cheerful class of people.[10]

Also, a new type of gun was developed by the Carron Iron Works in Scotland, one of the leaders in the industrial revolution that was taking place in Britain. The carronade was short and fat and fired about four times the weight of shot of a conventional gun, though over shorter ranges. It gave a great advantage in the short term, as French captains were shocked with the weight of fire coming out of a very small ship. It could not replace long guns, however, for it was soon found that an enemy could just keep out of range of the carronades. It was mainly used to supplement the guns on the quarterdecks of frigates and ships of the line. Coppering and carronades were both proving their worth as the centre of the naval war changed again.

Despite a good deal of success in reforming the navy and promoting new technology, the Sandwich administration at the Admiralty took much of the blame for the naval defeats. The North government fell from office in March 1782 and Sandwich went with it, just as British fortunes were about to take a

Sheathing and Coppering

A wooden ship's bottom was subject to two main problems. Weed and barnacles might grow on it to slow it down, and a fast ship had to be cleaned every four months or so. For this it needed a dry dock, which was only available in the Royal Dockyards in home waters, or it could be careened by hauling it down on one side and then the other, a difficult process that became more dangerous with larger ships. All this restricted the operational range of warships, especially those operating in the Mediterranean and West Indies.

The other problem was shipworm or *teredo navalis*, which was originally native to tropical water but tended to

transfer via the ships to some of the dockyards. It would eat its way along a timber or plank, weakening it almost imperceptibly until the hull was in a very dangerous condition.

By the beginning of the eighteenth century it was common to protect against weed by covering the hull in noxious compositions including black stuff, based mainly on tar, and white stuff, which included rosin, oil and brimstone. Worm was countered by sheathing, by attaching a thin, sacrificial layer of timber and isolating it from the rest of the hull by an unpalatable layer of hair and tar. Neither remedy was totally effective.

As early as the 1670s, ships going to the Mediterranean had been covered by sheets of lead, but it was found that the

ironwork of the hull, and crucially the rudder, decayed very rapidly. The Admiralty first tried copper sheathing on the frigate *Alarm* in 1761, but there was the same problem, which became identified as electrolysis between two different metals. When Lord Sandwich and Middleton decided to copper the whole fleet in 1780, every effort was made to separate the copper from the iron bolts of the hull, using tarred paper. This was enough to get the fleet through to the end of the American War, but after that it was necessary to develop copper alloys that were hard enough to be driven in as bolts. Every ship in the fleet had its underwater iron bolts replaced when it came in for repair, a process that took about 10 years and was completed in time for the next war.

ABOVE John Montague, 4th Earl of Sandwich.

RIGHT The stern of an elaborate model of the *Bellona*, one of the first of the new 74-gun ships. It is believed that this model was used by Sandwich and Middleton to demonstrate the principle of coppering to the King and it shows the technique in great detail.

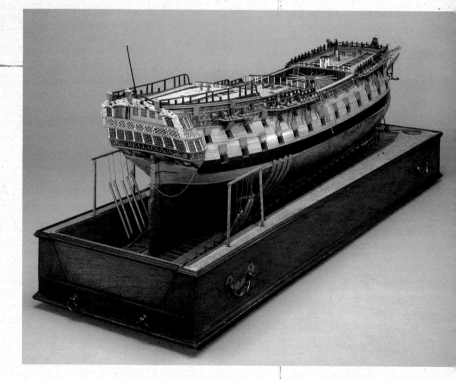

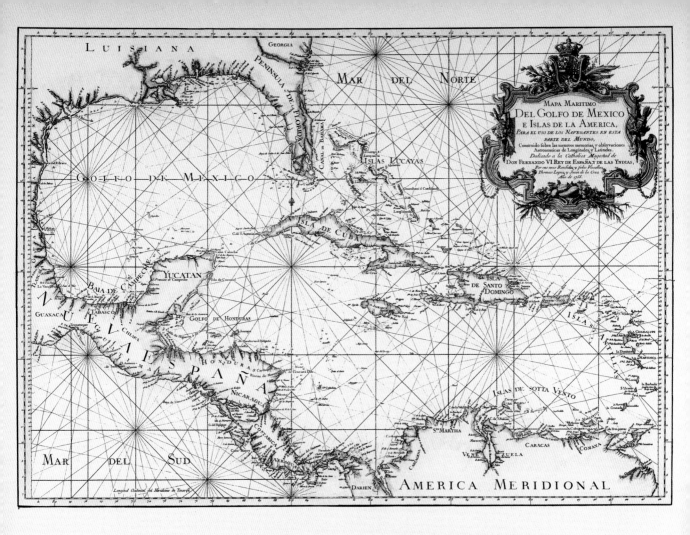

ABOVE A Spanish chart of the West Indies, dated 1760. The British possessions in the region were small compared with France and Spain, consisting of Jamaica and some of the small islands of the Lesser Antilles to the right; but they were highly profitable and fiercely fought over throughout the eighteenth century.

OPPOSITE ABOVE This statue of Admiral Sir George Rodney, at Spanish Town, Jamaica, celebrates his victory at the Saintes. In February 1783 the government of Jamaica commissioned John Bacon, a renowned British sculptor, to create the statue as an expression of the island's appreciation.

OPPOSITE BELOW In the Battle of Frigate Bay, St Kitts, Sir Samuel Hood's fleet at anchor in the bay fight off an attack by the French squadron, as seen from nearby Nevis. Painted by Thomas Maynard in 1783.

turn for the better. The war had now switched to the West Indies, which were vital to the economies of both Britain and France. The islands had three main advantages. Their climate allowed the growing of profitable commodities such as sugar, coffee and later cotton. They were close to the circular wind pattern of the North Atlantic, which allowed ships to travel in both directions between there and Europe. And they were all quite small, so that no plantation was far from the sea. This also meant that the nation that had sea power in the area had total control, and could move an army around to suppress a slave revolt, or to take an island from another colonial power. The islands accounted for about £3 million, a quarter of British imports, in 1772–3. About half of the ships of Liverpool traded there, while Glasgow's trade was also rising. As well as the vast profits to be made, the islands also provided a 'nursery for seamen' who would man the navy in wartime. They were even more vital in the French economy, accounting for nearly a

third of her foreign trade. Already in this war the French had taken seven out of ten of the largest British islands in the region.[11] If they could take Jamaica and perhaps Barbados as well, the British economy and the Royal Navy would be crippled.

Admiral Sir George Rodney was not a very attractive character, though he was affable enough in company. He was a compulsive gambler who had fled to Paris to escape his creditors in peacetime. His habit of appointing favourites to command was far from unusual, but his judgement of character was very poor and he once promoted his immature and incompetent son to captain at the age of 15. Nevertheless he was a good commander in battle, something that was desperately needed. He was appointed to command the fleet on the Leeward Islands Station in 1779. On the way out he paused to relieve Gibraltar from a Spanish siege, fighting at night against the common rules of warfare. When the Dutch declared war he took the opportunity to take the island of St Eustatius, rich from trading with both sides in the war. He became diverted by £3 million worth of plunder and neglected his operational duties. He ignored the laws of war, and the legal implications would dog him for years to come.

There had already been a series of indecisive actions between the British and French fleets in the West Indies. The most notable was off St Kitts, the oldest British colony in the region, in January 1782 when the French captured the island and were besieging Brimstone Hill, the 'Gibraltar of the Caribbean'. Admiral Samuel Hood's plans for a surprise attack on the French fleet collapsed and he took up a very clever defensive position in Frigate Bay, with his ships in a chevron formation pointing towards the prevailing wind. The French attack was driven off, but such defensive actions were never going to save the situation.

At last in April 1782, Rodney came up against Admiral De Grasse in the waters between Guadeloupe and Dominica, just off the small islands of the Saintes. There was an indecisive action on the 9th, but on the 12th the two fleets came together in the trade winds, with the French steering roughly south and the British forming up their fleet and heading in the opposite direction. As the fleets passed one another, Rodney's officers began to notice gaps in the French line just as the wind shifted in their favour. The Admiral, generally a tactical conservative, allowed his ships to break the line, perhaps urged on by his aide Sir Howard Douglas, or perhaps by accident. Admiral Hood did the same with his ships further down the line. The British were able to deploy their gun power in raking the enemy as they passed through and they cut off several sections of the French fleet and isolated a number of ships. They captured five ships of the line, including the great flagship *Ville de Paris*. The Battle of the Saintes showed that results could be achieved by abandoning the Fighting Instructions and breaking the line. Unlike Quiberon Bay and the two battles off Finisterre, the Saintes was fought against fleets whose formation was still largely intact and it showed the

way for the future. Rodney missed an even greater opportunity when he refused to pursue the defeated French, saying, 'Come, come, we have done very handsomely', but the battle removed any French threat to the British West Indies, and ruined their plans to take Jamaica.

Despite the victory, the loss of the Royal Navy's great flagship *Royal George* much nearer home at the end of August added to a sense of gloom. Almost certainly it was bad seamanship and a faulty command structure that caused her to capsize at Spithead with the loss of around a thousand lives (for no one knew how many sailors' 'wives' were on board), but it was blamed on faulty construction, another blow to the much maligned Navy Board.

At the Peace of Paris in 1783, American independence was recognised with ill grace by the British, who refused to turn up for the official painting. France seemed victorious though she had not won a major battle, and gained little in the colonial war. The British Empire, damaged but not destroyed, entered a new phase as the government began to look for colonies elsewhere. Independence was not the end of relations between Britain and the new United States of America, for British trade with the country flourished. In the early 1770s before the war broke out, British exports had averaged around £2.75 million per year. In the early 1790s they averaged £4.8 million, peaking at £6 million in 1796. Physical control of the country was no longer necessary for trade with it to expand.

THESE PAGES 'The Battle of the Saintes' by Thomas Luny. It shows the situation after the line was broken with several single-ship duels between the British and French ships of the line, including the flagship *Ville de Paris* under attack by the *Formidable* in the centre. It was a turning point in naval tactics, as well as the campaign in the West Indies.

Chapter 10
CRISIS AND MUTINY

Most British colonies were founded by private enterprise and defended by the help, however distant, of the Royal Navy. Potential naval bases such as Gibraltar and Minorca were often taken by the navy itself, but Australia was a unique case in several ways. Many reasons were put forward for colonising the continent, most of them maritime.

> This project of a settlement in that quarter has appeared in many Proteus-like form, sometimes as a halfway house to China, again as a check on the Spaniards at Manila and their Acapulco trade; sometimes as a place for transported convicts; then as a place of Asylum for American refugees; and sometimes as an Emporium for supplying our Marine Yards with Hemp and Cordage or for carrying on the fur trade on the N.W. Coast of America ...[12]

But it was the convict problem that caused the government to take action. It was no longer possible to send prisoners to the American colonies. They could instead be kept in hulks – old warships moored near the Royal Dockyards where the convicts could carry out hard labour – but these were becoming grossly overcrowded even by eighteenth-century penal standards, and a rebuilding of Newgate Gaol was not nearly enough to cope. According to popular theory there was a whole class of criminals, especially in London. Many of them preyed on shipping in the River Thames under picturesque names like 'scuffle hunters' and 'heavy horsemen' and it was estimated that millions of pounds worth of goods were stolen every year. Though the British now claimed to be masters of the seas, their more detailed control over their main trading river was very shaky; it is no coincidence that the Thames River

148

View of the JUSTITIA HULK, with the Convicts at Work, near Woolwich.

MORTELLA TOWER. Corsica.

A Middle Story
B Second Story
C Entering door
D Powder Room
E Kitchen
F Embrasures for 3 Guns
G Cistern
H Stand for employing the Cistern

ABOVE A diagram of the circular Mortella tower near St Florent on Corsica. Its defence of the bay made a strong impression on the British naval and army officers and it was a model for many later towers on the coast of southern and eastern England, and elsewhere.

Police, formed in 1798, was the first real police force in the country.

In contrast to this there was a new continent, peopled only by Aborigines who did not appear to live up to the intellectual ideal of the 'noble savage' and therefore deserved no consideration. The constant use of the death penalty had failed to deter crime in Britain, but would it be possible to transport a whole class to the other side of the world where they would remain in subjection, make good or perish?

The 'First Fleet' to Australia sailed from the Solent on 13 May 1787. It was commanded by Captain Arthur Phillip, a naval officer with few con-

nections, who had served in both the recent wars and had experience of convict transport with the Portuguese navy. His 11 ships carried 736 male and female convicts, along with their crews and guards. It was the first of many groups of ships, which would ultimately take 160,000 men and women unwillingly across the world. Not without reason the convicts feared a long voyage across barely known seas, to a land that even their gaolers hardly knew. They would spend months in the dark holds of tiny ships, confined by bars and fetters and subject to seasickness and pestilence.

> [We were] chained two and two together and confined in the hold during the whole course of our long voyage. ... we were scarcely allowed a sufficient quantity of victuals to keep us alive, and scarcely any water; for my part, I could have eaten three or four of our allowances, and you know well that I was never a great eater. ... When any of our comrades that were chained to us died, we kept it a secret as long as we could for the smell of a dead body, in order to get their allowance of provision ...[13]

The Royal Navy was indirectly responsible for the fact that North America became English-speaking. It was far more directly responsible for Australia. The habitable areas along the coast were discovered by Cook's expedition. The colony was largely founded to supply naval needs; the navy transported convicts who would be ther first settlers, and its marines guarded them. Its officers provided the first governors of New South Wales and later colonies.

Just as this extremely authoritarian society was being set up on the far side of the world, a new sense of liberty was developing much closer to home. When the French Revolution broke out in 1789, many in Britain welcomed it as a step towards the sort of parliamentary monarchy that already ruled Britain, but power soon fell into increasingly extreme hands. The intensive use of the guillotine during the Reign of Terror and the exe-

ABOVE 'The Glorious First of June' by Nicholas Pocock, himself a former seaman. This painting shows the *Brunswick* engaged with the French *Vengeur*, which suffered so much damage that she later sank.

LEFT The Union flag, used by Howe's flagship *Queen Charlotte* during the First of June battle, laid out on the floor of the Queen's House in Greenwich. It was probably made on board by sailmakers; hence the inaccuracy of its design. It does not show the Irish cross of St Patrick, which was only incorporated after the Acts of Union 1801.

cution of the King and Queen caused revulsion, though there was a strong body of middle-class opinion that supported the Corresponding Societies and other bodies devoted to extending the parliamentary franchise in Britain. Nevertheless, early in 1793 Britain joined a coalition of conservative forces and entered into a war with Revolutionary France.

At first the Royal Navy's task looked easy. The French navy had largely been run by aristocratic officers who had fled or been executed or deposed, and petty officers and merchant ship captains did not make good substitutes. There were revolts throughout the country, including one in Toulon which handed over the great naval base to coalition forces. But the allies failed to co-operate, Revolutionary forces were skilfully handled by a young artillery officer, Napoleon Bonaparte, and on withdrawal from Toulon the British failed to destroy most of the ships in the harbour. The British found another base when Corsica revolted from French rule, which had only been imposed a few decades earlier. In alliance with the nationalist Pasquale Paoli, they took over the island though they had to fight for three northern strong-points. At St Florent they had to defeat the Mortella Tower, which inflicted severe losses on British ships and troops. Bastia was taken after a siege and at Calvi the young Captain Nelson lost the sight of his right eye before the town was captured. A fine naval harbour was now available in Ajaccio, but the occupation was doomed without popular support. To the Corsicans it provided liberation from foreign rule, while the British saw the island as another Ireland to be ruled by them. Differences between the two concepts forced the British to withdraw in 1796.

On the Atlantic coast of France, the navy supported further unsuccessful revolts and blockaded French harbours. In 1794 a fleet was sent out to stop a French grain convoy returning from the United States, which stood between the country and starvation. It met the French 400 miles out in the Atlantic, the only great battle of the age to be fought out of sight of land. Six French ships were captured on what the British called The Glorious First of June, but the French could claim some kind of victory in that the grain convoy escaped. The navy settled down to a long blockade in the familiar waters of Brest. Lord Howe and his successors used a system of 'open' blockade. Most of the fleet would be resting in Torbay or the Solent, but frigates off the French port would follow the enemy if he escaped, while others would inform the main fleet.

The Prime Minister, William Pitt the Younger, was a great peace minister but was not noted for his strategic grasp and had few ideas for offensive action. He deployed large forces in the West Indies where, as in previous wars, highly profitable sugar islands could be taken by the nation enjoying naval superiority. This was helped by a slave revolt led by Toussaint L'Ouverture in St Domingue (later Haiti), but that was a two-edged weapon, as the British were not known for treating their own slaves well, and they made little progress in that country. Large military forces were committed to the region and some islands were indeed captured, but it was questionable whether a revolutionary regime could be defeated by what was essentially economic warfare.

There were two indecisive fleet actions in the Mediterranean under Admiral William Hotham in 1795, until Sir John Jervis took command of the fleet in the following year. The latter was a domineering character with strong views on naval duties and discipline. In the meantime Napoleon Bonaparte had taken command of the French army in Italy and was sweeping all before him. When Spain declared war on Britain in 1796, Jervis decided to evacuate the Mediterranean completely and station the bulk of his forces to face the main Spanish fleet off Cadiz. He had some success on 14 February 1797, when he encountered a Spanish fleet protecting a convoy off Cape St Vincent. His approach was too slow and would probably have allowed the Spanish to escape, until Commodore Nelson anticipated orders and took his ship out of the line for a more direct attack. The result was the capture of four Spanish ships of the line, including two very large ones – a much needed victory when the land war was going very badly. Jervis took the title Earl of St Vincent from the site of the battle.

One snag about the policy of open blockade was that sailors were underemployed during the long weeks in port. Mutiny was a longstanding tradition in the Royal Navy, but it nearly always took place when the ship was at anchor – the 1789 mutiny on the *Bounty*,

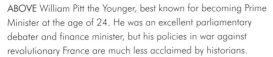

ABOVE William Pitt the Younger, best known for becoming Prime Minister at the age of 24. He was an excellent parliamentary debater and finance minister, but his policies in war against revolutionary France are much less acclaimed by historians.

ABOVE Sir John Jervis, the Earl of St Vincent, who took his title from the battle off the coast of Portugal. This is a copy of a picture by John Hoppner in the Royal Collection, which was painted around 1808, showing him wearing the uniform of a full admiral.

when Captain Bligh was deposed, was a notable exception. It was quite common for the seamen to refuse to raise the anchor if the ship was to be sent on foreign service without them being paid first, and there were perhaps hundreds of cases where the matter was settled without any recourse to higher authority.

By 1797 the seamen had more grievances than ever. They had fought four long years of war without any sign of victory and release. Their wages had not risen since the days of Oliver Cromwell, but now there was substantial price inflation which made it difficult to support a family ashore. There is no evidence that the seamen were much affected by the spirit of the French Revolution and nearly all of them were res-

olutely non-political, but underneath it all was an idea that old values were dying. There were many Irish seamen in the fleet, and it was easy for propagandists to link them with revolts in their own country, though that was not a decisive factor. The real issue was that the seamen, the men who made the navy work, who fought bravely in battle and waited patiently in port, were legitimately dissatisfied with their lot, neglected by politicians and the taxpayer. The standard of leadership among junior officers had perhaps declined due to the great expansion of the navy from 16,000 to 120,000 men, and the old system of almost feudal deference was dying out. The seaman had to suffer an increasing number of bad officers using what the Amer-

ABOVE Commodore Horatio Nelson leading a boarding party on to the Spanish ship of the line *San Josef*, showing his daring as well as his tactical skill. Boarding had largely fallen out of use as a tactic by this time, but Nelson was ready to do anything to get at the enemy.

icans might call 'cruel and unusual punishments', such as Lieutenants Hicks and Fitzpatrick of the *Glory*.

> *The former has in every means behaved tyrannically to the people with ordering them to be beat in the most cruel manner ... beating, blacking, tarring, and putting the people's heads in bags to the mortification of the whole ship's company ...*[14]

The crew of another ships complained, 'We might rather wish ourselves in prison or killed at once', while those of a third wrote, 'We are kept more like convicts than free-born Britons.'[15]

The seamen had an innate sense of justice and in 1797 the Channel Fleet, anchored at Spithead off Portsmouth, began to do something about it. In April they supported a petition to the Admiralty describing 'the many hardships and oppressions we have laboured under for many years, which, we hope, your lordships will redress as soon as possible'. In particular they objected to the low wages and demanded a rise 'that we might be the better able to support our wives and families in a manner comfortable'. They wanted to end the practice whereby a purser's pound was only 14 ounces, with the extra two going to the purser. They wanted flour and more vegetables in harbour, and better care for the sick. Finally, they wanted some guarantees of leave on shore,

> *...that we may be looked upon as a number of men standing in defence of our country; and that we may in somewise have grant and*

VOLUNTEERS.

G.   R. III.

God Save the King.

LET us, who are Englifhmen, protect and defend our good KING and COUNTRY againft the Attempts of all *Republicans* and *Levellers*, and againft the Defigns of our NATURAL ENEMIES, who intend in this Year to invade OLD ENGLAND, *our happy Country*, to murder our gracious KING as they have done *their own* ; to make WHORES of our *Wives* and *Daughters* ; to rob us of our Property, and teach us nothing but the *damn'd Art of murdering one another.*

ROYAL TARS
Of OLD ENGLAND,

If you love your COUNTRY, and your LIBERTY, now is the Time to fhew your Love.

R E P A I R,

All who have good Hearts, who love their KING, their COUNTRY, and RELIGION, who hate the FRENCH, and damn the POPE,

TO

Lieut. W. J. Stephens,

At his Rendezvous, SHOREHAM,

Where they will be allowed to Enter for any SHIP of WAR,

AND THE FOLLOWING

BOUNTIES will be given by his MAJESTY,
in Addition to Two Months Advance.

To Able Seamen,   - - -   *Five Pounds.*
To Ordinary Seamen,   - - -   *Two Pounds Ten Shillings.*
To Landmen,   - - . -   *Thirty Shillings.*

Conduct-Money paid to go by Land, and their Chefts and Bedding fent Carriage free.
Thofe Men who have ferved as PETTY-OFFICERS, and thofe who are otherwife qualified, will be recommended accordingly.

LEWES: PRINTED BY W. AND A. LEE.

The DELEGATES in COUNSEL or BEGGARS on HORSEBACK

ABOVE A print of mutinous sailors drawing up their demands while occupying the great cabin of a warship, a space usually reserved for captains and admirals. The print suggests anarchy, with Britannia upside down, orders torn up, and the parliamentary opposition, led by Charles Fox, 'at the bottom of it'.

LEFT A recuitment poster printed in Sussex at the height of the naval manning crisis of 1797. The 'rendezvous' was the local recruiting station, probably a hired room in an inn.

opportunity to taste the sweets of liberty on shore, when in any harbour, and when we have completed the duty of our ship, after our return from sea'.[16]

The crews of the Channel Fleet refused to raise anchor and elected delegates who took control of the ships. With its main armed force out of action and the French victorious on the other side of the Channel, the government chose conciliation. Seamen's wages were raised and there were concessions on some of the other issues.

Various ships were anchored at the Nore in the Thames estuary and they soon heard of the revolt and the success of the 'breeze from Spithead'. Admiral Adam Duncan of the North Sea Fleet dealt with a mutiny in his own ship by holding a ringleader over the side and saying, 'My lads, look at this fellow, he who dares to deprive me of the command of the fleet!' But in May the ships at the Nore revolted, demanding more concessions and displacing many of their officers. This time the government felt it had to draw the line and it took steps to isolate and starve the mutineers, who eventually gave up.

Some tried to blame the mutinies on a sudden influx of Quota men, 'Billy Pitt's men', who had been recruited by the local authorities to expand the navy quickly. Certainly these men, often unfamiliar with the sea and with a slightly higher standard of education, a midshipman. Parker was hanged, as were 28 other ringleaders from the Nore; more than 400 men were tried by court martial but most were pardoned.[17]

The mutinies were perhaps the most serious crisis of the British state in the whole of the Georgian period. The seamen had no intention of undermining the war effort or allowing the French to invade, but they did raise serious possibilities of defeat. Fortunately they were hushed up at the time and were over before the French had wind of them, but they may have influenced future French governments, who tended to believe that Britain was full of effete aristocrats, disaffected middle classes, discontented workers, Irish rebels and mutinous seamen.

For all its faults, the Royal Navy was the nearest thing to a meritocratic society outside revolutionary France. Certainly there was a strong aristocratic

ABOVE Richard Parker, the ringleader of the Nore mutineers, who had once been a midshipman but had fallen on hard times and entered the navy as a seaman. He was hanged after the affair.

RIGHT Sailors around a mess table, as drawn by Captain Marryat. The mess was the centre of the sailor's social life, and the ability to tell a good yarn was a cardinal social virtue. Note that the black sailor is accepted in this, the most domestic of naval settings.

OPPOSITE Admiral Duncan, with some of his officers standing behind him, receiving the surrender of the Dutch commander De Winter after defeating him in the Battle of Camperdown, as painted by Daniel Orme.

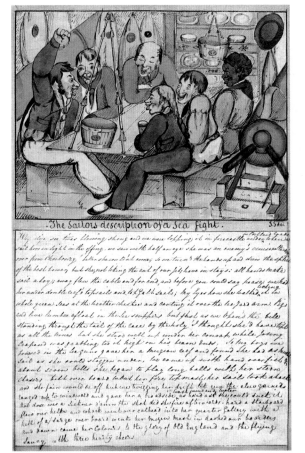

were an unstable element, but all the delegates at Spithead were able seamen or petty officers, often slightly older than average and perhaps with families to keep. It was a similar picture among those tried by court martial after the Nore mutiny. Such men were the natural leaders of the ship's company. True, the leader at the Nore, Richard Parker, had come in as a Quota man, but he was a former seaman who had once been

element in the officer corps, who expected fast promotion by means of friends and family, and Captain Basil Hall was tolerant of it as a way of luring the highest-born into the service, to bring their gentlemanly values with them. Without the 'rapid, or as it is called, unfair promotion of young men of family, ... such persons would speedily cease to exist in the Navy at all.'[18] But on the other side, Jane Austen knew the service well, for two of her brothers were officers. Her hypocritically snobbish character Sir Walter com-

plained of the navy, 'I have two strong grounds of objection to it. First, as being a means of bringing persons of obscure birth into undue distinction, and raising men to honours which their fathers and grandfathers never dreamt of; and secondly, as it cuts up a man's youth and vigour most horribly.'[19]

On the lower deck, crews were made up of men from many different nations: HMS *Caledonia* had Swedes, Frenchmen, Portuguese, North Americans, West Indians, Brazilians, Germans, Italians, Africans

and Russians on board.[20] There was little race distinction. Prints of the period quite commonly show black sailors doing their duty at the guns, taking risks in battle and even being accepted in the intimate world of the mess table. Frederick Marryat had even closer experience of the navy than Jane Austen, having served as a midshipman under Lord Cochrane. In his highly popular novel *Midshipman Easy* his black character Mesty is far superior in intelligence to the white seamen and is promoted to petty officer.

The wave of mutiny was not yet over and in September 1797 there was the most savage incident of all. Captain Hugh Pigot of the frigate *Hermione* was already known as a tyrant when one day in the West Indies he tried to sharpen up his crew's sail drill by ordering that the last men off the yardarm should be flogged. As a result two men fell to their deaths and Pigot ordered their bodies thrown overboard. That night the crew rose in revolt. They butchered most of their officers and took the ship into a Spanish port. This was deeply shocking to every naval officer and there was jubilation when HMS *Surprise* recaptured the ship from the Spanish Caribbean port of Puerto Cabello in October 1799, while some of the mutineers were tracked down and hanged.

In October 1797 there was no longer any doubt about Duncan's command of the North Sea Fleet, and he confronted a Dutch squadron off their own coast, near a place that the British came to call Camperdown. His fleet was made up of small ships of the line, mostly obsolete 64-gun ships and converted East Indiamen, but he sailed into action in two columns against the Dutch, ignoring the dangers of shallow waters and headlong attack. Eleven Dutch ships of the line were captured, providing an immense boost to national morale in very difficult times.

At home, the threat of invasion was revived as French forces were built up across the Channel. It was a far more terrifying prospect than previous invasions. The mass guillotining during the Reign of Terror was well known, and cartoons showed fire, execution and slaughter on a huge scale if the French should ever land. By the end of 1799 Napoleon Bonaparte had returned from his failure in Egypt and assumed political power in France as First Consul, at the age of 30. An all-conquering general and an autocratic leader, he was no less terrifying than the revolutionaries. Despite the threat the British were only just beginning to find a new unity, for the seamen were not the only people with grievances. The middle classes sought more political power through the Corresponding Societies, and the French tried unsuccessfully to ally with Irish nationalists such as Wolfe Tone. When volunteer units of soldiers were formed throughout the country they often used the word 'Loyal' in their title to show that they had a political as well as a military role. The publisher Rudolf Ackermann outlined their aims in 1799: 'To defeat the malice of our Country's common Enemy, and to crush the heads of Cerberian disloyalty; to preserve the good order of the Realm, and to protect our individual Property; and above all, for the safety of our Sovereign, and every branch of his august Family'.[21] But as the threat became more national and less political, the volunteers became more of a national and unifying force.

To pay for the increasingly expensive war, the government had to use its credit to the limit, and find more ways to raise taxes. Traditionally wars had been paid for by taxes on land, which were easy to collect as it was not possible to conceal a piece of ground, but put most of the burden on the traditional landowners. The government already levied duties on servants, carriages, ribbons and even windows – luxury items that were not easy to hide. In 1799 it had to take the very radical step of introducing income tax, which was the only realistic way of tapping into the growing monetary wealth of the nation. But this involved a considerable bureaucracy to assess and collect it, and intrusion into the affairs of every Briton who earned

LEFT A painting by Geoff Hunt, used as the book cover for *The Black Ship* by Dudley Pope, gives a sense of foreboding of the circumstances to come on the *Hermione*.

Consequences of a Suc————cessful French Invasion.

Nᵒ I. — Plate 2ᵈ. "We explain de Rights of Man to de Noblesse." — Scene. The House of Lords.

Description. — A Guillotine, which is placed on the Throne; the royal Chairs being removed, pour ac-commoder les Etrangers, (in English) To accommo-date the Strangers; Two Turkish Mutes, with strangling Bowstrings, each his Hand on his Mouth, stand as Sup-porters. The House empty of Peers. On a Board is written "Solitudinem faciunt, Pacem appellant." (in En-glish) They (that is, the French) create Solitude, and call it Peace." The Cap of Liberty above the Canopy, below which is painted in capital Letters "Confusion to all Order". A French Admi-ral, looking at the Tapestry, which represents the Defeat of ÿ Spanish invincible Armada, & the Portraits of the Immortal English Commanders, says "Me like not de Omen; destroy it". French Soldiers with Swords, Pikes, & several Bayonets, attack the Tapestry, on one side of the Room. A Sea Captain, on the Top of a Ladder, tears down ÿ Tapes-try from above; his Lieutenant sets fire to it below, & at the same Time pulls the Foot of the Ladder to break his Superior's Neck; saying "This is an easier Way of getting Preferment than de English Way". — Un Commandant en Chef, (in English) The Commander in Chief, in his full Republican Uniform, point-ing at the Mace, says "Here, take away this Bauble; but if there be any Gold, on "it, send it to my Lodging". A French Soldier carries it away on his Shoulder

Sir John Dalrymple, inv. *J. Gillray Nᵒ 27 Sᵗ James's Street.* *J. Gillray fecit.*

more than £60 per year. It was not long since Pitt himself had condemned income tax as 'an inquisition which would be generally invidious' but he hoped that it would raise £10 million a year. Some compared it with Ship Money, though in this case it was passed by parliament. When the tax was repealed at the end of the war, it was insisted that the commissioners' record be cut into small pieces and droped into the mash tub of a paper mill, so much was it hated.[22]

ABOVE The cartoonist James Gillray's vision of French rule, with the mace and tapestries of the House of Lords being looted and a guillotine set up over the woolsack.

OPPOSITE This Gillray cartoon of 1806 shows John Bull looking out of the upstairs window, as Charles James Fox and Henry Pett pay a visit in search of even more money to pay for the war.

Below decks in HMS *Victory*

HMS *Victory*, Nelson's flagship at Trafalgar, featured in Episode 3. Launched in 1765, she is the oldest warship in the world and the only surviving three-decked ship of the line. Although no longer afloat, today she is the flagship of the Second Sea Lord and Commander-in-Chief Naval Home Command and can be seen in No 2 dry dock at Portsmouth Historic Dockyard. Her iconic hull was painted in the 1803

rebuild at Chatham when, 'Victory's magazine was lined with copper, her figurehead and masts replaced and the paint scheme changed from red to the black and yellow we see today'.

Dan Snow explored the gun decks and the photographs below left show a wealth of detail of the tackles and ropes used to restrain the guns, and the carriages on which they could recoil and be rolled out through the gunports.

Filming also took place in the Hold in the bowels of the ship. Up to six months' supply of food and drink could be stored there. Most provisions were kept in barrels, which can be seen in the photograph below right, as well as the shingle ballast, which could be moved around the hold to alter the trim of the ship as supplies became depleted. Barrels could also be sunk into it, to prevent them moving around at sea.

LORD HOTHAM'S ACTION, March 14th 1795

Painted by T. Whitcombe

Published Sept 1 1816, at 48 Strand, for J. Jenkins's Naval Achievements.

ABOVE The aftermath of Hotham's action in March 1795 – a rather triumphalist print for an inconclusive action, showing the captured *Censeur* and *Ça Ira* with their tricolore flags hanging in low defeat after their capture by Nelson – but it was regarded as a great victory.

Engraved by I. Sutherland.

Chapter 11
NELSON AND THE
NEW TACTICS

Naval tactics, as used in great fleet battles, had developed by stages since the old days of Mathews, Byng and the Fighting Instructions. Anson had taken the first step towards a new order at Finisterre in 1747, when he had used a loophole to order a general chase and achieved a victory. Hawke had also used a chase at Quiberon Bay to get an even more spectacular result. Rodney had taken the most radical step of all at the Saintes when he broke the enemy line. He may or may not have been influenced by John Clerk of Eldin, a Scottish theoretical tactician who rarely went to sea and was never near a naval battle. He developed the theory of the attack 'from to windward', and the value of breaking the enemy line. His supporters claimed that he had a decisive influence on Camperdown and the *Edinburgh Evening Courant* reported, 'It is a most remarkable instance in the history of Admiral Duncan that he lived himself to illustrate the truth of the doctrine of his early friend, Mr Clerk, whose system of naval tactics he was the first to patronise, and to recommend to the British Navy.'[23] Nelson's friend, Captain Hardy, wrote later,

> Our departed friend, Lord Nelson, read Mr Clerk's works with great attention and frequently expressed his approbation of them in the fullest manner; he also recommended all the captains to read them with attention, and said that many good hints might be taken from them. He most approved of the attack from to-windward, and considered that breaking through the enemy's line absolutely necessary to obtain a great victory.[24]

One of Nelson's greatest assets was that he came fresh to fleet tactics in the mid 1790s. In his early career he had commanded small ships well away from the main force, and he had missed the great fleet battles of the American War. Even when in command of the ship of the line *Agamemnon* from 1793 he was mostly employed on other duties, until in March 1795 he was under Admiral Hotham in an indecisive action in the Mediterranean. He was responsible for the capture of two ships until the admiral recalled him. Nelson went on board the flagship and raged at the admiral, who answered calmly, like Rodney after the Saintes, 'We must be contented. We have done very well.' Nelson wrote to his wife afterwards, 'had we taken ten sail and allowed the 11th to escape when it had been possible to have got at her, I could ever have called it well done'. This statement, in favour of decisive, annihilating action, was the credo for the rest of Nelson's life. Sir John Jervis was an admiral much more to Nelson's taste, and it was under him that he had his first great triumph at the Battle of St Vincent in 1797. But Nelson was not the only officer to question the established tactical order by this time, and Duncan's tactics at Camperdown were not very different from those later used by Nelson.

Nelson had his first chance at independent command in 1798, when British intelligence reported an unusual build-up of land and sea forces in Toulon of which Bonaparte, the rising star of the French army, was taking charge. Nelson was given a small force of three ships of the line and three frigates to re-enter the Mediterranean and find out their intentions. Off Toulon he was struck by a gale and the rigging of his flagship, the 74-gun *Vanguard*, was seriously damaged. He carried out repairs off Sardinia but had lost contact with his frigates, whose captains had assumed that he would go back to Gibraltar for repairs. He was left with a force of three 74s, until he met a reinforcement of 10 more ships of the line off Toulon. Bonaparte had already sailed by this time with a great force of a dozen ships of the line, hundreds of transports and 31,000 troops to invade Egypt and open a land route to India.

Bonaparte stopped on the way to take Malta from the Knights of St John, and Nelson narrowly missed him after he sailed from there. Nelson had deduced correctly that the French were headed for Egypt, but in his impatience he overtook them and did not wait when he found they were not at Alexandria. Bonaparte landed soon afterwards, while Nelson searched the Mediterranean for him and replenished his ships at Syracuse. Soon he had reports from passing ships and other sources that the French had indeed landed near Alexandria.

Arriving off the port on 1 August, Nelson found that the French transports were safe in the harbour, but a fleet of ships of the line was anchored in a chevron formation in Aboukir Bay. The ships of the line were of an equal number in each fleet, but the French had one large 120-gun ship, *L'Orient,* and two 80s, whereas Nelson's ships were all 74s except for the inadequate 50-gun *Leander* and the tiny brig *Mutine.* Night was falling but Nelson had no hesitation in ordering an attack, against the conventional rules of naval warfare. He allowed his captains an unusual degree of initiative and it was probably Captain Thomas Foley, in command of the *Goliath*, who made the key tactical decision. He spotted that there was room between the shore and the French ship at the head of the line, and passed through the gap to attack on the inshore side. The French had not expected this, and their tactical preparations were generally very shoddy. Several more ships followed Foley until Nelson arrived in the *Vanguard* and began to engage the enemy on the other side. The ships at the head of the French line were already being beaten into surrender when battle developed around the great flagship *L'Orient.* Eventually she caught fire and was torn apart by a huge explosion that shocked and deafened all around. Nelson was already wounded and had been taken below, but his captains continued the fight throughout the night. Next morning, all but two of the French ships of the line had been taken, destroyed or driven aground. Tactically it owed nothing to the Fighting Instructions. The French, who had been in line of battle, had been crushed. The

ABOVE The French flagship *L'Orient* blows up at the climax of the Battle of the Nile, an event which deafened and traumatised all who saw it and brought the action to a halt for a while. Painted by George Arnauld.

British captains, Nelson's Band of Brothers, had attacked independently and won the most decisive naval victory of the age.

Its strategic importance was just as great. Bonaparte was isolated and eventually he would return home without his army. The British fleet was now in control of the Mediterranean, and this made it much easier to seek new allies against the French. Turkey and Russia soon joined in a new coalition, and Austria followed later. But these allies had different aims and ambitions, and eventually the coalition fell apart. Meanwhile Nelson became too closely involved with the affairs of Naples while he was recuperating there and repairing his ships. His friend Sir William Hamil-

ton was British ambassador there, and Nelson became increasingly and dangerously close to his wife, Emma. Suffering from a head wound and the strain of battle, Nelson made some very poor decisions and was eventually recalled home, where he was treated as a hero. The British continued to make some significant gains in the Mediterranean, taking Minorca in 1798, Malta in 1800 and Egypt in 1801.

In 1801 Nelson was appointed as second-in-command of a fleet under Sir Hyde Parker, to deal with a threatened alliance between Denmark, Russia, Prussia and Sweden, which might keep Britain out of the Baltic where she obtained much of her naval stores. The fleet was off Copenhagen by the end of March and the Danish fleet was formed up at anchor in a line, supported by floating batteries and shore forts. Nelson prepared meticulously for an attack by surveying the waters the night before, and began to sail in on 2 April. There were difficulties as a number of ships ran

Dreſses a la Nile respectfully dedicated to the Fashion Mongers of the day.

only one eye – I have the right to be a little blind sometimes ... I really do not see the signal.' The issue remained in the balance until the Danish Crown Prince offered a truce and negotiations. Before these were concluded it was found that Czar Paul I of Russia had died and the motivation for the alliance had collapsed. Copenhagen is regarded as one of Nelson's three great victories, but it is the only one in which the outcome was ever in doubt, and perhaps he needed a little luck to claim it as a success.

In 1802 William Pitt's government fell from office and a new one was formed under the far less effective Henry Addington – 'Pitt is to Addington as London is to Paddington', as the popular rhyme put it. With the usual situation of the British victorious on sea and the French on land, peace was concluded by the Treaty of Amiens, but Britain did not get a very good deal: the Cape of Good Hope, Egypt, Minorca and Malta were to

ABOVE LEFT AND RIGHT Nelson's triumph at the Nile was celebrated in many ways, and the public was eager for anything to commemorate the victory. 'Dress à la Nile', published very soon after the news of the battle reached London, shows a very spurious idea of Egyptian dress.

OPPOSITE Gillray's floating machine combines windmills, fortifications and paddle wheels to give a fantastic but rather frightening idea of what sort of craft the French might have up their sleeves during an attempted invasion. It was only one of a rash of ideas, including rockets, submarines and aerial bombardment by balloon.

aground and the enemy fought well. Hyde Parker, well offshore, signalled to Nelson to discontinue the action, but famously he put his telescope to his blind eye and commented to his captain, 'You know Foley, I have

be evacuated, though the last island was not in fact given up. St Vincent, now First Lord of the Admiralty, accepted the view that the peace was to be long-lasting and applied himself to the reform of the dockyards, which he believed were nests of corruption.

War resumed in 1803, because the British did not trust the French dictator and his ambitions. St Vincent carried out a mobilisation with characteristically ruthless use of the press gangs, even before the war started. At Harwich there was a 'man plunder' as the gangs took up every male in sight:

The Market house was to be their prison, where
a lieutenant was station'd with a guard of

Marines and before daylight next morning their
prison was full of all denominations, from the
Parish Priest to the farmer in his frock and
wooden Shoes. Even the poor Blacksmith cobler
taylor barber baker fisherman and doctor were
all dragg'd from their homes that night ...

The women of the town gathered round the
market house. 'Wives demanded their husbands, children their Fathers, and aged parents their Son
perhaps their only support.' Most would have to be
released as soon as it was established that they were
not seamen. A nervous lieutenant spoke to them.

I give you my word and honour that by this
day noon your husbands, Fathers and
Children shall be restored to your arms again,

AN ACCURATE REPRESENTATION of the FLOATING MACHINE
Invented by the FRENCH for INVADING ENGLAND. and Acts
on the principals of both Wind & Water Mills. carries 60-000 Men & 600 Cannon.

only such as are entitled to serve their king
owing to being able Seamen or gain their living
by the Salt water such as Fishermen &c. Every
other will be liberated as soon as my brother
Officers can all meet here ...[25]

Despite all this effort, the government had no
strategy for attacking the enemy. At the same time
Bonaparte (who was to crown himself as Emperor
Napoleon in 1804) could only attack the King's other
realm in Hanover, while building up a fleet of barges at
Boulogne for an invasion of England. The British
countered with the usual strategy of blockade.
Admiral Lord Keith was put in charge of the North Sea
Fleet, which also covered the eastern end of the

ABOVE The blockade of Boulogne. A line of small French ships is
behind the sandbanks close to the shore, with British sloops and
brigs in mid Channel and larger ships, including two-deckers, in the
foreground.

OPPOSITE A nineteenth-century example of a cat o'nine tails, which
some believed was at the core of naval discipline. In fact the picture
was far more complex. There were a few tyrannical captains, such
as Pigot of the *Hermione*, but others hardly used the cat at all.

English Channel and would face the main invasion
force if it were launched. 'Billy Blue' Cornwallis took
command of the Channel Fleet, whose main task was
the blockade of Brest. Nelson at last became a fully-
fledged commander-in-chief on the Mediterranean
Station and his main focus was the blockade of

Toulon. Unlike the close blockade St Vincent would have operated, Nelson preferred to spend much time away from the port at his tenuous bases in Sardinia, hoping he might lure the enemy out.

This stalemate lasted for two years. For much of the time the seaman's life was relaxed on blockade service. In 1805 John Powell wrote,

> We keep watch the same here as at sea, ie four hours up and the same down. I am in the starboard watch so that when the larboard watch is on in a morning we can sleep till 7 or 8 o'clock and sometimes longer. Some days we have but little to do but on others nobody would believe that is unused to the sea what a hurry we are all in. As a proof of it, last Monday I ate one part of my breakfast upon deck, another in the mizzen top and finished it on the mizzen topsail yard.[26]

Strict discipline was felt to be necessary to keep the men in order in a confined space. William Robinson describes a flogging.

> All hands now being mustered, the captain orders the man to strip; he is then seized to a grating by the wrists and knees; his crime is then mentioned, and the prisoner may plead, but, in nineteen cases out of twenty, he is flogged for the most trifling offence or neglect.[27]

Pitt resumed office in 1804 but he still had few ideas. After several fiascos off Boulogne, Napoleon began to realise that there was no chance of his invasion succeeding unless the French ships of the line could take control of the Channel and drive the British frigates and sloops away. He conceived a plan by which Admiral Villeneuve would evade Nelson (which was not particularly difficult) and escape from Toulon to lure him across the Atlantic to the West

Indies and attempt to lose him. Villeneuve would unite with the forces there and re-cross the ocean to pick up Spanish forces at Vigo and Cadiz, then the French fleet at Brest in order to overwelm the British Channel Fleet. All went well at first in the early days of 1805; Villeneuve escaped, Nelson was confused about his destination but followed and almost caught up with him in the West Indies, until false intelligence sent him south instead of north. When he realised that the French were heading back, he sent a fast frigate across the Atlantic to warn the government. Her captain, George Bettesworth, spotted the French and saw that they were going too far north to re-enter the Mediterranean and realised they must be headed for the Channel. Bettesworth dashed home and informed the new First Lord of the Admiralty, Lord Barham, formerly Sir Charles Middleton. Barham just had time to put together a squadron off Cape Finisterre under Admiral Calder. It fought an action with Villeneuve's fleet, in which two French ships were captured. This was indecisive by Nelsonian standards, but it was enough to convince Napoleon that his invasion plan was never going to succeed, and he took his army away from Boulogne to fight the Austrians.

After that Villeneuve's fleet moved from port to port, growing like a snowball and consuming supplies like a cuckoo in the nest. It ended up in Cadiz with a potential force of about 40 ships of the line, if all were serviceable at once. To counter this, Barham began to build up a strong British fleet off the port, and Nelson was recalled from leave to take command.

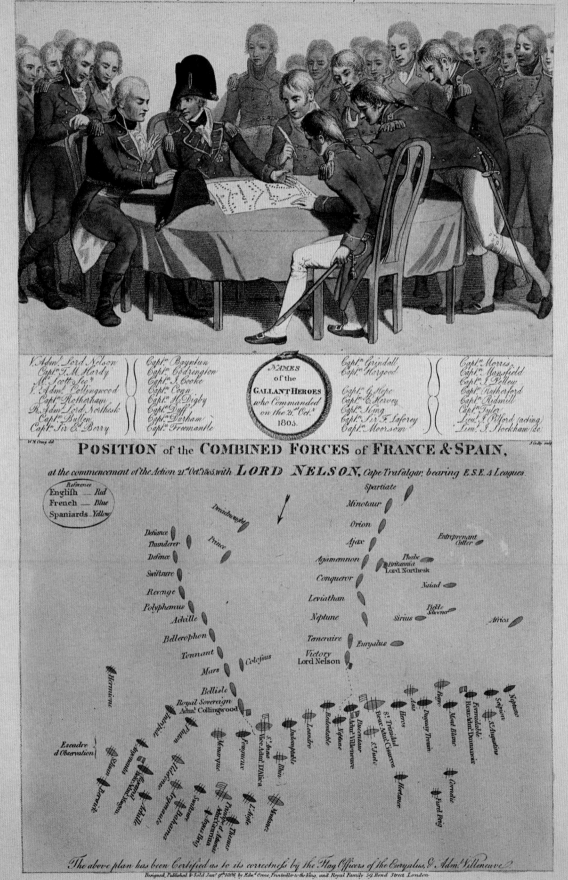

England expects every Man to do his duty.

LORD NELSON explaining to the Officers the PLAN of ATTACK previous to the BATTLE of TRAFALGAR.

Names of the GALLANT HEROES who Commanded on the 21.st Oct.r 1805.

V.l Adm.l Lord Nelson
Capt.n T. M. Hardy
M.r Scott Sec.y
V.l Adm.l Collingwood
Capt.n Rotheram
R. Adm.l Lord Northesk
Capt.n Bullen
Capt.n Sir E.d Berry

Capt.n Baynton
Capt.n Codrington
Capt.n I. Cooke
Capt.n Conn
Capt.n H. Digby
Capt.n Duff
Capt.n Durham
Capt.n Freemantle

Capt.n Grindall
Capt.n Hargood
Capt.n G. Hope
Capt.n E. Harvey
Capt.n King
Capt.n Sir F. Laforey
Capt.n Moorsom

Capt.n Morris
Capt.n Mansfield
Capt.n I. Pelley
Capt.n Rutherford
Capt.n Redmill
Capt.n Tyler
Lieu.t I. Pilford (acting)
Lieu.t I. Stockham do.

W.m Craig del.

POSITION of the COMBINED FORCES of FRANCE & SPAIN,

J. Godby sculp.

at the commencement of the Action 21.st Oct. 1805 with LORD NELSON, Cape Trafalgar, bearing E.S.E. 4 Leagues.

References
English — Red
French — Blue
Spaniards — Yellow

The above plan has been Certified as to its correctness by the Flag Officers of the Euryalus, & Adm.l Villeneuve.

Designed, Published & Sold Jan.r 9.th 1806, by Edw.d Orme, Printseller to the King, and Royal Family 59 Bond Street London.

SUBSCRIPTIONS for a SPLENDID ENGRAVING of the DEATH of NELSON, SIZE 23 by 17.th are RECEIVED at 59 BOND STREET.

He had thought a good deal about tactics during three brief weeks ashore. If his fleet was big enough he planned to divide it into three squadrons, two of equal strength. One, led by Nelson himself, would cut the enemy line of battle 'about one-third of their Line from their leading ship'. The other would attack the part of the line that had been cut off and create 'a pell-mell battle' in which the British would have a great advantage in gunnery. The smallest group, under an officer of great initiative and including the fastest sailing ships, would be placed 'in a situation of advantage', and would attack where it seemed most useful.

A day after arriving off Cadiz, Nelson described his ideas to the captains of the fleet in the great cabin of the *Victory*.

> *... when I came to explain to them the 'Nelson touch', it was like an electric shock. Some shed tears, all approved – 'it was new – it was singular – it was simple!'; and from the Admirals downwards, it was repeated – 'It*

> *must succeed, if they will allow us to get at them! You are, my Lord, surrounded by friends whom you inspire with confidence.'*[28]

Nelson tried to lure the enemy out as he had done off Toulon. He kept his ships 50 miles offshore so that the enemy would never know his strength, with a line of frigates to report enemy movements. When a new ship or squadron joined it was ordered not to fire a gun salute, which would alert the enemy. However, Nelson had to send squadrons in turn to Gibraltar to replenish, and on 19 October he had 27

OPPOSITE The Nelson Touch. The Admiral explains his tactics to his astonished captains; but in fact the tactics used on the day of Trafalgar were not quite what he had planned, partly because his fleet was smaller than he expected, but also possibly because Collingwood rushed into battle too fast.

BELOW Nelson's Trafalgar signal, 'England expects that every man will do his duty', was made with a new system that allowed individual words to be spelled out when necessary.

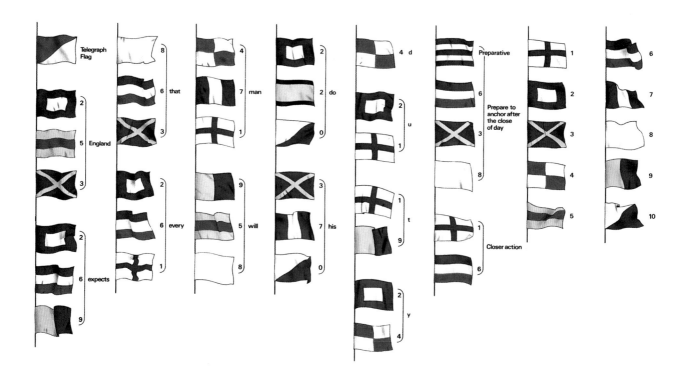

ships of the line when it was reported that the enemy fleet of 33 French and Spanish ships of the line was coming out.

Villeneuve had decided to take his force into the Mediterranean before he was dismissed by Napoleon. It took some time to get them out, but the great fleet was sailing south-east on the morning of 21 October 1805 when Villeneuve realised he was going to be intercepted by Nelson and turned round to try to run back into Cadiz. Nelson's fleet was smaller than he had hoped and his plans had to be adapted. He attacked on two columns, one led by himself, one by his old friend Vice Admiral Cuthbert Collingwood. It was a dangerous tactic, for on the approach his ships would be exposed, one by one, to the full force of the enemy broadsides and would barely be able to reply. It was only made possible because of the lack of practice of the enemy ships, which were arranged in a rather disorderly line of battle. Even so, the first ships of Collingwood's line

suffered heavily as they approached the enemy, as did the first two of Nelson's line, including the *Victory*. But once each ship was ready to cut through the line it would gain an advantage, firing its full broadside into the bows of the enemy astern, and the vulnerable stern of the ship ahead. After that, the ships settled into gunnery duels in groups of two, three or four.

In the *Victory*, Lieutenant Louis Roteley found a scene of horror.

> *A man should witness a battle in a three-decker from the middle deck, for it beggars all description. ... There was fire from above, fire from below, besides the fire from the deck I was upon, the guns recoiling with violence reports louder than thunder, the deck heaving and the side straining. ... Lips might move, but orders and hearing were out of the question: everything was done by signs.*

It was even worse in the cockpit as Lieutenant Paul Nicolas of the *Belleisle* found.

My nerves were but little accustomed to such trials, but even the dangers of the battle did not seem more terrific than the spectacle before me. On a long table lay several anxiously looking for their turn to receive the surgeon's care, yet dreading the fate which he might pronounce. One subject was undergoing amputation, and every part was heaped with sufferers: their piercing shrieks and expiring groans were echoed through this vault of misery; ... what a contrast to the hilarity and enthusiastic mirth which reigned in this spot the preceding evening![29]

The *Victory* found herself in a duel with the *Redoutable*, whose Captain, Lucas, had trained his men in musketry rather than the great guns. Nelson was hit in the shoulder by a musket ball fired from the tops,

OPPOSITE Pocock's view of the beginning of the Battle of Trafalgar shows the ragged Franco-Spanish line stretching diagonally from left to right. Collingwood's line is in the background; Nelson's is closer, heading from right to left.

BELOW The melée at the end of the battle with some ships dismasted, the *Superbe* on fire and other French and Spanish ships captured, while some of them escape in the background.

FOLLOWING PAGES Nelson is shot on the deck of *Victory* to the horror of Captain Hardy, while a midshipman fires into the rigging of *Redoutable* where the shot came from. The painting, by Denis Dighton, also shows much detail of gun crews at work and marines in action.

RIGHT Nelson's funeral procession up the Thames, showing the line of official naval barges in the centre of the river with other boats following, and people crowded on lighters and along the banks. St Paul's, the site of his burial, is in the left background.

An accurate View (*drawn & etched by J.T. Smith, Engraver of the ANTIQUITIES of* London & Westminster) *Greenwich to Whitehall; comprehending not only the First Barge covered with black cloth. The Standard, borne by Capt. Sir Fra. Laforey Bt Supported by Lieut. Barker an The Guidon, borne by Capt. Baynton (in the absence of Capt. Durham) supported by 2 Lieut. Rouge croix and pursuivants. ——— Second Barge, covered with black Cloth; Heralds of Arms, bearing the Surcoat, Target & Sword Crest & the Gauntlet & Spurs of the deceased: The Banner of the deceased, as K.B. borne by Capt. Rotheram. supp The great Banner, with the augmentations, borne by Capt. Moorsom, supported by Lieut. Keys & N. Tucker. ——— Thir with black Velvet, black plumes &c. Capt. Yule, Atkinson (Master of the Victory) Capt. Williams, Lieut. Brown & Pa The BODY: Norroy K. of Arms (in the absence of Clarenceux, indisposed) Union Flag: Attendants on the B*

which punctured his lung and passed through his spine. He was carried below in great agony and died slowly over the next three hours. There was little more he could have done by that time, his ships were fully engaged and the action was running their way. In the end 18 French and Spanish ships were sunk and one burned. The rest escaped into Cadiz, or were captured by another British squadron two weeks later. But a storm was brewing as Nelson had observed before his death. He urged that his ships be anchored after the fight, but most had their anchors shot away, and their crews were exhausted.

The three-day storm was worse than the battle for some. In the *Belleisle*,

The hours dragged tediously on, and death appeared in each gust of the tempest. In battle the chances were equal, and it was possible for many to escape; but shipwreck in such a hurricane was certain destruction to all, and the doubtful situation of the ship kept the mind in a perpetual state of terror. In this horrible suspense each stroke of the bell, as it proclaimed the hour, sounded as the knell of our approaching destiny, for none could expect to escape the impending danger...[30]

Many of the officers and men were traumatised by the battle.

... the action will be by the nation conceived a very glorious one but when the devastation is considered how can we glory in it? How many orphans and fatherless has it made? How many has it made sad and how few (concerned) has it made glad? In the Victory we do not feel it a victory. The loss of our chief has thrown a gloom around that nothing but the society of our friends and families can dispel. That quarterdeck which was formally crowded is emptied. The happy scenes we formerly witnessed are now laid aside, the theatre, the music, the dancing which accompanied the dull part of our time is now laid aside. We look to the seat of an old

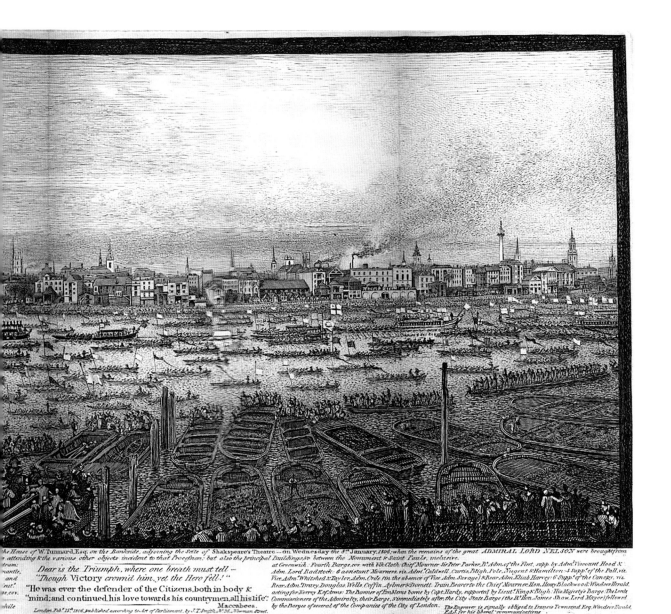

he House of W. Tunnard, Esq. on the Bankside, adjoining the Site of Shakspeare's Theatre — on Wednesday the 8.th January, 1806; when the remains of the great ADMIRAL LORD NELSON were brought from
attending & the various other objects incident to that Procession; but also the principal Buildings, &c. between the Monument & Saint Paul's, inclusive.

tram: *Dear is the Triumph, where one breath must tell —*
nantle,   "Though Victory crown'd him, yet the Hero fell!"
and
est: "He was ever the defender of the Citizens, both in body &
er, cov.   "mind; and continued his love towards his countrymen, all his life".
while   Maccabees.
London, Feb. 15.th *1806, published according to Act of Parliament, by J.T.Smith, N.º 31, Newman Street.*

at Greenwich : Fourth Barge, cov. with blk.Cloth. Chief Mourner Sir Peter Parker, B.t Adm.l of the Fleet, supp. by Adm.l Viscount Hood &
Adm. Lord Radstock : 6 assistant Mourners, viz. Adm.l Caldwell, Curtis, Bligh, Pole, Nugent & Hamilton. 4 Supp.rs of the Pall, viz.
Vice Adm.l Whitshed & Taylor. Adm. Orde (in the absence of Vice Adm. Savage) & Rear Adm. Eliab Harvey: 6 Supp.rs of the Canopy, viz.
Rear Adm. Drury, Douglas, Wells, Coffin, Aylmer & Domett. Train Bearer to the Chief Mourner, Hon. Henry Blackwood: Windsor Herald.
acting for Norroy K.g of Arms: The Banner of Emblems borne by Capt. Hardy, supported by Lieut.t King & Bligh: His Majesty's Barge. The Lords
Commissioners of the Admiralty, their Barge, &immediately after, the City State Barge (the R.t Hon. James Shaw, Lord Mayor) followed
by the Barges of several of the Companies of the City of London. The Engraver is signally obliged to Frances Townsend Esq. Windsor Herald,
E.A.S. for his liberal communications

*messmate and find he is gone – we ask for such
and such a man – he was killed, sir, in the
action, he lost a leg – we ask for no-one for fear
of a similar reply one hundred and fifty killed
and wounded. I am alive without a wound.*[31]

The triumph at Trafalgar did not prevent an invasion, which had already been postponed, but it did

establish British sea power for almost a century. At
home, the news of the battle and Nelson's death
caused a peculiar combination of delight and grief.
His funeral, in London early in 1806, was a combination of those of Winston Churchill and Princess
Diana, of the warrior who had saved his country and
the beloved icon with a flawed private life, and it
inspired similar outpourings of grief.

Horatio, Viscount Nelson (1758–1805)

Horatio Nelson was born in the vicarage at Burnham Thorpe, a remote village in Norfolk where his father was rector. He was one of a large family but was devastated when his mother died when he was 10, leaving a huge gap in his life that was perhaps never filled. Though he was considered rather delicate as a boy, he was invariably brave and there was an opportunity when his uncle, Captain Maurice Suckling, was appointed to the command of a ship after a period on half-pay. In the event the *Raisonable* did not go to sea but the 12-year-old Nelson made two voyages to the West Indies in merchant ships, learning how to sail the oceans as part of a small crew. On his return he took charge of one of the boats of his uncle's new ship, the *Triumph*, moored at Chatham, and he learned navigation and seamanship on the Medway. He volunteered for an expedition to test the idea that the Arctic Ocean might have less ice than previously thought and could offer a route to the Pacific. Serving in the converted bomb-vessel *Carcass* under Captain Skeffington Lutwidge, he was

said to have fought off a polar bear and certainly played a useful role in command of one of the ship's boats. Later, on a voyage back from India, he had a religious experience as he recovered from illness and remained very devout for the rest of his life.

His uncle, now an official of the Navy Board, supervised his training and arranged suitable appointments for him to develop his inborn genius as a seaman and leader. When war began with the American colonists he was appointed acting lieutenant of the 64-gun *Worcester* and passed his examination in the following year; he was only 18 though the regulations demanded that he should be at least 20. He was promoted to commander of the brig *Badger* in 1778 and to full captain the following year, at the age of 20. He spent the rest of the war commanding small ships on both sides of the Atlantic, and led the naval side of an expedition in Nicaragua, which failed and devastated his health for a time.

In 1784 he was appointed captain of the frigate *Boreas* and sailed to the West Indies, where he became the senior naval officer in the Leeward Islands, with Prince William, later King William IV, under his command. His attempts to enforce the Navigation Acts and ban trade in American ships made

him many enemies, but he found solace with the niece of the Governor of Nevis, Frances Nisbet, whom he married in 1787. He returned to England and was at his father's home in Norfolk for the next five years.

As war with revolutionary France began in 1793 he was recalled and given command of the 64-gun *Agamemnon*, a ship that delighted him. He took part in the British expedition to Corsica and lost the sight of his right eye at the Siege of Calvi. He had his first taste of fleet battle under the over-cautious Admiral Hotham in 1795. He much preferred Sir John Jervis when he took over the fleet, but Jervis decided to withdraw from the Mediterranean and Nelson, now in command of the 74-gun *Captain*, had to complete the evacuation of Corsica. Nelson had his first success in battle on St Valentine's Day 1797 when he anticipated Jervis's order and took several ships off Cape St Vincent. Nelson lost his right arm during a catastrophic attack on Tenerife, and was laid low for several months. He was given command of a squadron to re-enter the Mediterranean and he had perhaps his

greatest success at the Battle of the Nile. But after a triumph, there was nearly always a setback in Nelson's career. Repairing his ships in Naples, he became too close to the regime there and at some stage he began an affair with the Ambassador's wife, Lady Emma Hamilton. Recalled to London, he soon found that he was a popular hero, but ended his marriage in brutal fashion. He was appointed as second-in-command under Sir Hyde Parker and had another, though slightly more ambiguous, triumph at Copenhagen. Then he launched an unsuccessful attack on Boulogne, before the war ended with the Treaty of Amiens.

Nelson spent the short peace touring with Emma and her husband in a strange ménage à trois, and began to set up

home with her at Merton just south of London when he was recalled to lead the Mediterranean Fleet. He spent two years on the blockade of Toulon, before chasing the French across the Atlantic and back again. He had just

three weeks at home before being recalled again to take charge of a force to counter the great Franco-Spanish fleet at Cadiz. The enemy came out to fight the Battle of Trafalgar on 21 October 1805 and Nelson was mortally wounded. His funeral early in 1806 was one of the greatest and most emotional pageants that London has ever seen. Nelson was a dedicated officer, a charismatic leader, a good seaman, a skilled and original tactician and a resolute and fearless fighter.

LEFT Portrait of the Admiral by Lemuel Abbot.

THESE PAGES Gillray expressed the popular mood after the Nile, showing Nelson as 'The British Hero Cleansing ye Mouth of the Nile' by destroying the 'Revolutionary Crocodiles'.

Chapter 12

THE TRIUMPHS AND LIMITATIONS OF SEA POWER

After Trafalgar there was yet another 'elephant and whale' situation, with the British victorious at sea while Napoleon had won stunning victories against the Austrians and was all-powerful in Europe. This time there was no question of going back to a compromise peace, which had failed last time, so Napoleon tried another tactic to ruin the trade of what he called 'a nation of shopkeepers'. The Continental System, established in the Berlin Decrees of 1806, banned British trade from ports under Napoleon's influence. It was an attempt to fight a sea war and apply a blockade without a navy. The British replied with a series of Orders in Council which banned trade with any ports applying the decrees. This demanded a new kind of Royal Navy. Up until now it had been successful in defending convoys with frigates, and blockading a few major naval ports with ships of the line. Now it had to be ready to blockade any port, however small, that was considered to be complying with the Berlin Decrees. New classes of small ship were built in great numbers. The 18-gun brigs of the *Cruizer* class had originally been designed in the 1790s, but more than 90 of them were ordered in the early 1800s. The navy continued to expand and had more than a thousand ships by 1812. It also developed the world's first mass production by means of machine tools. Marc Isambard Brunel, father of the great Victorian engineer, designed a series of machines to make rigging blocks in the Royal Dockyard at Portsmouth.

The navy had not lost all its bad officers. Captain Robert Corbet of the *Nereide* was tried by court martial for unauthorised punishments as one of his men testified.

THE LANDING OF THE BRITISH ARMY AT MONDEGO BAY.

He then sent for Moses Veale, the boatswain's mate, to beat me. He gave me six or eight strokes. I could not stand, and Captain Corbet then told me if I did not stand he would seize me up to the Jacob's ladder. I was then seized up and beat as long as he thought proper.

Later, in command of the *Africaine*, Corbet was killed in action and it was suggested that his own men had fired the fatal shot. But officers like him were exceptions by that time. Most had come to respect the seamen and would have agreed with Captain Anselm Griffiths' remark that, 'Seamen are nowadays a think-ing set of people and a large proportion of them possess no inconsiderable share of common sense ...'[32]

A traditional colonial war was carried out on the fringes of the great European conflict. Sir Home

Popham took the Cape of Good Hope from the Dutch in 1806 with little trouble. This protected the route to India, and it added a colony that would attract a great deal of British settlement over the years, as well as con-flict with the better-established Dutch. While there, Popham heard that the Spanish forces in the River Plate were very weak and the people would welcome liberation. He sailed there on his own initiative and took Buenos Aires; but the Spanish soon discovered British weakness and revolted against them, making the affair an expensive fiasco.

The possible revival of the French navy could never be ignored, and eventually they were able to build up substantial forces of ships of the line largely in occupied Mediterranean ports, though it was never clear how they were to be manned with battle-hard-ened seamen.

In the meantime there was a very real fear that they might acquire ships through allies and conquests. When Denmark came under French control at the Treaty of Tilsit in 1807, there was also the worry about keeping the Baltic open. Rather like the Gulf today, the sea was a main source of strategic goods, including timber floated down the rivers of Poland and Russia, and of Stockholm tar. A large expedition was mounted under Sir James Gambier, and forces

were landed to besiege Copenhagen while the city was bombarded by Gambier's ships. Eventually the Danes agreed that the British could take possession of the Dockyard for six weeks, to remove all ships and stores, according to the terms of surrender. They returned with 70 captured ships, including 18 of the line. Admiral Sir James Saumarez, once Nelson's second-in-command at the Nile, led fleets into the Baltic over the next four years, in alliance with Sweden. The great supply route was kept open, and eventually links would be made with the Russians.

The British were also looking for a way onto the continent of Europe using their great naval advantage. In 1809, forces were landed on the Dutch island of Walcheren to take pressure off Britain's allies, the Austrians, and close the entrance to the River Scheldt and the port of Antwerp. In traditional fashion the two

OPPOSITE Some of Wellington's troops, equipment and horses landing at Figuera da Foz in Modego Bay, Portugal, in 1809, to start their involvement in what became the Peninsula War.

BELOW The town and bay of Corunna, with numerous transports at anchor ready to take off Sir John Moore's army, and the town and citadel behind them. The Roman lighthouse is on the far left. Nearly all the troops were withdrawn, despite the tragic death of their leader.

SOUTH VIEW OF CORUNNA FROM THE HEIGHTS NEAR THE CONVENT OF St MARGARET.

ABOVE Thomas Cochrane, Earl of Dundonald, who was a colourful character. He is shown wearing a naval uniform down one side of his body and prison dress on the other – a reference to his imprisonment in 1814 for an alleged Stock Exchange fraud.

OPPOSITE Cochrane's chart of the Basque Road affair, made to demonstrate his point that a potentially devastating attack on the French fleet by fireship only failed because he was not backed up by the commander, the over-cautious Lord Gambier.

Napoleon's brother. This led to a Spanish revolt, and the cruelties of the French occupiers were depicted by the painter Goya. British troops under Sir Arthur Wellesley were sent out to join what became the Peninsular War and the navy soon became involved. The 74-gun ship *Alfred* was detached from the squadron blockading Lisbon to land a few hundred marines in support of a local revolt at the town of Figueira da Foz in Portugal. Meanwhile a large fleet of transports left Cork carrying 9,000 troops under Wellesley. They sailed to Corunna where the Spanish rebels refused to let them land, so they went south to use the tiny harbour at Figueira, and were joined by 4,000 more. They marched south to Lisbon, with the *Alfred* and other ships maintaining communication and providing supplies. When more troops arrived they were landed on the beaches, showing the advantages of having a harbour such as Figueira. One of the soldiers describes his landing by boat.

> There were twenty to thirty British sailors on the shore, all quite naked, who, at the moment the foremost breakers withdrew, dashed like lightning into the surf, and after many efforts ... at last succeeded in casting a long rope to us, which we were able to seize. Then with a loud hurrah, they ran at top speed through the advancing breakers up the beach, dragging us with them, until the boat stuck fast ... Finally ... each of them took a soldier on his back and carried him thus to the dry shore.[33]

After defeating the French at Rolica and Vimeiro, Wellesley's army took Lisbon, which served as a base for the remainder of the war. But his newly appointed superiors negotiated a deal with the French that allowed them to withdraw on very favourable terms.

In the meantime, Captain Thomas Cochrane, Earl of Dundonald, was raiding enemy commerce on the Mediterranean coast when he heard that the Spanish had switched sides. He was already famous for having fought perhaps the greatest single-ship

commanders, Sir Richard Strachan for the navy and the Earl of Chatham for the army, failed to co-operate and 4,000 men died from malaria before the attempt was abandoned.

But already, almost by accident, the navy had found another route to the continent. In 1808 the Portuguese, long-standing allies and trading partners of Britain, had refused to operate the Continental System. The French demanded to send an army through Spain to crush them. When the Spanish demurred their king was overthrown and replaced by action in history, when he captured a Spanish frigate four times the size of his own, and as a radical Member of Parliament. Now he increased his campaign against the French with great energy and ingenuity, raiding signal stations, attacking strongpoints, firing rockets and defending Fort Trinidad in Rosas Bay when others were about to give it up. Cochrane conceived a plan to defeat the French in Spain, using an island base off the French coast, plus Minorca which was now in the hands of friendly Spanish forces. Ships and marines based in these places would cut off French communications along the coasts and force them to use the much more difficult paths over the Pyrenees, while the Spanish and Portuguese guerrillas would defeat them with minimum help from regular troops. Cochrane was indeed sent on an expedition to destroy the French

ships in the anchorage at Basque Roads off the west coast of France, but he soon fell out with his commander, Lord Gambier, and the plan came to nothing.

In the meantime General Sir John Moore began an advance from Lisbon into the interior of Spain. This time he was opposed by Napoleon himself, though he never met him in battle. Moore retreated to Corunna to have his army withdrawn, but he was killed in battle and buried on the outskirts of the town; 'Not a drum was heard, not a funeral note, As his corse to the ramparts we hurried'. There was dismay when no transport ships were to be found in the harbour, for they had gone to Vigo. There was terror when some soldiers blew up a powder magazine, not realising it was connected to a much larger one, and horror as cavalrymen were ordered to kill their horses by cutting their throats –'Wounded horses, mad with pain, were

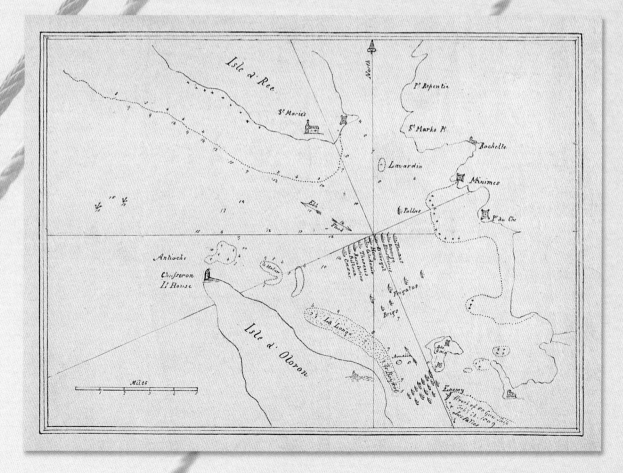

The Techniques of sailing

A sail operates on the same principle as an aeroplane wing. The wind passes on both sides of it, but because of the curve it moves slightly faster on one side than the other. This makes the air pressure slightly less on that side, and it tends to suck the sail towards it. If the wind is directly behind it, the sail operates more like a parachute, but again the pressure is less on one side than the other. This is less efficient and ships do not sail best with the wind directly behind them.

The sail is trimmed at about 15 degrees to the angle of the wind. One component pushes the ship forward, and one sideways, known as leeway. This is largely counteracted by the shape of the hull, which is designed to move forwards rather than sideways; but every sailing ship makes a certain amount of leeway.

A ship sails on one tack or the other – if the wind is coming over the starboard side she is said to be on the starboard tack. The wind is stronger higher up, so each of the sails is set at a slightly different angle. The officer of the watch had to be constantly aware of changes in the wind. If it varied in direction he had to order the crew to pull on the braces to alter the angle of the yards. If it got stronger he had to get them to take in sail, starting by furling the uppermost ones, such as the topgallants and royals. Then he might furl the lower sails, the courses. Finally he could reef the topsails, sending men aloft to haul up and stow upper parts of the sail as required. Only in extreme weather would he furl all the sails at sea, operating 'under bare poles.'

At best a square-rigged sailing ship can sail about two points, or 22½ degrees, into the wind, which means that 135 degrees of the compass are not available to it at any given moment – though with the effects of leeway a sailing ship can make no progress at all against a strong wind – hence the sailor has to be careful not to be trapped in a bay or heading for a lee shore.

A ship can beat into the wind, sailing as close as possible and turning occasionally to bring the wind on the other side, which can be done in two ways. It can turn its stern to the wind and move through 225 degrees or more, known as wearing. In a three-masted ship the foresails are used to power the ship, the others are shivered, that is they are kept with their edges pointing into the wind so that they have no effect. Wearing is much easier than tacking in difficult conditions, but it takes a good deal of time and distance.

Otherwise a ship can tack, by turning its bows towards the wind. The main and mizzen sails are brought round to the opposite angle, the fore sails stay the same to help push the bows round. When the wind is on the other side of the ship, the fore sails are brought round and the ship is ready to sail on the new tack. This might fail if it is too light, or the waves are too high and the ship might be stuck in irons, unable to pay off on either tack.

ABOVE Sailor aloft on the *Phoenix*.

ABOVE The USS *Constitution* engaging HMS *Guerriere* in August 1812, painted by Thomas Birch. The victory of the American ship caused a good deal of soul-searching in the Royal Navy.

to be seen running through the street, and the ground was covered with mangled carcasses of these noble animals'.[34] At last the transports appeared; the navy had worked out a detailed plan for loading the men, which was ruined by fog, so some ships were almost empty, some grossly overloaded. Many of the merchant ship captains in charge of the transports had no experience of warfare or of navigation outside their local areas. Some fled when the French fired guns from a hill above the harbour. Many of them barely found their way back to southern England, but overall the evacuation was a great success.

Wellesley returned to Lisbon and gained the title of Duke of Wellington after a series of victories. He relied on naval support to keep his armies supplied and prevent the French from doing the same with theirs, a payback from the Battle of Trafalgar. In 1812 he advanced deep into the interior and Commodore Sir Home Popham was sent to the north coast to support him and co-operate with local guerrillas. Popham raided various points along the mountainous and indented coastline, keeping large numbers of French troops occupied. He took the port of Santander as Wellington became bogged down in the siege of Burgos 70 miles to the south. He sent supplies to Wellington, but the army was eventually forced to retreat back to Portugal. Popham's campaign had proved highly useful, but he had not captured one of

the key points such as San Sebastian, which could be used to cut communication between France and Spain. In the following year Wellington was able to advance across Spain and into France, while at the same time Napoleon's great empire was under threat with the failure of his war on Russia. Often Wellington's complaints about naval co-operation were rather mean-spirited, but his final assessment was generous. 'If anyone wishes to know the history of this war, I will tell them that it is our maritime superiority gives me the power of maintaining my army while the enemy are unable to do so.'[35]

Already by this time, the Royal Navy was distracted by another war on the other side of the Atlantic. Many British seamen, including deserters from the Royal Navy, had joined American merchant ships and it was very difficult to separate out their nationalities in an age of minimal record keeping. The Americans objected to their ships being stopped and

searched for British sailors to man the navy, and there were several violent incidents before war was formally declared on 18 June 1812. Blockade was the main British strategy. The Americans depended heavily on seaborne trade and if their ports could be closed they would be forced to make peace. The Americans could hit back by invading Canada, or they could use their own navy to break the British blockade.

The Continental Navy of John Paul Jones's day had virtually disappeared after independence, but a new force was set up to protect American shipping against the Barbary corsairs. It included three very large and very fine frigates, the *United States, Constitution* and *President*, as well as a number of smaller frigates, sloops and brigs. But the United States Navy was very small, with 14 operational ships when the war started and a little over 5,000 men, some of them employed in forts and dockyards. As Secretary of the Navy Jones put it,

President's House, after its destruction by the British.

Our great inferiority in naval strength, does not permit us to meet them on this ground without hazarding the precious Germ of our national glory – we have however the means of creating a powerful diversion & of turning the Scale of annoyance against the enemy.[36]

ABOVE The 'President's House' in Washington, almost derelict and scarred by flames after its burning by the British in 1814. It was restored to become the White House.

OPPOSITE The Battle of Lake Erie in September 1813, showing the American leader, Captain Oliver Hazard Perry, leaving his badly damaged flagship *Lawrence* for the much smaller *Niagara*. Nevertheless, it was an American victory.

New ships were put in hand, including 74-gun ships of the line, which would outgun British ones but never outnumber them.

The USS *Constitution* had a narrow escape from a British squadron in very light winds off the Jersey coast in mid July, but a month later she defeated the British frigate *Guerriere* due to her heavier firepower. This began a run of American successes in which the sloop Frolic defeated the *Wasp*, the *United States* captured the *Macedonian*, and the *Constitution* the *Java*. After long years of war in which they had assumed that any of their ships could defeat an enemy of up to

50 per cent greater force, the British had a shock. These losses were not nearly serious enough to disrupt Britain's war with either France or America, but they caused a huge loss of prestige. In July 1813 the Admiralty warned ships not to attack unless they were sure of victory.

.. they do not conceive that any of His Majesty's Frigates should attempt to engage, single handed, the larger Class of American Ships; which though they may be called

*Frigates, are of a size, Complemant and weight
of Metal much beyond that Class, and more
resembling Line of Battle Ships.*[37]

Already one captain, Philip Broke of the *Shannon*,
believed that he had found the answer to American
superiority, through better gunnery. He trained his
men incessantly, in aiming as well as rapid fire, for the
Nelsonian system had assumed close action in which
accuracy was not important. In June 1813, while
blockading Boston, he issued a direct challenge to
Captain James Lawrence of the *Chesapeake* which he
knew was in the port. 'As the Chesapeake now
appears ready for Sea, I request you will do me the
favour to meet the Shannon with her, ship to ship, to
try the fortune of our respective Flags'.[38] He promised
him that the two ships were of roughly equal force and
assured Lawrence that the proposal was 'highly
advantageous' to him. In fact Lawrence had already
sailed and did not receive the letter. The two ships met
in a short, sharp battle in which the *Shannon*'s broadsides defeated the *Chesapeake* in six minutes. Some of
her timbers were incorporated in a mill in Hampshire
and are there to this day.

If the Americans were to retaliate by attacking
Canada, they would have to secure naval control of the
Great Lakes. Both sides built up substantial forces there,
including full-sized ships of the line. The British ships
were largely manned by auxiliaries and army troops and
were defeated by Admiral Perry on Lake Erie in 1813.
Commodore James Yeo was sent with a force of Marines
and 900 seamen to support the campaign in 1814, but
the control of the lakes was never fully resolved even
after several battles. In the meantime the American
frigate *Essex* was ranging much further afield raiding
British shipping in the Pacific and using the Galapagos
Islands as a base. Finally she was captured by HM ships
Phoebe and *Cherub* off Valparaiso in March 1814.

In the summer of 1814 Admiral Cockburn led a
major assault on Chesapeake Bay, after previous raids
had shown how weak the defences were. When they
landed at the new American capital of Washington,

they felt they were avenging a raid on the Canadian
capital, York, two years earlier. They were careful to
confine their attacks to public buildings and the
troops and sailors did not pay any special attention
when they burned what they called 'the President's
palace'. According to legend they would create the
new name of what has become the most famous building in the world, for when it was rebuilt it was painted
to hide the burns, and was soon known as 'The White
House', though in fact it had been white since its com-
pletion in 1798. The war was settled by negotiation in
1815, without either side gaining a clear advantage.

While the American war continued, Napoleon
was defeated by the advancing Russian, Prussian, Aus-
trian and Swedish armies in the Battle of the Nations
near Leipzig. The following year he was forced to abdi-
cate as emperor and accepted the sovereignty of the
tiny island of Elba off the coast of Italy. He was taken
there in the British frigate *Undaunted* but escaped ten
months later to resume his rule in France. After his
final defeat at Waterloo, he surrendered to a British
naval squadron off Rochefort, led by Captain Thomas
Maitland in the veteran 74-gun ship *Bellerophon*. Even
in the face of defeat Bonaparte took an interest in
everything around him and according to Maitland,
'He conversed a great deal, and showed no depression
of spirits'.[39] But he lost his composure when he was
told that he was to be exiled to the far-flung outpost of
St Helena, where escape was far less likely. Midshipman Charles Abbot visited him there with a party of
naval officers in 1817.

*He is not so fat and unwieldy as he is generally
represented to be and appeared to be in very
good health but is much dissatisfied with his
present condition, of which he complains bitterly,
and in many instances with great injustice, as Sir
Hudson Lowe shows him every civility that he
thinks compatible with his security.*[40]

After 22 years of almost continuous war, the
Royal Navy had reached a high point in its life. It had

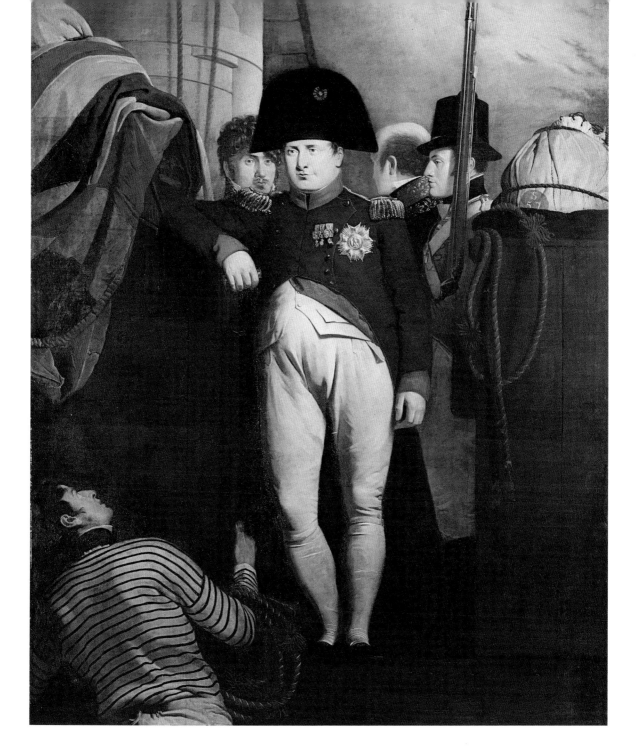

ABOVE Napoleon puts a brave face on his defeat at Waterloo and the prospect of banishment to the almost inaccessible island of St Helena. He is on board the 74-gun ship *Bellerophon*, commanded by Captain Maitland, in Plymouth Sound in 1815. Painted by Sir Charles Eastlake.

fought against almost every nation with any kind of modern navy, and nearly always emerged victorious.

It had ranged across the seas and oceans of the world, taken colonies in Africa and Asia and briefly in Latin America. It had supported the army very effectively in Spain and now it was to guard the defeated Napoleon on his isolated island. It was to face new challenges in the long years of peace that were to follow, both in technology and in society.

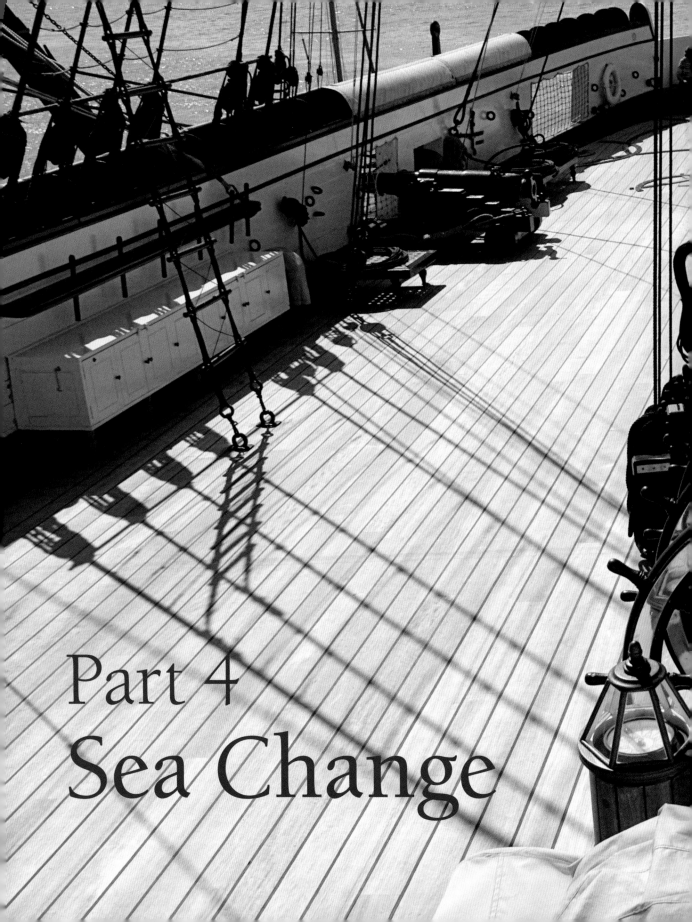

Part 4
Sea Change

BELOW Lord Exmouth's bombardment of Algiers in August 1816 by George Chambers. The ship in the centre is the *Impregnable*. Though he did not paint it until 1836, Chambers went to Portsmouth to sketch the ships that had taken part. The town of Algiers is seen ablaze in the background wth shells exploding.

Chapter 13
THE EFFECTS OF
A LONG PEACE

After the long wars the greatest fleet in the world was reduced from 1,009 ships in 1813 to 179 in 1826 and only a few of these were in commission. From 145,000 men in 1810–13, parliament voted for 23,000 in 1826. Officers who had begun their careers in the boom years found themselves on almost permanent half-pay, with little prospect of employment and even less of prize money. Lieutenant Thomas Chrystie knew that 'there would be no chance of promotion for an officer who had little or no interest'. He joined the merchant navy, hoping that 'the system of favouritism, particularly on account of corrupt Parliamentary reasons, may not continue to blot on the honourable government of this noble country'. Lieutenant John Fullarton wrote of his past, 'Nothing but the common occurrences of services. Health broken from climate and hurts received, like a thousand others upon the active list. As Jack says, "not worth a single damn".'[1]

This was a smaller navy, less close to British society, whose main actions would be away from home waters, acting as a kind of 'world's policeman' – even if Britain did not have a regular domestic police force of its own when the period began. The first action was a comparatively large affair, the bombardment of Algiers in 1816. Lord Exmouth had already taken a squadron to the city twice during the year. The first time he paid heavy ransoms for the release of some Neapolitan and Sardinian slaves; his second visit resulted only in the arrest of the British consul and retaliation against British subjects. This compared very ill with American successes the year before and Exmouth was sent back with a fleet of five ships of the line, frigates and a few smaller ships. On the way he joined forces with a Dutch squadron on a similar mission and the combined

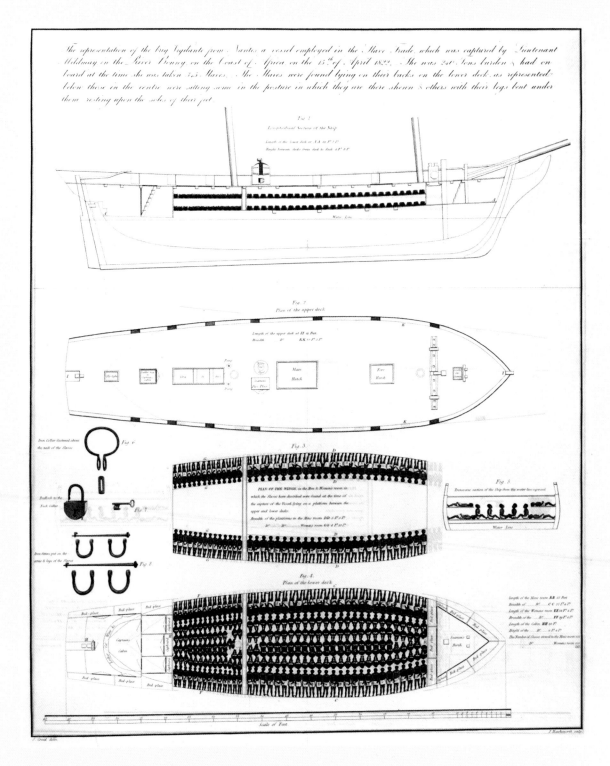

ABOVE Deck plans and sections of the slave ship *Vigilante*, captured off
the African coast in 1822, showing some of the irons used to restrain the
slaves. The ship had fine lines for speed in the hope of evading pursuers.

force had a total of 632 cannon, half of which would be on the wrong side of the ships during an engagement. This compared rather poorly with the 1,000 shore-mounted guns of Algiers. When the Algerians refused Exmouth's demands, he began a bombardment as described by the American consul.

> *The cannonade endures with a fury which can only be comprehended from practical experience; shells and rockets fly over and by my house like hail. The fire is returned with constancy from several batteries situated at the north-west corner of the town and from four heavy guns directly below my windows ... At half past seven, the shipping in the port is on fire ... The upper part of my house appears to*

> *be destroyed, several shells having fallen into it, whole rooms are knocked to atoms.*[2]

The Algerians gave up and agreed to release 1,642 slaves, 18 of whom were British and 28 Dutch. According to Lieutenant James Hall,

> *On being put on board the Transport they ascended the rigging and yards and seemed to be in a delirium of joy. The transition from slavery to liberty was so sudden a thing, so*

BELOW A steam pinnace used for chasing slave ships off the coast of Zanzibar in 1880-82. She was attached to the old battleship *London*, which was based in the port. Painted in watercolour by Lieutenant E F Inglefield, one of the ship's officers.

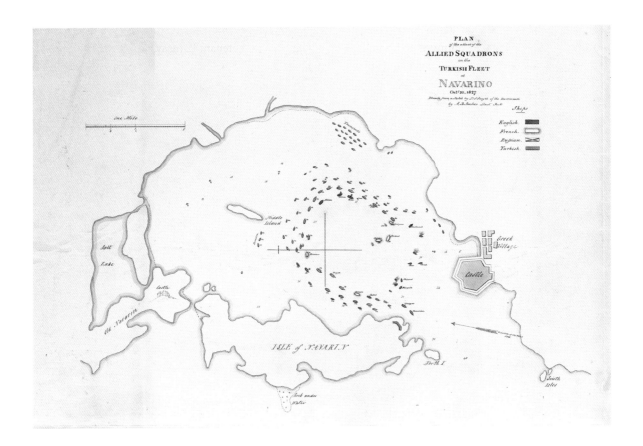

unexpected, that it seemed to these poor men as a dream. ... They all looked healthy, were very clean and well clothed. Very different from what we expected to see, and infinitely superior to prisoners in England or France.[3]

The Algerians also agreed, 'the practice of condemning Christians to slavery was formally and for ever renounced by Algiers'. Exmouth was voted the thanks of parliament and loaded with honours, but the Algerian issue was only solved when the French invaded and colonised the country in 1829.

The Algiers affair had strong resonances with another of the navy's major peacetime activities. The trade in slaves from Africa had been abolished by parliament in 1807, though many other countries did not support the ban. Moreover, the actual ownership of slaves was still legal in British colonies until 1834, and much longer than that in the United States and parts

ABOVE A chart showing the Battle of Navarino in 1827, produced by A B Becher of the Hydrographic Office from information supplied by Lieutenant Smyth of the *Dartmouth*. The British, French and Russian squadrons sailed into the middle of the crescent formation adopted by the Turkish fleet in Navarino Bay, and battle followed, with great loss to the Turks.

OPPOSITE The paddle frigate *Gorgon*, built at Pembroke Dock and her engine at Deptford in 1838. She represented a major advance in design, as she was much faster than previous paddle steamers. As well as six heavy guns, she could carry up to 1,600 troops. Many others were built to a similar design over the next decade.

of Latin America. The navy had few resources to enforce a ban before 1815, though two ships operated off the African coast in 1807. After that, normally 2–7 ships were involved, including two frigates, but the effort was fraught with difficulties. Spain, Portugal and the United States still imported large numbers of slaves, and it was difficult to stop ships under foreign flags without incurring legal difficulties, at least until treaties were signed with the individual governments. As a result export of slaves continued to boom in the 1830s and '40s even after Britain abolished slavery. There were some who suggested that attempts to suppress the trade just made things worse in the slave ships that tried to evade the ban, for example one stopped by HMS *Tartar* in 1821. The slaves below decks were,

> *...clinging to the gratings to inhale a mouthful of fresh air, and fighting with each other for a taste of water, showing their parched tongues, and pointing to their reduced stomachs as if overcome by famine, for although the living cargo had only been completed the day before, yet many who had been longer on board were reduced to living skeletons ...*[4]

Two of the most successful ships were the *Black Joke* under Lieutenant Ramsay and the *Fair Rosamund* under Lieutenant Huntley; between 1830 and 1832 they captured nine slavers, compared with two for the rest of the squadron. Some officers enjoyed the thrill of the chase and the satisfaction of conferring freedom: 'The men were bound together in twos by irons riveted round the ankles. On arrival these chains were removed, and they appeared much gratified.'[5] But more often the officers were bored by the monotony of the coast and the lack of comforts. The lower deck enjoyed it more, despite the huge death rate: 54 men died for every 1,000 on the West Coast of Africa per year, compared with 18 in the West Indies, which had once been regarded with horror, and less than 10 in home waters. In compensation there was the payment of head money for every slave liberated, which was

H.M. STEAM FRIGATE GORGON.

welcome in the days when prize money was no longer available. In all more than a thousand ships were stopped and nearly 150,000 slaves were liberated and landed. It came to an end following agreements with the governments of Brazil and Cuba, and when the American Civil War of 1861–65 ended the demand.

The sailing navy was not completely finished with fleet battles. Eleven years after Algiers, the navy was involved in another action against the Muslims in the Mediterranean. As the Greeks revolted against Turkish rule, a French, Russian and British squadron of 22 ships encountered a much larger Turkish fleet at Navarino Bay off the west coast of Greece. Seaman Charles McPherson witnessed the beginning of an action from the 78-gun *Genoa*.

> *The pipe went to bring the ship to anchor, and to furl sails. I was sent to the fore topsail yardarm ... I here had a grand bird's eye view of the whole harbour. ... In the Bay, and round about us, were ranged in a triple line the Turco-Egyptian fleet ... We could see in a moment the situation our ship was placed in – a situation more perilous than any other ship in the whole three squadrons. Right abreast of us, and bringing nearly every gun to bear upon us, lay two of the enemy's line of battle ships: a little further ahead on our starboard bow now lay another two deck ship, and three double-bank frigates were so placed on our larboard bow and ahead, that they could gall us severely with their shot, while a large frigate lay athwart our stern that raked us with success for some time, till a French ship hove down and relieved us from her fire.*[6]

Superior training and skills soon prevailed and all but eight of 78 Turkish vessels were destroyed or captured, clearing the way for Greek independence. This was the last great sailing ship action, for the development of the warship was about to move into new territory.

By 1815, the experience of a long war was beginning to combine with the proto-Victorian concept of improvement to produce new ideas in sailing ship design. Robert Seppings had already redesigned the bows of ships so that they could take more punishment, such as they had received during the approach at Trafalgar. In 1811 he launched the 74-gun *Tremendous*, fitted with an internal diagonal structure that supported the building of much larger ships without their bodies 'hogging' or sagging at the ends. As a result, the largest three-deckers in the navy in 1815, the *Nelson* class of 1806, were measured at 2,601 tons; the *Prince of Wales* class of 1848 were measured at 3,185 tons as originally built. But Seppings' redesign of the sterns of warships proved far less popular. For centuries they had been very weak in structure, composed largely of glass and with fragile galleries. Seppings created the new 'circular stern' which was much stronger but reduced both beauty and comfort, qualities that were highly regarded by peacetime officers. In 1832 Pepys' old Navy Board was abolished as part of a far-reaching reform and Seppings was replaced by Sir William Symonds, a naval officer whose battleships were based on the principles of the sailing dinghy and offered greater speed. His designs came in for much criticism from the growing profession of naval architects who were beginning to supplant the old shipwrights in the drawing offices. They had deep draught and made very poor gun platforms, and naval officers came to realise that they were not a success. But in the meantime, a much greater change was beginning to engulf the navy.

As First Lord of the Admiralty from 1812–30, Lord Melville is often falsely accused of stating, 'their Lordships feel it is their bounden duty to discourage to the utmost of their ability the employment of steam vessels, as they consider the introduction of Steam is calculated to strike a fatal blow at the supremacy of the Empire.'[7] On the contrary, he did a good deal to encourage steam power and he wrote in 1823,

*There is every reason to believe from the purposes
to which Steam Vessels are now applied that they
would be found very useful in the protection of our
trade in the Channel ... It will be proper now to
provide Steam Engines for at least six vessels ...
and I therefore desire that you will take the
necessary steps for that purpose.*[8]

The Royal Navy had paddle warships from 1821,
initially as harbour tugs and river craft. From about

BELOW The tug of war between the paddle steamer *Alecto* and the
screw ship *Rattler*, staged in April 1845. It was largely a publicity
stunt, the Admiralty already knew that the screw was more efficient,
but the *Rattler* towed the *Alecto* against the power of her engines
and paddles.

1830 it became increasingly common to arm them,
though there was an inherent difficulty in fitting
broadside guns to a paddle vessel. Moreover, the
engines took up a huge amount of space amidships
despite efforts to develop types for shipboard use; and
at sea, a ship would become very difficult to steer if
one paddle was damaged in action or out of the water
in large waves. The screw propeller was developed by
several individuals in the late 1830s and the
Archimedes, the first seagoing screw ship, soon
attracted Admiralty notice as did Isambard Kingdom
Brunel's huge *Great Britain* of 1843. The screw had
obvious advantages for the navy and in 1845 the navy
staged a famous tug-of-war between the paddler *Alecto*
and the screw-ship *Rattler* of equal size and horse-

H.M. STEAM SLOOPS "RATTLER" AND "ALECTO" TOWING STERN TO STERN,
for the purpose of testing the relative powers of the Screw Propeller and the Paddle-Wheel.

power. It was largely a public relations exercise; the Admiralty had already made up its mind in favour of the screw. An old ship of the line, the Ajax, was converted to screw propulsion in the following year, though it was a blockship for harbour defence rather than a true ocean-going steamship. In 1850 when the French went a stage further with the ominously named *Napoleon*, the British followed with the *Agamemnon*, their first purpose-built steam battleship. But steam was still an auxiliary to sail, the telescopic funnel was raised and the screw lowered into position only when the wind died down or it was necessary to enter or leave a harbour without the assistance of wind or tugs.

Each ship still carried a full complement of seamen to man its guns and sails, and the engineers and stoker were fitted uneasily on board. The first engineers came with the engines and were employees of the firms that supplied them. In 1836 the first regular naval engineers were appointed, ranking just after more traditional warrant officers such as carpenters; but it was necessary to attract a good quality of skilled mechanic, and they were far better paid than carpenters. In 1847 the most senior members of the branch were appointed by commission, though they were called 'inspectors of machinery afloat' rather than being given a more military title. The engineer was accompanied by large numbers of stokers, who started as unskilled, muscular landsmen who shov-elled large quantities of coal into the hungry furnaces. It soon became clear that a certain amount of skill was needed to keep a fire going efficiently, while the stokers gradually took on simple maintenance duties in addition.

In general, conditions had got much better for the seamen. John Bechervaise, who entered the navy as a seaman in 1820, admitted that in the past, 'The dread of a man of war was next to a French prison' but things had much improved by the 1820s.

> *... the wonderful improvements which have taken place render the navy superior beyond compare to any merchant vessel. It is possible the pay may be a little less, that I allow, but taking into consideration the regularity of diet, routine of duty, and comfort of the whole system, it makes up for everything, and pensions for old age.*[9]

The biggest step of the age was to set up the navy's first real system of shore training. The defeats in the American War had shown the defects in gunnery, just as Broke's success against the *Chesapeake* had inspired some captains to see the possibilities of improvement. Meanwhile General Sir Howard Douglas watched Popham's ships firing off the north coast of Spain in 1812, an experience which, he wrote, made him tremble for the laurels of the navy. He published an influential book on naval gunnery in 1820. The most practical suggestion came from Commander George Smith in 1829. He proposed,

> *... to place the ship at Portsmouth, off the North end of the Dockyard, for the purpose of firing at Targets, representing Ships' sides. Masts, Yards, etc, made of old hammock cloths, stretched on Spars, and placed in the direction of the Collegians fire: thus affording the means of trying Men's skill and various experiments in Gunnery.*[10]

MR. T. P. COOKE, AS "WILLIAM," IN "BLACK-EYED SUSAN."

ABOVE The actor T P Cooke in his most famous role as William in *Black Ey'd Susan*. He continued to play this part for many years. Here he is seen in typical seaman's dress of around 1850 with an early version of the square collar, and the Naval General Service medal, issued in 1848, to which he was entitled.

HMS *Excellent*, an old 74 that had fought at St Vincent, was chosen for the task and Smith was appointed to the command. John Bechervaise studied on the course there and wrote, 'Here I passed 16 months in comfort, learned the art of naval gunnery in all its various branches, and on leaving her to join the Melville obtained a certificate class No. 1, endorsed as to conduct etc.'[11] As well as training men for the one major skill they were unlikely to learn in the merchant service, the *Excellent* tended to reinforce the idea they were in the navy on a more permanent basis, and not just for a particular war or a single commission.

There was a rash of post-war memoirs, including ones from the lower deck such as those by Jack Nastyface (William Robinson), John Bechervaise and John Nicol. Deprived of their original livelihood, some officers turned to creative writing, including most famously Captain Frederick Marryat, who virtually founded naval fiction and became the most popular author of his day, between Sir Walter Scott and Charles Dickens. His novels were often quite close to his own experience as a midshipman under Lord Cochrane and they recounted adventures of young seamen, unlike the later novels of C S Forester and Patrick O'Brian, which tended to feature captains on detached service. Marryat's books said very little about the modern steam navy, but they kept the service in the public eye with stories of fearless action and adventure.

Theatre was increasingly popular due to the introduction of gas lighting, and the navy was well represented. The best known playwright was Douglas Jerrold, whose 1829 melodrama *Black-Ey'd Susan* told of a seaman who rescued his girlfriend from the attentions of his captain and was only saved from hanging at the last moment. It had an unprecedented run of 300 nights in the Surrey Theatre, followed by Covent Garden and then Drury Lane. The favourite actor was T P Cooke, who had served in the navy at the Battle of St Vincent and was said to bring the bold, active and romantic nature of the British tar to the stage. He excelled as Long Tom Coffin in *The Pilot* in 1827, bringing suggestions of 'thoughtfulness and mystery, of deep-toned passion and pathos' to the part, even if his persona was about to become outdated in the age of steam.[12]

William IV, the 'sailor king' who ruled from 1830 to 1837, had served as a captain under Nelson in the 1780s and signified a revived royal interest in the navy, the first since the days of James II. Queen Victoria followed this, for she toured the country in a series of Royal Yachts named *Victoria and Albert* and trav-

BELOW The taking of Chusan by a force led by Rear-Admiral Sir William Parker in the *Wellesley*, during the First Opium War, illustrated by Edward Hodges Cree.

elled to her favourite home, Osborne on the Isle of Wight. She launched many ships for the navy, leading to the tradition that a woman should launch a ship, and she sent several of her sons into the navy.

From any moral standpoint, the Opium Wars between 1840 and 1860 were among the least attractive of the Royal Navy's activities – condemned by the young William Gladstone when he told parliament, 'a war more unjust in its origin, a war more calculated to cover this country with permanent disgrace, I do not know'. China had long provided the west with desirable items such as silk, porcelain and tea, but there was nothing the Chinese people wanted in return, except silver and illicit opium. When Commissioner Lin Zexu tried to bring an end to the trade by destroying the stocks of the drug in Canton in 1840, the British invaded. Britain had the great new technological advantages of steam power and iron ships, and penetrated a long way up the Yangtze River as well as destroying coastal towns. A key battle came on 7 January 1841 when British forces approached the

entrance to the Canton River. The Chinese defended from forts equipped with guns mounted on solid blocks which could not be elevated or depressed, and with very poor quality gunpowder. A small fleet of their junks was stationed in the river. The iron paddle frigate *Nemesis* under Captain William Hall approached the junks and fired a lucky shot with a rocket. One of them exploded with a force that reminded watchers *L'Orient* at the Nile 43 years ago. With less than 6 feet draught of water, the *Nemesis* was able to attack the other junks over a sandbank and destroyed or captured them all. She rounded off the day by attacking a small town up-river. It was a battle between old and new, and the Chinese were given a very graphic illustration of the potential of British sea power.

BELOW The *Nemesis*, accompanied by the *Sulphur*, *Calliope*, *Starling* and *Larne*, attacks the Chinese junks in Anson Bay in January 1841, providing a dramatic demonstration of the combination of steam, iron and gun powder.

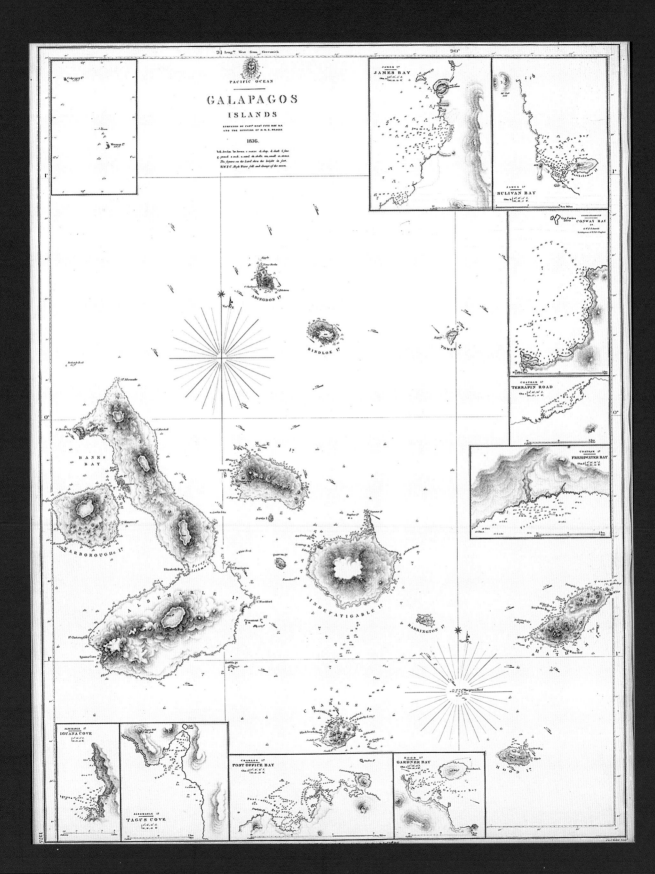

After two years of war the British gained the possession of Hong Kong and were given trading rights in four other ports. Captain Charles Elliot, formerly of the Royal Navy and now the chief superintendent for trade in china, had been a great advocate of Hong Kong, but it was a huge disappointment for the first 10 years of British possession. According to a report of 1844, 'the number of Chinese on the island was computed at 19,000, of whom not more than 1,000 are women and children. In the census are included ninety-seven women slaves, and female attendants on thirty-one brothels, eight gambling houses, and twenty opium shops &c'.[13] But trade soon picked up and it became a great entrepôt, while a naval base was developed. A second war, in 1856–60, opened up ten further ports but the whole affair left a long-lasting bitterness towards British imperialism.

This kind of activity demanded a good knowledge of the world, in the form of chart-making as well as intelligence. Behind much of this was Sir John Barrow, the Second Secretary to the Admiralty, who promoted scientific voyages in the Arctic and Africa and was a founder of the Royal Geographic Society. In the past, the Dutch and then the French had made far better charts than the British. Despite Cook's great skill before and during his voyages, it was 1795 before the Admiralty Hydrographic Department was set up, largely to collect what was available and issue them to ships. When Sir Francis Beaufort took office as Hydrographer in 1829 he was already a very experienced naval captain at the age of 55. Over the next quarter century he commissioned 1,500 new charts, setting new levels of accuracy and establishing the Admiralty

Chart as the standard for the rest of the world. Some were still in use a century and a half afterwards.

The peacetime navy sponsored many scientific expeditions, including one by the sloop *Beagle* between 1831 and 1836, Charles Darwin was on board. Beaufort recommended him for the trip although Darwin was not yet 'a finished naturalist, but amply qualified for collecting, observing, & noting anything worthy to be noted in natural history'.[14] Darwin was not a seaman and played no part in the running of the ship but used the opportunity that only sea travel could give, to study creatures in different environments; a visit to the Galapagos Islands, with their unique life forms, helped inspire him towards his theory of evolution, perhaps the most radical and controversial idea of the nineteenth century.

Darwin had originally gone as companion to the captain of the *Beagle*, Robert FitzRoy, and the voyage was intended to have a religious dimension with a missionary on board. FitzRoy was to make his own contribution to science. After the voyage he served unsuccessfully as governor of New Zealand and in 1853 he was appointed

LEFT Admiralty chart of Galapagos Islands completed by Robert FitzRoy during the *Beagle* voyage of 1831 and 1836.

RIGHT Robert FitzRoy was always deeply concerned about the large numbers of ships and boats lost in bad weather. His barometer was designed to be set up on shore to warn fishermen about impending storms. The panels on either side describe the consequences of rising and falling pressure, and there is also a thermometer and humidity gauge.

The Steam Engine

The first steam engines, such as those developed by Thomas Newcomen in 1712, were atmospheric engines: steam was condensed inside a cylinder by contact with water, and that created a vacuum which drew the piston towards it. James Watt developed the separate condenser by 1769: the steam to be condensed was extracted to a separate compartment, avoiding the waste of energy involved in constantly heating and cooling the cylinder, thus doubling the efficiency. With the invention of devices to translate the up and down action of the cylinder into a rotary motion which could power a paddle, it was now possible to use the steam engine in a ship. Early successes included Robert Fulton's *Clermont* on the Hudson and Henry Bell's *Comet* on the River Clyde in 1812.

For the next half century steam was considered an auxiliary to sail. The main problem for the designer was to fit the engine into the confined space of a ship, and types such as the steeple, beam and side-lever were used. It became clear that high-pressure steam would be more efficient, but much of it would be wasted in a single cylinder. The answer was to fit a second cylinder to re-use the steam at lower pressure, creating the compound engine first used in warships in 1872. This was followed by the triple-expansion engine, which used a third cylinder for even greater efficiency, and made the ocean-going steamship practicable.

Newer engines used higher-pressure steam, and this could be generated more efficiently in a rotary motion than the reciprocal movement of pistons. The turbine engine took up less space on board ship, it was capable of higher speed and it needed less maintenance as it had fewer moving parts.

It comprised a series of rotors inside a long tube, fitted with numerous blades. Steam was fed in at one end to drive the turbine blades round. The speed was usually too high for practical use at sea and gearing was necessary to reduce it. Most ships had separate, smaller engines for reversing.

BELOW The engines of the paddle frigate *Retribution*, which was launched in 1844.

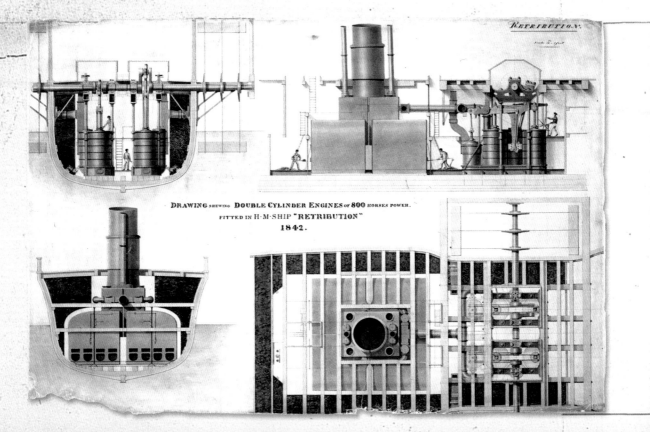

DRAWING shewing **DOUBLE CYLINDER ENGINES** of **800** horses power.
FITTED IN H·M·SHIP "**RETRIBUTION**"
1842.

to collect weather statistics for the Board of Trade. Far exceeding his brief, he had telegraph messages sent to him in his office, where he developed the 'synoptic chart', which is still the basis of weather forecasting today. He designed barometers to forecast bad weather, and set up beacons at the ports to warn fishermen. His ideas were well in advance of the means available as a forecaster, and he was always an unstable character. Criticism of his forecasts contributed to his suicide in 1865.

Attempts to discover the North-West Passage round the north of Canada were far less successful than the *Beagle* voyage, but attracted just as much attention. Though Cook and George Vancouver had found nothing of value in the previous century, Sir John Franklin set out on a voyage in February 1845. A veteran of Trafalgar, he was already a hero of Arctic exploration and was known as 'the man who ate his boots' from an earlier escapade. His expedition learned from the experiences of James Clark Ross and others who had found parts of the route; it used strengthened steamships and was well equipped with canned food and a fine library. Nevertheless it disappeared and more than 30 expeditions were mounted to look for it, some financed by the Admiralty, some by Franklin's wife and her supporters. The public refused to accept that 129 men had been lost and did not believe the Inuit reports that bodies had been found showing evidence of cannibalism.

In 1854, after nearly 40 years of general peace, a dispute over the control of the holy sites in Jerusalem (then part of the Turkish Empire) led to war between Russia on one side and Britain, France and Turkey on the other. It was decided to attack Russia and clearly a naval mobilisation was needed for this. The press gang had never been abolished, but the world had changed since it was last used in 1815. The Navigation Acts had been repealed and it was no longer safe to assume that the crew of British ships were all British, while concepts of civil liberty had advanced. It might just have been possible to impress men if British security was directly threatened, but this war was far away,

in alliance with France, the second-strongest naval power. The Royal Navy had built up small reserve forces in dockyard riggers and the Coastguard which was made up of former Royal Navy men, but despite the war fever that gripped the country it was difficult to find enough men to fit out expeditions to both the Baltic and the Black Sea. The navy was forced to take on men of all descriptions, 'even to butchers' boys, navvies, cabmen, etc. – not men of the standard of the Guards'. Ships were sent out again as soon as they arrived from foreign stations; Swedes and Norwegians were recruited though the two nationalities had historic differences and 'would not pull together in the same ship'. One ship sailed with only eight able seamen in a complement of 850, and the navy was able to fit out far fewer ships than it had hoped. As one ship owner put it, 'The Lord have mercy upon the British Fleet should we again have the world in arms against us!'[15]

Although British naval forces operated in the Baltic under the volatile Sir Charles Napier, the main emphasis of the war was to be in the Crimean Peninsula, as it was decided to harm the Russians by destroying their great naval base at Sevastopol. The Russian navy was not very efficient and the British and French fleets had no difficulty in convoying the troops to Turkey and then into the Crimea. A landing on the peninsula was agreed under the command of Rear Admiral Sir Edmund Lyons. At two in the morning of 14 September 1854 a rocket was fired from the French flagship and was answered by one from her British counterpart. Three hundred and fifty-seven ships' boats began to land 26,000 British infantry, who were soon on shore unopposed. It took another three days to complete the landing among surf then they marched south to fight a bloody battle to cross the River Alma. It was decided not to attack Sevastopol from the north but to head round the city and set up positions to the south; the city was never really besieged, as the northern side remained open. A small landlocked harbour at Balaclava was used to keep the allied forces supplied – its defence against

ABOVE The bombardment of Sevastopol by John Wilson Carmichael. The large warships on the left are partly de-rigged, as they will be towed into action by steamships. The bombardment already seems to be having some effect and the sailors in the boats are cheering, but in fact its effects were disappointing.

OPPOSITE The Diamond battery at the siege of Sevastopol, manned by the naval brigade, with officers and ratings standing by for action. It shows a large naval gun with much of its equipment, and the naval uniform of the time, which was not formally adopted until just after the war. By William Simpson, the first official war artist.

Russian counter-attack led to the great battle of October 1854, which saw both the 'thin red line' and the charge of the Light Brigade, symbolising the bravery of the British soldier and the stupidity of his officers.

Meanwhile on 17 October, the two navies tried their best against the open mouth of Sevastopol Harbour. On a calm day, sailing ships that had not yet been fitted with engines were moved into position by steam frigates lashed alongside and more than a thousand allied naval guns opened fire against 73 Russian guns on shore. But the Russians had explosive and incendiary shells while the allied hulls were all wooden. Five of the British ships were set on fire and another ran aground before the force was obliged to withdraw. Only six Russian guns had been dismounted and they had suffered fifty casualties, compared with 310 British and French killed and wounded. The dangers of fighting forts with ships were never better illustrated. There was no longer any prospect of a quick victory, and the allies settled into a long siege of Sevastopol.

Sailors often went ashore as part of naval brigades to fight alongside the army. To support the siege the navy landed 3,700 sailors and marines, along with six 68-pounder guns, fifty 32-pounders and 680 rockets. Sailors soon found that life ashore was not a perpetual holiday as they imagined. 'Up to my neck in mud in all weather, and doing my natural sleep every night in a puddle of water ... for my own part I have given up all hopes of being dry again.'[16]

Sevastopol eventually fell in September 1855 and the war, largely pointless from the start, was settled by 1856. The Crimean War was the beginning of a new age in many respects. In this more populist age came the first medal issued to all ranks for gallantry, the Victoria Cross. Lieutenant C D Lucas was the first to be gazetted for the award, and Commander H J Raby was the first to receive it in a presentation by the Queen in June 1857. Prints showed the recipients lining up before Her Majesty, with ordinary sailors standing just behind officers. The war saw the real foundation of the profession of nursing and modern military medical services. The wounded and sick in the hospital where Florence Nightingale made her name, both soldiers and sailors, were brought in by the navy, and an army officer, Lord Arthur Hay, suggested improvements.

> *There are, by today's statement, 4,600 rank and file in Scutari Hospital; the whole of these men have been landed in ship-boats by driblets, carried through every weather in open litters ... Without any difficulty half-a-dozen boats, made purposely for landing the sick,*

> *could be constructed; any number of covered litters might be made, and any number of Turks ... might be hired as coolies to carry.*[17]

In operations, the war saw the first use of mines, and even a primitive form of human torpedo. It had almost the first war photographs, and a picture of a grossly overcrowded Balaclava Harbour provided a graphic image of the difficulties of supply in a modern war, even with the aid of the steamship. The Admiralty commissioned one of the first official war artists, William 'Crimean' Simpson. It was also in the Crimea that the first modern-style war correspondents appeared. William Howard Russell's dispatches for The Times let the navy off fairly lightly, for it was more professional than the army and was less heavily engaged. Nevertheless reform was still needed in the navy. Manning the fleet had not proved easy and moreover this was the first steam war, and the end of the purely sailing navy.

ABOVE A watercolour of *Britannia* (formerly the *Prince of Wales*) moored off Dartmouth late in the nineteenth century, with her tender, the *Hindustan*. Sailing boats for training are seen alongside. The ships were becoming increasingly unhealthy by this time and were replaced by a college on shore in 1905.

Chapter 14
STEAM, STEEL AND SHELLFIRE

For centuries the naval officer had learned his trade through apprenticeship to a particular captain, but in 1857, after the success of training boy recruits, the Admiralty turned over HMS *Illustrious*, an old 74-gun ship of 1803, to the training of naval cadets as potential officers. The first 23 cadets arrived in August. More accommodation was needed as the intake expanded and on the first day of 1859 the cadets moved to the old three-decker *Britannia*. Haslar Creek near Portsmouth proved unhealthy and the ship was taken to Portland, then in 1863 to the beautiful and sheltered harbour of Dartmouth in Devon.

Britannia was now the main, almost the only, means of entry to the navy as an executive officer. Mark Kerr joined in 1877.

We slept in hammocks, and our clothes were stowed in a sea-chest, which later accompanied us when we joined a sea-going ship. On shore, at the bottom of the hill, was the gymnasium, and at the top were the cricket, hockey and football grounds, and also a tuck-shop. Attached to the Britannia was a small-sailing ship called the Dolphin, in which the senior terms took short sea cruises under sail. There were many cutters with sails and oars, in which we were instructed in the arts of pulling and sailing.

We were brought up in a naval atmosphere, surrounded by bluejackets and marine, the latter being employed as out valets, and we were taught our seamanship by warrant officers and petty officers. There were still among the watermen who used to convey us ashore and bring us off again ... an old fellow called Yeo, who claimed to have been a youngster at the Battle of Trafalgar.[18]

The officers' uniform evolved slowly after 1815, from the relatively free and easy dress of wartime to a stiffer Victorian style. The most significant change was the addition of gold stripes on the cuffs or shoulder straps to indicate rank – one for a lieutenant, two for a commander and three for a captain. In 1863 the rank of sub-lieutenant was recognised and given one stripe, with each rank above being given an additional stripe, so a captain from then on had four. This was a custom which spread to most other navies in the world, then to merchant ship masters and finally to the senior pilot of a civil aircraft. Symbolically at least, a senior pilot – even of a small aeroplane – claims the same authority as the captain of a major warship with perhaps two hundred to a thousand men under him. The navy itself is much more reluctant to issue stripes, and today most warships are headed by commanders with only three of them.

The 1850s also saw the transformation of the naval rating's conditions of service. Until then he had probably been an ex-merchant seaman, taken on for a single voyage only and dressed in his own clothes or those sold to him by the ship's purser. In the 1850s it was decided to recruit most potential seamen as boys and train them from the beginning in naval ways. They were offered permanent service for 10 and later 12 years, and a pension after 22 years. The naval seaman began to diverge from the merchant seaman, with his own style, culture and dress; a uniform for the lower deck was established for the first time in 1857. It adopted the navy blue that officers had worn for a century or more, but otherwise it had nothing in common with the officers' dress. The ratings' uniform already had its square collar and bell-bottom trousers, adapted from what was fashionable among seamen. It began to evolve over the years, mainly due to the customs of seamen themselves,

BELOW Seamen at gun drill on board the training ship HMS *Excellent* around 1840. This was the first systematic shore training adopted by the Royal Navy, and it helped to create a permanent body of seaman-gunners to become the core of the regular navy .

RIGHT King Edward VII and his son, the future George V, wear officer's uniforms during a naval visit, while the royal children are in the sailor suits worn by children of all classes in those days.

as they embellished the regulation dress. Martinet officers might try to enforce the rules, but the seaman still had to pay for his uniform and felt he had a moral right to modify it. Occasionally an Admiralty committee looked into the matter and nearly always adopted what the seamen were already wearing as standard.

The ratings' uniform, known as 'square rig' because of the shape of its collar, has always been the subject of much myth – its three stripes were not in memory of Nelson's battles as legend suggests. It had a curious interaction with children's clothing and one of the earliest examples was a suit worn by the Prince of Wales on board the Royal Yacht in 1846. Sailor suits became very popular with children, especially since one of the alternatives was the much more formal 'Lord Fauntleroy' suit. This also symbolised the image of the sailor – popular and loveable, but rather childlike.

Petty officers such as boatswain's mates and quarter gunners had always been seen as the backbone of the lower deck, leading the crew and forming the link between officers and men. But their status was very fragile; each man was appointed by a particular captain and might give up his rating if he moved to another ship or his captain changed. Petty officers were given anchor badges in 1827, and their rating was made more permanent. The rating of leading seaman was introduced below them, to encourage able seamen to become better qualified. The chief petty officer was brought in above, with higher pay, separate mess and eventually an officer-style uniform. The sailor now had a regular career structure to encourage him.

The seaman has always been a common character in fiction, though his popularity in real life was in inverse proportion to the exposure to his drunken exploits ashore. From a slightly greater distance the seaman was a holy fool like Parsifal or Crocodile Dundee. There was never any doubt about his courage and competence in his own element, where he braved the storms and defeated his country's enemies. On land he was generous and open-handed, and hated

injustice. He applied the rules of the sea to the land, often with startling effect, as a thousand broadsheets and cartoons showed. Sailors had long enjoyed the free issue of tobacco for chewing and for pipes, and they began to make it into ropes which could be cut to form cigarettes. John Player and Sons of Nottingham was already using a sailor of 'HMS Hero' on its pipe tobacco when it began to produce Players Navy Cut cigarettes in 1888, and the association of sailors and cigarettes survived until the middle of the twentieth century.

In 1887 the First Lord of the Admiralty told the House of Commons,

> *The Navy now seems to be a very popular service. A high standard and restrictions on the number of entries have been imposed to prevent an undue influx of boys, but the competition is, notwithstanding considerable. It is worthy of note that, simultaneously with the growing popularity of the Navy with parents as a career for their sons, there is a dread of dismissal from the Service which previously did not exist.*[19]

The navy preferred country boys for its recruits, but in practice most came from the cities of the south of England. In 1875 Sam Noble was a rare recruit from Scotland, taken on by a Royal Marine sergeant.

> *He then drew such a picture of the sea: how I should have nothing to do but sit and let the wind blow me along: live on plum-pudding and the roast beef of old England: lashings of grog and tobacco: seeing the world the while and meeting and chatting with princesses and all the beautiful ladies of other lands – ah! It was a gay life...!*[20]

A boy who joined the training ship *Impregnable* in 1885 found that she was,

> *... one of the old 'wooden walls.' She had three gun decks besides the upper deck with its raised poop and forecastle. She had five decks in all – upper, main, middle and lower and, above the holds the orlop deck where the bags, etc were stowed. There were three masts, that is, three lower masts with topmasts and topgallant masts above each; and, during the sail-drill season she had the sails, ropes and gear of a full-rigged ship.*[21]

LEFT The Players Navy Cut packet featured a sailor on its design from 1888. The name of the ship on his cap changed to *Invincible* and then *Excellent* and the uniform was modernised over the years. It was a classic image of masculinity and world travel.

RIGHT The boys of the training ship *Impregnable* at Plymouth man the yards and ratlines in honour of distinguished visitors seated in the foreground. Climbing skills and balance were still highly valued in the navy in the 1890s, as gunboats on remote stations continued to use sail on occasion.

RIGHT The first mastless battleship, the *Devastation* of 1871, is seen here firing a salute from her forward turret in honour of a visit by the Shah of Persia in 1873, painted by E W Cooke. The ship was a milestone in battleship development, but never saw action, being broken up in 1908.

According to the regulations, a fiddler was available to give the boys the opportunity of dancing and to 'promote cheerfulness'. The ship's police were to 'check bad language and violent conduct'. Discipline was to be light and subtle: flogging was only to be used 'in cases of theft or highly immoral character' and the cane would 'rarely be required'.[22] The reality was rather different. Charles Humphreys joined HMS *Boscawen* at Portland in November 1870. 'I cannot describe those 12 months of learning discipline. We were very often short of food and many a rope's end did I feel. Our instructors were very cruel, but I suppose it was mainly because we had a very stern captain.'[23]

The naval world was changed in 1859 by the launch of the French ironclad *Gloire*. After a number of armoured floating batteries in the Crimean War, and radical developments in iron merchant ships, the French were the first to take the most dramatic step in warship design. The British soon followed with the much superior *Warrior*, launched at Blackwall on the Thames in 1860. She was much larger at 9,210 tons and actually built of iron rather than just 'iron-clad'. She still had much of the form of an old wooden ship, with a full set of masts and most of her guns on the broadside, but this was only the start of a new revolution; there was to be no stability in ship design for the next 30 years. The ram bow was quickly adopted by the *Warrior*'s successors, and its effectiveness seemed to be confirmed during the Battle of Lissa between the Austrians and the Italians in 1866. Meanwhile the battles of the American Civil War showed the advantages of putting guns in turrets, but this was very difficult in a seagoing sailing ship. Another solution was the central battery ship, in which a small number of large guns were placed in an armoured citadel and could be moved on rails from one gunport to another. The *Captain* of 1870 attempted to combine sailing rig

with turrets and was soon lost in the Bay of Biscay. The *Devastation* of 1871 took the radical step of abandoning sail power altogether, though her reliance on her engines meant that her range was short and she was most useful for coastal defence. Ten years later, the *Admiral* class replaced the turret with the barbette, which protected the magazines and the routes to them, rather than the guns. Armour plate was devel-

oped, while gun power was greatly increased. It was impossible to form an effective line of battle during this period, as technological change created a great variety of ships. Types in service in the mid-1880s included broadside ironclads like the *Warrior*, central battery ironclads, armoured rams, coast defence ships, mastless turret ships such as the *Devastation*, and barbette ships. With the instability in technology

and the constant threat of a new weapon appearing, there were doubts about whether the navy was the most effective defence of the country. The army gained new prominence and popularity, while the Palmerston forts (or follies) were built to defend the great naval bases.

Ships no longer carried their guns on several decks, so the old term of frigate as used for a single-

Iron and Steel Shipbuilding

The coming of iron and later steel gave the shipbuilder many more options, once he had learned to use it. In the private shipyards (which built many warships after the Naval Defence Act of 1889) the shipwright was largely supplanted and confined to lining up the erection of the ship. His place was taken by specialist metalworkers such as blacksmiths, boilermakers, platers and riveters. In the Royal Dockyards the shipwrights adapted to the new order and kept their jobs.

Ships were still built on slips at an angle, as in the days of wood. The basic structure was still made up of a keel, frames and an outer and inner skin, but the details had all changed. It was unusual for the vertical keel to protrude below the hull, rather it was incorporated in the internal structure as just another longitudinal member. The horizontal keel plates, laid directly on the blocks, were the first sections to be fitted. Frames were now cut out from steel plates, with L-section bars riveted to them to fix them to other parts. Deck beams were usually made of iron bars with bulb-sections at the ends, and bent into shape using jacks on a slab fitted with pegs to give the form. Ships' hulls were now covered with rectangular steel plates rather than long wooden planks. Each was riveted to the ones above and below and on either side, giving a far more rigid structure: it was referred to as shell plating and was the most important part of the structure.

Shipbuilders had to add extra strength in midships to support the engines and boilers. The propeller shafts, leading aft through the lower stern at an angle, had to be made watertight and be totally straight, or the engines would never work properly. The rudder was no longer attached to the stern post so several options were available for the shape of the stern, including raked, cruiser and flat or transom. Instead the rudder was balanced, that is pivoted about or near its centre, so that the force needed to turn it was much less. Nevertheless a larger ship needed the assistance of engines to turn it. At the other end of the ship the ram bow was common in battleships and many cruisers, with a large forged frame forming its centre. The whole structure was held together by rivets of various types, perhaps countersunk to create a smoother surface, and sometimes the plates were joggled or depressed in the area of the join for the same reason. Iron and steel shipbuilding needed much more capital than wooden shipbuilding had done, and by 1914 warship building was concentrated in fourteen main firms.

BELOW The section of an armoured ship of around 1900 showing the main armour belt marked O. Angled armour is fitted inside, designed to protect the engines, magazine and steering system from shellfire.

RIGHT ABOVE Making engines at the Keyham steam factory at Plymouth in the 1860s.

RIGHT BELOW HMS *Achilles*, an iron screw ship of nearly 10,000 tons, under construction in No.2 Dock at Chatham in 1862, showing how the system of framing was adopted from wooden shipbuilding techniques.

Fig. 4.—Midship Section of a Large Armoured Ship.

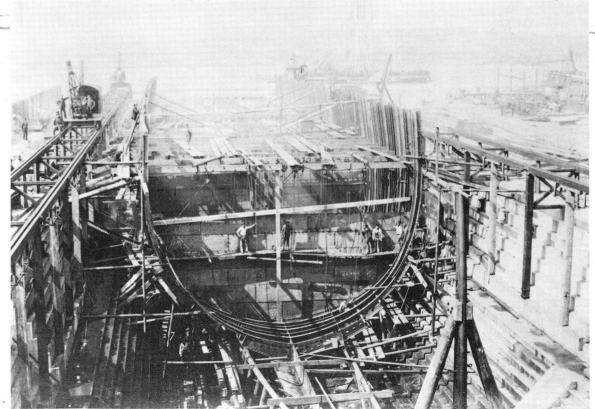

decker became meaningless. It was replaced in the role of medium-sized, fast, long-range warship by the cruiser, which was intended to patrol trade routes and control the empire. Armoured cruisers evolved almost accidentally with the *Shannon* of 1875, and protected cruisers were being built by the late 1880s, with restricted armour and the coal carefully distributed to keep out enemy shot.

From 1863 onwards the navy began to stage annual cruises round the ports of the British Isles. In an earlier age it would not have been possible to withdraw so many ships from the English Channel in case political crises developed before they could get back, but now the electric telegraph allowed instant recall when the ships were in port, and steam power allowed them to return in almost any weather conditions.

Before the first cruise involving five brand-new ironclad battleships and frigates, Captain Arthur Cochrane of the *Warrior* addressed the crew. The task was,

> *To show the people of Britain our new navy the squadron have been given a special duty. Over the next three months we shall be visiting ports on the east and west coasts of England and Scotland, culminating in Dublin. Visitors will be allowed aboard and where possible leave will be given. I need hardly warn you that leave breaking and misconduct will be treated severely.'* [24]

The squadron's warmest reception was in Liverpool, which took the navy to its heart. Forty ship owners contributed £10 each to entertain 800 sailors and 200 marines, and more than 57,000 people visited the *Warrior* alone. One of them described the scene.

> *Along the broad white deck, which looked like a great broad street, men were seen rope making, carpentering, making hammocks, and hand ropes, & c. Sentries were walking their quiet rounds as silently as if there was no*

> *crowd around them. Going down the ladder to the main-deck, the ear was greeted with the bleating of sheep, and the cackle of domestic fowls in spacious coops, and the animals seemed quite at home among plenty of clean fodder and food. Large quantities of butcher's meat hanging up ready for cooking. Cooks busy at work in the galley, preparing all sorts of dishes – the smell set up is savoury, and calculated to give one an appetite.* [25]

The great communications revolution of the age was the electric telegraph, which made it possible to send a message by Morse code instantaneously. Many land lines had already been set up by 1851, when the first successful line was laid across the English Channel between Calais and Dover. It was followed by others across the sheltered but deep waters of the Mediterranean, and lines connecting British colonies. The most difficult and useful underwater cable was across the Atlantic, which would use the shortest route and link the British possessions in Ireland and Newfoundland, and join to the network in the United States. In the spring of 1858 the British screw battleship *Agamemnon* met the American frigate *Niagara* in mid Atlantic, each carrying enough cable to traverse half the ocean. After delays due to storms, the two ends were spliced together on 16 June; the two ships then proceeded eastwards and westwards. There were several failures and the operation had to be started again, but the *Agamemnon* reached Valentia Bay in the southwest of Ireland on 4 August and the first transatlantic message was set on the 17th. But it was a false dawn, the cable only worked for 20 days before it gave up. In 1865 a more successful cable was laid by Brunel's giant ship, the *Great Eastern*.

The telegraph was essential in the development of Britain's merchant shipping fleet, which was increasingly dominant in the world after their main rivals the Americans, declined during their civil war. Ships were now divided into liners, which ran regular routes carrying both goods and passengers, and

H.M.S. 'AGAMEMNON' LAYING THE ATLANTIC TELEGRAPH CABLE IN 1858 A WHALE CROSSES THE LINE

tramps which relied on the telegraph to pick up cargoes all around the world. Steam progressed in the merchant service at almost the same pace as in the Royal Navy. It was 1884 before steam tonnage overtook sail on the British register but progress was fast after that as the new triple-expansion engines allowed much greater economy. By the end of the century there were 7 million tons of British steamships compared with 2 million tons of sailing ships, but of course the steamships did far more work.

Free trade was at the centre of British economic policy after the abolition of the Corn Laws in 1846. The country was in a strong position as the world's only major industrial power until the 1870s. The country relied on imports far more than ever, not just luxury goods for trade as in the past, but foodstuffs. Exports of coal, a vital factor in the economy, totalled 5.6 million tons in 1856 and more than 22 million tons by 1884.

ABOVE The screw battleship *Agamemnon* laying the Atlantic telegraph cable in 1858, showing the apparatus rigged across the stern to let the cable out. This shows a moment of tension as a whale crosses the cable.

All these imports would have to be protected by the navy in wartime. Strategists tended to see the problem in terms of individual raiders that would have to be hunted down, rather than the less exciting work of protecting convoys. For a protection role the navy developed the cruiser, a large warship that could also be useful scouting for the fleet and for 'showing the flag' in the empire. Like the battleships of the late nineteenth century they carried no sails and had armour and a mixture of guns, with a long hull for speed. By the end of the century they had several engines and often four funnels, which gave a distinctive, though not attractive appearance.

Meanwhile another navy served in the rest of the world and among the British colonies. The steam gunboat, evolved during the Crimean War, was a small vessel designed to fight in shallow and restricted waters, either among the Åland Islands off Finland, or in the Sea of Azov near the Crimea. It found a new lease of life after the war, in policing the world on behalf of the British Empire. A colonial governor, a consul or a group of merchants could use the new electric telegraph to communicate with the nearest naval headquarters or with London, and a cheap and small gunboat might be sent. More than a hundred requests were received in five years between 1857 and 1861, and the great majority were complied with. Not all involved aggressive action, or indeed any kind of violence at all. In February 1858, for example, the *Iris* was sent to the New Hebrides to investigate a murder, though it is not clear what training the sailors had for this. The Board of Trade asked for a ship to help with the erection of a lighthouse at Cay Lobos in the Bahamas, assistance was given to Dr David Livingstone and his Zambesi expedition, and two vessels were sent from China to assist the Governor of New Zealand 'as a check to the natives'.[26] The gunboats were a key element in 'Pax Britannica', which supporters claimed had succeeded the ancient Roman Empire in spreading law and order around the known world.

The navy was also a factor in European politics, especially in the Mediterranean. Though essentially a conservative organisation, it was often used in support of liberal foreign policy. In 1860 the great Italian leader Giuseppe Garibaldi led a successful revolt in Sicily against the repressive regime of Naples. When he crossed to mainland Italy, a Royal Navy squadron stood by to protect him from the Neapolitan navy. The eventual result was the unification of Italy.

The great European crisis of the period came after a revolt in the Balkans was crushed by the Turks, much to the horror of the Liberals led by William Gladstone. When the Russian army began to invade Turkey it was the Conservatives, led by their Prime Minster Benjamin Disraeli, who were horrified at the possible threat to the balance of power should Russia get a naval base in the Mediterranean. The Royal Navy sent a force under Sir Geoffrey Phipps Hornby through the Dardanelles as a warning. The Russians offered no opposition and a conference was arranged in Berlin. According to Disraeli this led to 'peace with honour'.

Seaman James Wood found himself in boats off Zanzibar chasing Arab dhows and trying to prevent the slave trade – though he had doubts when he found that the slaves actually lived a comfortable life but were subjected to hazards and hardship during and after a chase by the British navy.[27] The 1860s and '70s were also a golden age for the naval brigades, with around 16 major operations, from New Zealand to Dominica, and South Africa to Egypt. They gave the seaman experiences of many different kinds of warfare. Petty Officer William Jenkin of HMS *Shah* faced a Zulu charge in 1879.

The enemy sighted by our scouts 6 am. Order 'man the trenches, every man in his place in three seconds'. Zulus commenced fire at 6.30 pm, advancing in horseshoe formation, estimated number of Zulus 1500 to 3000. Gatlings and 6 pdrs opened with shell at 800 yards. Enemy advance courageously and ignorantly to within thirty yards of our trenches, one man throwing his assegai at a Gatling gun.[28]

Sloops and gunboats were far more conservative in design, usually with wooden hulls that could be repaired away from the facilities of a dockyard, and they combined sail and steam power because coal was scarce in the outposts of empire. These still deployed the traditional skills of the sailors and shipwrights as well as the newer expertise of engine room artificers who might have to do repairs or make new parts on their own initiative.

The British were slow to react when the French engineer Ferdinand de Lesseps opened the Suez Canal in 1869, but they soon came to see its importance on the route to India. In 1875 Disraeli bought a large shareholding from the bankrupt Egyptian government. In 1881 the Egyptian army revolted against foreign influence, and in the following spring a joint European force was sent to deal with it. The arrival of the force off Alexandria caused anti-Christian riots and in July a British fleet of eight battleships and other vessels began to bombard the town. Seaman Thomas Holman is rather cursory about the bombardment itself. 'The game was a very one-sided one from the first, and soon ended without very much loss on our side, but with a much larger death role on theirs.' The most dramatic naval incident was when the gunboat *Condor* rescued HMS *Temeraire* after she was grounded, then sailed within 1,200 yards of Fort Marabout to engage it and force its surrender. This earned the famous signal 'Well done Condor' and established the career of her captain Charles Beresford. Thomas Holman gives further detail about the occupation of the city after this incident.

After finishing the sailor's part of the business then, we had to buckle on blankets and water bottles, and do what we could to prevent those skulking Arab thieves from looting the town. So, with a naval officer installed as head of police, we landed, and with machine guns, rifles and bayonets, and even fisticuffs if required, we beat and bullied those dogs into some sort of obedience and civility.[29]

After landing an army and fighting several battles ashore, the British took Egypt as a protectorate and the Suez Canal was secure.

The role of the engineer officer was changing, now that modern warships depended entirely on them for their source of power. Each battleship or cruiser carried several commissioned engineer officers, though they were not recognised as the equals of the executive officers who commanded the ship and took charge of watches. From 1880 engineer officers were given full professional training in a college at Keyham in Plymouth dockyard. But as officers they were not expected to get their hands dirty, unlike merchant ship engineering officers, so a new class had to created. Engine room artificers were skilled men recruited direct from civil life, and from a very different background to the seamen and stokers.

On board ships of war they find themselves surrounded by men who have been brought up to a different system from boyhood, and who cannot therefore understand that the habits of their own ordinary course of life may prove a hardship to others, who for many years have been accustomed to a different mode of living.[30]

RIGHT The composite screw sloop *Gannet*, built at Sheerness in 1878 and currently being restored at Chatham Historic Dockyard. She was a typical colonial gunboat, with both sail and steam power and a metal frame with wood planking.

ABOVE A Whitehead torpedo around 1890. The original cigar shape is beginning to become more cylindrical. The tube from which it is fired can be seen in the background.

OPPOSITE The bombardment of Alexandria in 1882. The gunboat *Condor* under Captain Charles Beresford engages Fort Marabout at close range to earn the signal, 'Well done *Condor*' from the admiral, and fame for her captain. This is an early work by W L Wyllie, who went to Alexandria to make drawings for the picture.

Naval superiority was threatened in 1869 when Robert Whitehead, a Briton living in Austria, demonstrated his self-propelled torpedo. Launched by a small and fast craft, it could strike a large ship underwater and damage it fatally. The British responded with increased defences for their capital ships and their own torpedo boats from 1876, creating a new kind of navy. The torpedo boats were quite small, with a complement of up to 25, and were not regarded as independent commands – some were designed to be carried by capital ships like ship's boats.

Imperialism was not particularly fashionable in the middle years of the century: in 1859, for example, the *United Services Magazine* carried an article 'On the Necessity of Contracting the British Empire'; and the island of Corfu was given back to Greece in 1864. Nevertheless, the navy continued to build up its network of overseas bases, all the more important now that warships had to take on coal. Bermuda, Hong Kong, Halifax, Gibraltar, Malta, Jamaica, the Cape of Good Hope, Ascension Island, Trincomalee, Vancouver and Sydney all saw increased naval building and presence.

Imperialism was popular again by the last decades of the nineteenth century, more so than ever before. The term 'jingoism' arose during the Russian Crisis of 1877–8, with the music hall song,

We don't want to fight, but by jingo if we do,
We've got the ships, we've got the men, and
we've got the money too

All classes and many different political groups were united in support of imperialism. Joseph Chamberlain, the radical mayor of Birmingham, transferred his allegiance to the Conservative Party in support of it. From the extreme left H M Hyndman of the quasi-Marxist Social Democratic Federation believed in the future of the British Empire and the need for a strong navy. The role of the navy in national defence had never been questioned, and its work in creating and defending the empire had almost equal public support by the end of the century. Inland colonisation was now increasingly possible due to the use of steamships on rivers, and in the longer term the building of railways. At the same time the new nation of Germany, left behind in the colonial race, demanded her 'place in the sun'; this began the 'Scramble for Africa' in 1885–5 when most of the remaining parts of the continent were taken over by the European powers.

The navy had enjoyed a comparatively undisturbed existence since the end of the Crimean War, largely serving abroad and unnoticed by press and parliament. This began to change during the 1880s, as new nations began to seek naval power and British complacency was shaken. W T Stead, one of the apostles of the 'new journalism', published a series of articles on 'The Truth about the Navy' in the *Pall Mall Gazette*. Stead took his cue from a remark by William Gladstone, whose triumphant election campaign of 1880 he had helped to engineer. The strength to Britain, Gladstone postulated, was 'not to be found in alliances with great military powers' but 'in the sufficiency and supremacy of her navy – a navy as powerful now as all the navies of Europe'. Stead argued that this was no longer true, that colonial expansion since then, the increased need for foreign commerce and the growth of other navies had made Britain especially vulnerable. In particular he was concerned about the new steam fleet's dependence on overseas coaling stations round the world, most of which were undefended against attack. His naval contact was the young captain of the gunnery ship *Excellent*, John Fisher, who was presented to him as 'the one man we have who can be compared to Nelson'. Stead's campaign was not the last piece of journalism to contain little more than a grain of truth, but public opinion forced the government to add £3½ million to the naval estimates.[31] And the campaign began a new age in Britain's naval history.

Technology on HMS *Warrior*

The most dramatic symbol of the nineteenth-century Royal Navy is moored just outside the Victory Gate of the Royal Navy Dockyard in Portsmouth. She provided a fitting location for Dan Snow and the team for Episode 4. Launched in 1860 and first commissioned into the navy on 1 August 1861, HMS *Warrior* was 'the largest, fastest, strongest and most powerful warship in the world'. She was a response to the French warship *Gloire* (1859), although she was some 60 per cent larger and much more advanced. Whereas the French ship's wooden hull was merely clad in 4½-inch thick iron, *Warrior*'s was made entirely from it. Indeed *Warrior* has been credited as the greatest single development in the history of warship design, fully harnessing for the first time the possibilities of iron and steel as structural ship-building materials.

Warrior was described as a frigate, but she had the ability to defeat an enemy single-handedly. Her design centred around a long single gun deck, as opposed to the three decks of a conventional wooden ship of the line. *Warrior* carried 26 awesome muzzle-loading 68-pounder guns complemented by 10 of the newly adopted 110-pounder Armstrong breech-loading rifled guns including two on upper-deck slide and pivot carriages (a replica is shown on the right). Sadly these latter guns proved unexpectedly unreliable and unsafe.

The ship was not only revolutionary in terms of structure and armament; she was the first ship to incorporate a steam drying room – it took five hours to dry 120 hammocks or 320 other items of clothing – amongst other attempts to improve the lot of the Victorian seaman.

Rescued as a hulk from Milford Haven, *Warrior* underwent a stunning restoration in the 1980s, and a notable feature of the preserved ship is the high level of detail and accuracy of her structural elements and fittings. Of particular difficulty for the restoration team was the location and relationship of movable items and fixtures. Much of this was resolved when a midshipman's logbook, containing a sketch plan and views of all the decks, was found in the Royal Naval Museum. It allowed the team to recreate the pristine Enfield rifles and Colt Navy revolvers seen in the racks (left) and the shot held in iron bars (overleaf) on the main gun deck.

1. Dan Snow loads a 110-pounder Armstrong breech-loading gun on Warrior.
3. The shot and powder charge are pushed through the hollow screw and the vent piece is replaced.

2. The breech screw is loosened and the large vent piece hauled out.
4. The handles are used to tighten the breech screw and provide the necessary gas tight seal before firing.

BLACK&WHITE.

A WEEKLY ILLUSTRATED RECORD AND REVIEW, WITH WHICH IS INCORPORATED "THE PICTORIAL WORLD"

No. 127—Vol. VI. [Registered at the G.P.O. as a Newspaper]   SATURDAY, JULY 8, 1893   [PRICE SIXPENCE By Post 6½D

THE "VICTORIA" DISASTER—THE LAST MOMENTS OF ADMIRAL SIR GEORGE TRYON

Chapter 15
ROAD TO WAR

In 1889, in response to the growing navies of other countries, parliament passed the Naval Defence Act. This gave extra money to build ships, and set up the two-power standard, which stated that the Royal Navy was to be kept up to the strength of the next two greatest powers. This was the beginning of a naval arms race that would see fleets greatly increased over the next quarter of a century. One of the first casualties was William Gladstone, now a veteran prime minister. In 1894 he resigned the office for the fourth and last time at the age of 84, over the demand for yet more warships. He claimed, 'that this competitive action of ours would accelerate some great European catastrophe: these vast armaments must lead to some flare-up'.[32]

This coincided with the publication of *The Influence of Sea Power upon History* by Captain A T Mahan of the US Navy. Mahan's aim was to persuade the United States to invest more in her fleet, but nearly all the historical examples he used, apart from a few classical ones and the Battle of Lepanto in 1571, were from Britain's wars with the Netherlands, France and Spain. He argued for the timelessness of sea power and that nations could only flourish with strong navies. He claimed that the French guerre de course against merchant shipping had shown its futility through the years and that the essence of naval power was a strong battlefleet. Mahan's works became immensely popular in Britain, Germany and Japan and he was seen as the apostle of the 'new navalism'. Others were already beginning to argue that sea power was less important in an age when railways could open up continents, and the submarine was about to give the guerre de course a new lease of life. But in the long run, the navy that deployed submarines as the main naval weapon lost two wars; and the great international struggles of the twentieth century, including the Cold War, were won by the maritime rather than the continental powers.

and men in the water. Then there was a further upheaval, which appeared to be the boilers exploding, causing a swell of water, carrying with it spars and other forms of wreckage and making the efforts of rescue by boats most difficult. Many poor fellows, evidently seriously injured, were seen to drown within a few yards of my boat, which was unable to reach them through the wreckage.[33]

As well as its humanitarian effects, the disaster was used to discredit a looser system of fleet control that had been developed by Vice-Admiral Sir George Tryon, who perished in the disaster. The court martial of the surviving officers exonerated Rear-Admiral Albert Markham of the *Camperdown* who had failed to use his initiative and take avoiding action. Like the courts martial of the mid-eighteenth century it tended to reinforce rigid fleet discipline and led to greatly increased centralisation – something the navy would pay for later.

The Imperial role continued and Winston Churchill, then a young army officer and war correspondent, watched the gunboats fight their way up the Nile during General Kitchener's expedition of 1898.

At about eleven o'clock the gunboats ascended the Nile, and now engaged the enemy's batteries on both banks. Throughout the day loud reports of their guns could be heard, and, looking from our position on the ridge, we could see the white vessels steaming slowly forward against the current, under clouds of black smoke from their furnaces and amid other clouds of white smoke from the artillery. The forts, which mounted nearly fifty guns, replied vigorously; but the British aim was accurate and their fire crushing. The embrasures were smashed to bits and many of the Dervish guns dismounted.[34]

Britain's largest war of the age was against the Boers, the South African Dutch who had moved into

ABOVE Naval gunboats towing local sailing craft up the River Nile as part of General Kitchener's campaign of 1898. Each gunboat is armed with a variety of weapons.

OPPOSITE Queen Victoria's Diamond Jubilee Naval Review at Spithead in June 1897. To the left is a line of what later became known as 'pre-Dreadnought' battleships of the *Majestic* class headed by HMS *Renown*, all 'dressed overall' with celebratory flags. The Queen is in the Royal Yacht *Victoria and Albert* on the right.

The greatest naval disaster of the age occurred when the battleship *Camperdown* accidentally rammed and sank HMS *Victoria* off the coast of Lebanon in 1893.

Vast quantities of spars, wreckage, etc., shot up to the surface, wounding many who were fortunate to get away from the ship, and were now struggling in the great upheaval of water. Then, and not until then, we in the boats were ordered to proceed to the succour of Officers

Transvaal and the Orange Free State to escape British rule. As with the Crimean War 45 years earlier, it was a war in which the navy was not really tested. The army got the blame for failures during the first year, while the navy was praised for its energy and initiative in landing guns. Time and again, at the Siege of Ladysmith and many other battles, it was only the naval 12-pounders and 6-inch guns that could match the Boers' 'Long Toms' supplied by Germany.

With British naval supremacy, there was never any real prospect of a foreign power intervening on behalf of the Boers, but there was no doubt about where European sympathies lay. British atrocities against the Boers were reported and greatly exaggerated, especially in Germany. The British were shocked at the depth of the hostility, and found that their foreign policy of 'splendid isolation' was not as successful as they had hoped. This was not helped in the autumn of 1899, when Germany passed a new Navy Law which would double the size of her fleet. In 1903, to add fuel to the flames, Erskine Childers published his novel *Riddle of the Sands*, in which two intrepid yachtsmen foil a German plan to invade England. British opinion had not been hostile to the new state of Germany, founded by Bismarck as recently as 1871. But Germany began to see that it had been left behind in the colonial race and demanded its place alongside the other great powers. To the Germans, a great battlefleet was just one of the aspects of great power status; to the British, it could only be aimed against them, their trade and their colonial empire

Naval progress was now assisted by two inventors. Charles Parsons took his boat *Turbinia* to Queen Victoria's Diamond Jubilee Naval Review in 1897 to demonstrate a new principle of steam power. Instead of cylinders pumping up and down, Parsons had developed the turbine, which deployed high-pressure steam to create a rotary motion; he was successful in attracting attention and in a short space of time the navy's destroyers were powered by turbines. John Philip Holland was Irish-born like Parsons but had opposite views on the British Empire. A US resident, he developed his *Fenian Ram*, the first practical submarine whose title showed where his sympathies lay. In 1901, in a supreme irony, the British Government ordered its first submarine known as *Holland No 1*, just before Germany built its first U-boat. There was fast development after that and many advanced naval

ABOVE Parson's *Turbinia* at high speed. She was built in 1894 solely to demonstrate the speed that could be attained by a turbine engine, which she did very successfully. She made her last voyage in 1907 and is now preserved in Newcastle.

officers were well aware that the submarine had great potential as a weapon of war.

When 'Admiral 'Jackie' Fisher became professional head of the navy as First Sea Lord in 1904, his main task was to reduce expenditure. He soon focused on the gunboat fleet spread around the empire. He divided the ships into four main categories. 'Fighting ships' included all modern battleships, cruisers and destroyers. Obsolete cruisers and torpedo boats were 'of doubtful value'; there was a large group of 'utterly useless ships for fighting purposes' which might or might not find roles as depot ships and so on and required 'most careful consideration'; and 'absolutely obsolete vessels' which required 'none at all! Break them up!'[35] When the Royal Tournament began in 1907, one of its highlights was the field gun race where representatives of the naval divisions at Chatham, Portsmouth and Plymouth took a gun to pieces and carried it over a series of obstacles. It was already nostalgic, for Fisher's new navy was far less keen to get involved in that kind of warfare; sailors were concentrated closer to home waters, and great fleets were built up to defend the country.

In fact the navy and the general public were obsessed with the number of ships, particularly battleships, compared with the other naval powers. The Navy League was formed in 1895 to campaign for greater public interest in the navy. It wanted to appeal to all classes, particularly the working classes who were beginning to turn towards socialist parties of pacifist inclination. It pointed out that the country was now dependent on imports for most of its food-stuffs and raw materials, and command of the sea was more important than ever. It was to be highly success-ful over the next 20 years.

Up to this point ships were developing very diverse armaments: 12 and 13.5-inch guns with longer range and great hitting power, large numbers of 6-inch because of their higher rate of fire, light Hotchkiss guns against torpedo craft as well as the intermediate 9.2-inch which was just enough to penetrate the latest armour of the 1890s. According to Fisher a battleship had 'representatives of all calibres' as if 'you were peo-pling the Ark'.[36] Captain Percy Scott developed the idea of firing by salvoes so that the fall of shot could be observed and corrected if necessary. This would be much easier if all the guns were of the same calibre. Fisher decided to incorporate all this in a new battle-ship design, carrying an armament of ten 12-inch

guns, with a secondary battery against torpedo craft. He also fitted her with turbine engines to give greater speed, for he constantly quoted, or misquoted, Mrs Glasse's famous cookery book –'first catch your hare'. The new ship, named the *Dreadnought*, was built very rapidly in just a year, about a third of the normal time for a battleship. When completed in 1906, she was faster and far better armed than any capital ship afloat. All the rest were obsolete; in future, naval power would be measured by the number of Dreadnought battle-ships available. As Fisher had hoped, the Germans were wrong-footed. Their first Dreadnoughts would not be started for 18 months and they would be infe-rior, with reciprocating engines and lighter guns.

In fact the *Dreadnought* was not Fisher's first love. He was well aware that Britain was totally dependent on

BELOW The *Dreadnought*, from a German postcard. The building of the first all-big-gun, turbine-powered battleship created huge interest in all the navies of the world.

England Linienschiff „Dreadnought." 1906.

John Fisher, Baron of Kilverstone (1841–1920)

Fisher was born in Ceylon, and later his enemies would spread rumours that he was part Chinese. His father was an army captain who soon left to become a coffee planter and played no further part in his life; Fisher was sent to England at the age of 6 to be brought up by his godmother. When he joined the navy in 1854 it was before cadet training began at Dartmouth and in a purely sailing ship that soon proved its ineffectiveness in the Baltic campaign against Russia. He was a moderniser for the rest of his career. He was an acting lieutenant by the end of the Second China War and took part in the bombardment of the Peiho Forts in 1859.

Back home he passed the navigational examination with flying colours but specialised in gunnery in HMS *Excellent*. He won the coveted appointment as gunnery officer of the new *Warrior* and made a special study of mines, later becoming a pioneer of torpedoes. In 1874 he was one of the officers sent to study the Whitehead factory in Fiume. Promoted to captain, Fisher commanded several of the new armoured ships, usually as flag captain under the direct orders of a leading admiral. He took part in the bombardment of Alexandria in 1882 but was struck down with dysentery ashore, from which he took four years to recover. He began to develop his press relations, including the carefully planted leak, during a navy scare in 1884, and at the Admiralty as Director of Naval Ordnance he was responsible for adding quick-firing guns to the fleet's armoury for use against torpedo boats. In 1894 he was a vice admiral and commander-in-chief in the West Indies, when there was a crisis with France and he conceived a characteristically daring plan to rescue the falsely imprisoned Captain Dreyfus from Devil's Island.

In 1899 he took command of the Mediterranean Fleet, still the best job in the navy. He renewed its interest in gunnery and tactics, but had a poor relationship with his second-in-command, Sir Charles Beresford, which came to a head when, in front of crowds on shore, he ordered Beresford to go round and do a mooring again in Grand Harbour,

imported foodstuffs and raw materials and wanted a class of cruiser that could defeat anything the enemy might send on the high seas. Armoured cruisers were already almost as large as battleships, but now Fisher designed the battlecruiser, which had the armament of a Dreadnought but greater speed and range – it paid for this by using lighter armour. The first three of the type, the *Invincible* class, were in service by 1908, while *Dreadnought* was the only modern battleship in commission. But soon Fisher, against his better judgement, would be caught up in a fervour for more Dreadnoughts.

The building of the *Dreadnought* cancelled out the huge number of old battleships that Britain had amassed over the years, and in the medium term it gave the Germans some hope of catching up. This began a new phase in the naval arms race, which soon entered popular consciousness. The Liberal Party was in power, committed to reducing naval expenditure and to a programme of social reform which included national insurance and old age pensions. In 1909 the Navy League organised successful demonstrations for more Dreadnoughts with the slogan, 'We want eight and we won't wait'. Sylvia Pankhurst, the most radical of her Suffragette family, published a newspaper called the *Women's Dreadnought*; when she moved into Labour politics she re-named it the *Workers'*

him many enemies. His supporters and favourites were said to be in the 'Fishpond' while Beresford became leader of the opposition to him and was castigated as a 'reactionary', though he had many good ideas of his own.

Fisher retired from the Admiralty in 1910 but was recalled at Churchill's instigation a few months after the First World War began. Even a huge department like the wartime Admiralty had no room for two such colossal egos, and Fisher resigned in 1915 over the Dardanelles campaign. He joined the board of invention and research and had a role in developing Asdic, which would eventually be the main means of detecting submerged submarines. He remains a controversial figure to this day, his great efforts at naval reform being undermined by the divisive nature of his rule.

OPPOSITE Sir John Fisher as a vice admiral.

Malta. He became Second Sea Lord in charge of naval personnel in 1902 and executed many reforms, including the Selborne Scheme to integrate engineer officers with the executive.

In 1904 he became First Sea Lord, initially intending to reduce naval expenditure. Though he was tempted by the idea of the submarine as the main defence of the homeland, he sponsored the building of the *Dreadnought* in a year, and was even more enthusiastic about the battlecruiser. He carried out numerous reforms, though his combatant manner, reinforced by his terse, heavily underlined and italicised letters, made

ABOVE LEFT The battlecruiser *Invincible*.

Dreadnought. The combination of naval expenditure and social reform was causing great strain to the financial system. Lloyd George's budget of 1909 imposed taxes on the rich and was rejected by the House of Lords. This led to a constitutional crisis in which the power of the Lords was curbed. The Liberal Party had traditionally opposed large expenditure on armaments. After Winston Churchill became First Lord of the Admiralty his cousin wrote to him, 'you are in danger of becoming purely a "Navy man" and losing sight of the far greater job of a great leader of the Liberal Party.'[37] She predicted accurately that Churchill would eventually be drawn back to the Con-servative Party, and indeed the Liberal Party would decline after this, never to form a government again.

As the arms race intensified, there was a rapid growth in the size of new Dreadnoughts laid down. The *Dreadnought* herself was of 17,900 tons with 12-inch guns. The *Orion* class of 'super-Dreadnoughts', ordered in 1909, were of 22,000 tons with 13.5-inch guns. The mighty ships of the *Queen Elizabeth* class, begun in 1912, were of 33,000 tons and had 15-inch guns. Forty Dreadnoughts and battlecruisers had been built or were under order for the Royal Navy by August 1914, a massive financial investment in the navy. This was matched by great improvements in the accuracy of naval gunnery, under the guidance of Percy Scott. Gunnery results for the fleet were published, and a cartoon in *Punch* magazine had Britannia (the goddess not the ship) showing an astonished Kaiser Wilhelm how results had improved from 42 per cent in 1904 to 71 per cent in 1906 – possibly the only period when the press treated naval exercises with the same attention as sporting events. But there was more to come. Japan's victory against the Russians at Tsushima in 1905 had shown the value of long-range gunnery, and the director system was developed so that a single tower high in the ship could control the aim of all the big guns, tending to great accuracy. Unfortunately the

Admiralty chose to use the fire-control system developed by Lieutenant Frederick Dreyer, rather than a much superior system produced by the talented amateur inventor, Charles Pollen.

As First Lord of the Admiralty from 1911, Winston Churchill was well aware of the growing problems of the lower deck.

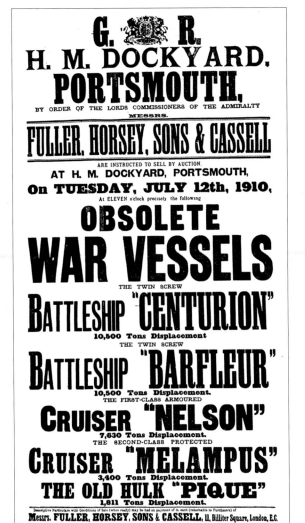

The sailor's life is one of exceptional hardship. Service in a ship of war is not only strenuous but more uncomfortable than twelve or fourteen years ago. Instead of seeing something of the world, the young sailor knows nothing but the North Sea and a few war anchorages round the coast. The construction of the modern warship renders it extremely uncomfortable and even unhealthy as a living place. Nothing is possible in the nature of a recreation room on board, nor are there facilities for any kind of rest, privacy or amusement. A man has only the mess deck to go to, where he is herded with several hundred others in messes of about sixteen. If he wants to read and write in quiet there is no place for him. Now that armour has been carried to the upper deck, he has to subsist on artificial light and ventilation. If he wants to smoke or see the daylight he has to go on deck, where there is scarcely any shelter. When the majority of ships were abroad in good climates this would not have mattered so much; but the life of the bluejacket and stoker in our finest ships of war around the British coasts and in the North Sea is one of pitiable discomfort, which cannot, while the present competition in armaments continues and the present types of war-ship construction prevail, be effectively alleviated.[38]

But with so much money taken up in building battleships and in social reform, there was nothing left to improve lower-deck conditions, which had remained largely the same for 40 years.

Rigoy House Winston Churchill M.P. First Lord of the admiralty on board H.M.S. Enchantress, 1912.

ABOVE Winston Churchill as First Lord of the Admiralty on the deck of the Admiralty yacht *Enchantress*. He spent a great deal of time on this vessel, visiting naval bases at home and abroad and keeping in touch with the fleet.

OPPOSITE The sale of old warships in 1910, including two battleships built in 1892 and rapidly made obsolete.

FOLLOWING PAGES The end of sail made it necessary for sailors to take some exercise despite the crowded conditions on board ship. Commander William James used some interesting ideas on board the *Dreadnought*, *Neptune* and battlecruiser *Queen Mary* in 1910–13. From *New Battleship Organisations*.

The final demise of naval sail led to an identity crisis among the traditional seamen. As the First Lord of the Admiralty quoted to the House of Commons in 1903,

Everything in the modern Fleet is done by machinery, be it steam, hydraulic, compressed air, electricity, to which will probably be added in the near future, explosive oil and liquid air. Not only are the ships propelled solely by machinery, but they are steered by machinery. Their principal arms – gun and torpedo – are worked by machinery. They are lit by machinery, the water used by those on board for drinking, cooking, and washing is produced by machinery; messages which were formerly transmitted by voice-pipe, now go by telephone. The orders which the Admiral wishes to give to the Fleet could formerly only be made by flags in the day and lamps at night; they are now made by electricity, that is by wireless

1. Tug of War.
2. Jump.
3. Buck.
4. Wall Bars.

5. Horizontal Climbing Rope.
6. Vertical Climbing Ropes.
7. Trapeze (Coaling Derrick).
8. Horse.

9. Travelling Rings (Awning Jackstay).
10. Vertical Climbing Ropes.
11. Rings (Coaling Derrick).
12. Parallel Bars.

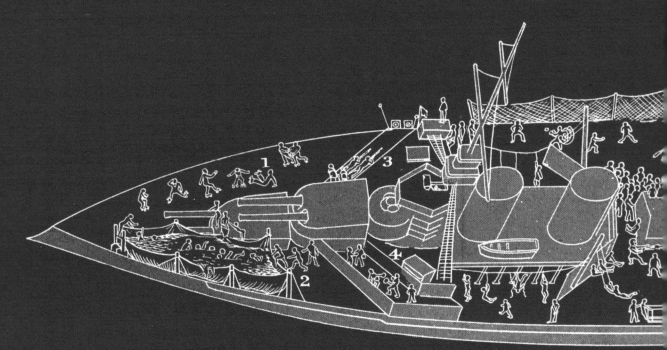

1. Roller Skating.
2. Large Swimming Bath (Fxle Awning).

3. Morris Tube Range.
4. Boxing.

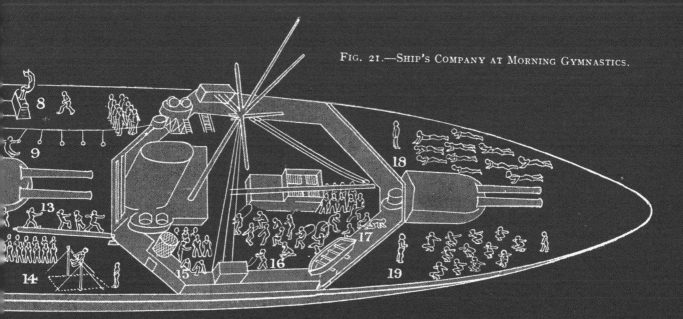

Fig. 21.—Ship's Company at Morning Gymnastics.

13. Balancing (Coaling Derrick).
14. Horizontal Bar.
15. Shelf Drill.
16. Skipping.

17. Shelf Drill.
18. Swedish Drill.
19. Swedish Drill.

[To face p. 164

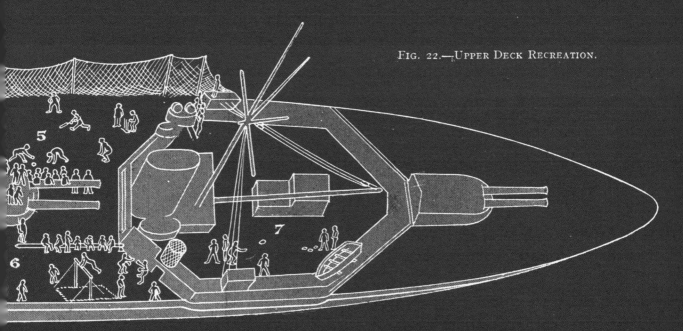

Fig. 22.—Upper Deck Recreation.

5. Cricket.
6. Gymnastics, Bayonet Fighting, etc.

7. Officers. Quoits, etc.

[To face p. 172

telegraphy and electric flashing signal lamps.
Orders which were formerly written out by
hand are now produced by typewriter or by the
printing machine. Formerly the Admiral visited
another ship in his pulling barge; now he goes
in a steam-boat. The anchor, formerly hove up
by hand, is now worked by an engine. The live
bullocks which were formerly taken to sea are
now replaced by frozen carcasses maintained
in that condition by machinery. If a fire breaks
out in the ship the steam pumps drown it. If
the ship springs a leak, steam pumps keep
down the water. The very air that those on
board between decks breathe is provided by a
fan driven by machinery.[39]

The navy was increasingly becoming a collection
of specialists, which was reflected in the badges worn
by sailors. Already the petty officer wore crossed
anchors or a single anchor surmounted by a crown,
and the leading seaman had a single anchor. Seamen
were also awarded chevrons for periods of good
conduct and were immensely proud of them – the
three-badge able seaman became a figure of legend, a
man who had spent at least 13 years in the navy and
kept out of trouble but had never sought promotion.
Those who had passed the course at *Excellent* or
another gunnery school wore a gun badge, but in
1890 there was a rash of new badges. The torpedoman
was finally separated from the gunner, and badges
were awarded to sick-berth attendants, signallers,
naval police artisans and gymnastic instructors. The
latter became important with the final demise of sail
after 1900, for the seaman no longer had the obvious
means of exercise. As Fisher wrote in 1903, 'We are as
"Babes in the Wood" compared with foreign countries
in the matter of gymnastic exercises – so important for
health and physical development. Observe our
slouching boys and pot-bellied Petty Officers.'[40]

If anything, the navy had become more class-
ridden over the years. In the days of Nelson it was not
unusual for a seaman to earn a commission, for many

had been recruited though the merchant service in the
first place, and some had a good education. This
became less common in Victorian times, except for
warrant officers who might rise very slowly to the rank
of lieutenant but would be too old to expect any further
promotion by that time. Otherwise, all commissions
went to cadets from Dartmouth College but entry there
was restricted to those with a combination of money
and naval connections. Henry Capper campaigned to
open up commissioned rank to the lower deck and was
approached by the mother of a sub-lieutenant who said
to him, 'I have the greatest sympathy with you person-
ally in your desire to rise, but you have chosen the
wrong service. The Navy belongs to us, and if you were
to win the commissions you ask for it would be at the
expense of our sons and nephews whose birthright it
is.'[41] Fisher tried to open up officer rank to promising
young seamen, and in 1912 Churchill started a scheme
by which selected men could train for commissions at
an early age, but it was difficult to study on the lower
deck and numbers were never large.

The navy had begun to move ashore in the 1890s,
as parliament voted money to build shore barracks at
the main bases of Chatham, Portsmouth and Plymouth, and most of the antiquated hulks, often left
over from the days of Nelson, were replaced. The most
dramatic reminder of the era was the Naval College at
Dartmouth, overlooking the town and replacing the
aged wooden ships of the line. Just as grand was the
new officers' mess at Portsmouth, built in Flemish
style with turrets and a Tuscan-style entrance porch.
Inside, the visitor was likely to be impressed by the
grand staircase carved with the names of Britain's
naval victories. There was a great dining hall with a
hammerbeam roof, and numerous battle scenes by
the marine artist W L Wyllie.

Fisher was determined to integrate the engineer
officer into the naval structure, and under the Selborne
Scheme, started in 1903, all officers including Royal
Marines were to be trained in common. Later they
could specialise in engineering, navigation or gunnery.
As they reached higher rank, all would be eligible to

command ships and for promotion to admiral. But ultimately the scheme failed, and the engineer remained a specialist on the fringes of the navy.

The turbine engines were not much more fuel-efficient than the older engines, and their great horsepower demanded large quantities of coal, which had to be manhandled by the crew. Ships normally coaled up as soon as they came back from operations, when the men were already tired. It was a filthy, laborious business involving almost everyone on board. As Commander William James wrote, 'the one maxim which is always true is that every soul who can possibly take part should do so for large coalings.'[42]

Life was as hard as ever for the stoker. The new ships also needed great numbers of them to load the coal into the fires, and by about 1910 they outnumbered seamen in the navy. They were recruited to lower standards and did not have the early disciplinary training of the seamen, which led to problems. In 1906 Lieutenant Collard was in charge of a party of dissident stoker recruits when he ordered them to go 'on the knee'. This was a normal naval order to give the men in the rear ranks a better chance to see what was going on, but Collard was known to have used it as a punishment, and his manner was unfortunate to say the least. The stokers refused to obey and there were riots in Portsmouth – a hundred people were injured and marines were called in to restore order. This was only one of at least two dozen cases of mutiny or 'collective indiscipline' between 1900 and 1914, but it was the most reported and even reached the pages of the *New York Times*.[43]

Technology would reduce the need for stokers, though only in the long term. It was already well known that oil was a far more efficient fuel than coal for a steam engine. It gave better endurance and performance for the same weight of fuel, speed was easier to increase suddenly, and the operation of coaling ship could be abolished – all that had to be done once the oiler had come alongside was for a few stokers to

ABOVE Stokers at work in the boiler room of a coal-fired ship, carrying out hard labour in intense heat.

OPPOSITE Kiel Regatta Week, 1914. A German Zeppelin passes over the new 'super-Dreadnought' battleships *King George V*, *Ajax*, *Centurion* and *Audacious*, and the ships of the 2nd Cruiser Squadron.

connect the pipes and the fuel was pumped on board. This also raised the possibility of refuelling at sea, though that was not exploited for the time being. Oil fuel could be moved easily about the ship to improve trim, and it could be stored in almost any compartment. It also meant that the great regiments of stokers were no longer needed on board, so they could be greatly reduced in numbers and concentrate on maintenance tasks, while a large amount of accommodation was freed up. Against this, oil did not provide the protection against enemy gunfire that coal had done, and it had to be imported, with huge long-term impact on

Britain's strategic needs. Churchill consulted with Sir Marcus Samuel, the founder of Shell Oil, and signed an agreement with the Anglo-Persian Oil Company to guarantee supplies. Fuel storage tanks were built at all the dockyards, new ships were to be built to use oil and older ones were to be converted in turn.

From 1905 onwards there was a series of crises that raised international tension; most had a strong maritime dimension, notably in 1911 when Germany sent the gunboat *Panther* to enforce her claims to a protectorate over Morocco. But it was an event on land that led to the final crisis. The Archduke Franz Ferdinand, heir to the Austro-Hungarian Empire, was assassinated in Sarajevo and the Austrians blamed the Serbs. This led to the involvement of the Serbs' protectors, the Russians, and then of France who had an alliance with Russia. Britain had an entente rather than a formal alliance with France and Russia and was not obliged to go to war at this stage. But the German plans demanded that they defeat France quickly before the 'Russian steamroller' had time to galvanise, and the only way to do this was by attacking through Belgium, whose independence Britain had guaranteed since 1830.

Against this background, four new Dreadnoughts and four cruisers under Admiral Sir George Warrender made a courtesy visit to Germany during the Kiel Week Regatta in June 1914. It was a significant occasion, as the Kiel Canal had recently been widened to cope with the new Dreadnoughts. Warrender's fleet had orders to find out all they could about the German navy, including gunnery and torpedo equipment and techniques, and signalling practices. On the surface all was friendly. George von Hase of the

German Navy noted, 'At all the balls and dinners the young English officers could be seen getting on famously with the German officers and flirting zealously with the German ladies.' Sub-Lieutenant Stephen King-Hall of the cruiser *Southampton* found out more about the sociology than the weapons of the Germans. The ratings, he observed, were better educated and smarter than those in the British navy, but once out of the eye of their officers they tended to behave like schoolboys away from their teachers. He noted that their officers were charming and polite but none regarded his ship as his home, for each had a cabin in the barracks ashore. 'If we ever cross swords', he concluded, it will be with gallant opponents.'[44]

Chapter 16

THE TEST OF WAR

When Britain declared war on 4 August 1914, the fleet was already mobilised for exercises and Churchill simply kept the men in service as the war began. There was great jubilation in the navy, the army and the general public at the start of war, but that was only because few people understood either the limitations or the enormous destructive power of modern weapons. Admiral Sir John Jellicoe took over command of the fleet from the ageing Sir George Callaghan. The main force, now named the Grand Fleet, moved to the great anchorage at Scapa Flow in the Orkneys where it had enough room for exercise and gunnery practice, and would be able to prevent any German breakout into the Atlantic. The menace of the submarine was emphasised right from the beginning when a U-boat sank three cruisers, the *Aboukir*, *Cressy* and *Hogue*, in a single day. Scapa Flow was clearly unsafe as anchorage and the Grand Fleet was homeless for several months while defences were prepared.

The new Dreadnought battleships, about two dozen of them, were at the core of the Grand Fleet. In battle formation they were preceded by a squadron of about half a dozen battlecruisers, intended for scouting and as a highly mobile part of the battlefleet. Around and ahead of these were light cruisers, which would be the first to sight the enemy and needed some gun power of their own. As Fisher put it, 'a scout that has to run as soon as she sights three funnels is useless to obtain any information except the number of funnels of the first ship she sighted!'[45] The force was protected by flotillas of destroyers, which would beat off torpedo attacks and launch attacks of their own. Fleet tactics were far more complex than they had been in Nelson's day, and the line of battle was considered more important than ever. The battle was not expected to descend into a mêlée as Trafalgar had done, and the admiral anticipated keeping control of his

fleet throughout. This led Jellicoe into over-detailed tactical planning, the opposite of Nelson's system.

The navy and the public, with no good reason, expected a quick Trafalgar, but the Germans had no wish to sacrifice their smaller fleet in this way. Instead they mounted a series of bombardments of east coast towns, hoping to lure out and ambush small British squadrons and reduce the deficit. Jellicoe resisted this pressure but the battlecruisers, under the command of Vice-Admiral Sir David Beatty, were moved south to the Firth of Forth and given the title 'Battle Cruiser Fleet', which tended to give him ideas of independence. Beatty met a small enemy force on the Dogger Bank in January 1915 and it only escaped because of poor gunnery and signalling by the battlecruisers. Nevertheless Beatty had good looks and a hunger for publicity. He became known as the dashing operational leader, while Jellicoe was the cautious commander back at base.

The continued failure to have a great battle was a disappointment to the press and public. The navy had failed in 'expectation management': it had allowed this heroic and unrealistic picture to be built up, and the Grand Fleet settled down to years of boredom at its remote anchorage – for very few young sailors appreciated the islands' delights of archaeology or natural history. Lieutenant Stephen King-Hall claims that 'Scapa Flow has some magnificent scenery but of those who spent some time in that part of the world it has been said that they passed through three stages. First, they talked to themselves; then they talked to the sheep; and lastly they thought the sheep talked to them.'[46] According to Lieutenant Angus Cunningham-Graham,

> For the officers, at any rate those who were country-bred, there was more to do. There were two or three trout lochs within reach: the distance we could go was limited by the notice for steam that we were at, normally four hours, never more. It was also possible to catch sea trout at the mouths of the burns: I was never clever enough to get even one. [47]

Due to expansion in numbers over the last quarter of a century, the navy was considered fully

examinations were begun there in 1916. At its peak in November 1917 the navy had 420,301 men in service. The army was a much greater consumer of men in this war. It began with just over a quarter of a million regulars and just under half a million reservists. During the conflict it recruited nearly 5 million men, nearly a fifth of the adult population of the United Kingdom, plus more than 3 million dominion and colonial troops. The army had to go much further in accommodating itself to the general population, and commissions were given to men of far lower social status than would have happened before the war.

In February 1915 the Germans looked to their new and untried weapon, the U-boat. They had already had success in sinking the three cruisers in 1914, but now they were to turn them in an unexpected direction, against British merchant shipping in the North Sea. The laws on this kind of warfare were largely unwritten, but in general the Geneva Convention demanded that a merchant ship should be stopped, her status as a belligerent established, the safety of her crew assured, and then she could be either sunk or taken as a prize. Such rules were applied in the very early days of the war. The first merchant ship to be sunk was the *Giltra*, which was stopped by *U-17* in October 1914 off the Norwegian coast. The Germans put her crew into lifeboats and even towed them part of the way towards the shore, before sinking the ship by gunfire. But such practices were not consistent with submarine warfare, which demanded concealment. On 4 February 1915 the Germans proclaimed that all waters around Great Britain were a war zone and any ship in them was liable to be sunk without warning. At the time German had only 37 submarines to enforce this, and only about a third of these could be at sea at any given time, but it proved surprisingly successful. Churchill confused the

manned when the war began – so much so that Churchill sent the amateur seamen of the Royal Naval Volunteer Reserve off to fight in Flanders, where they soon became bogged down in the trench warfare of the Western Front. Unlike the Second World War, the navy of 1914–18 did not reach very far into the civilian population for growth. It had been expanding at a steady pace for the previous 25 years, and comprised 146,000 men in 1913 – as much as the highest wartime number a century earlier. Lord Brassey, an enthusiast for naval reserves, wrote in 1906, 'Never before has the British Navy been in such a condition of immediate preparedness for war as at the present time. The Navy is in fact being maintained in peace time on a war footing.'[48] It had been assumed that the war would be brief, which made planning much easier in the short term. Instructors and half-educated trainees were taken out of the training schools on the outbreak. This caused problems as the war dragged on and there was no supply of freshly-trained men but it was mitigated by the fact that the main force was largely static at Scapa Flow. Training courses and

issue by fitting out Q-ships, warships disguised as merchantmen, which would only show their armament when a U-boat surfaced to attack by gunfire; this gave the Germans the excuse that they could not tell whether a ship was a warship or not, and were obliged to sink it without warning. The greatest problem for Germany was that the policy was highly offensive to neutrals, especially the United States. The *Lusitania* was a British ocean liner sunk by *U-20* off the south coast of Ireland on 7 May. There is still controversy about whether she was carrying enough arms to make her a legitimate target, but the important fact was that 128 Americans were lost when she went down. The Germans were forced to modify their policy, then to abandon it after other incidents with passenger liners. Britain had won the first round of the submarine war, though the navy had hardly been involved and still had no real answer to the U-boat.

The stalemate in the North Sea matched the situation on the Western Front in France and Belgium, where armies of millions of men faced each other across hundreds of miles of trenches, and where advances could only be made at great human cost. Inventive as always, Churchill conceived a new plan. Russia had huge numbers of men but little to equip them with, while Turkey was by far the weakest of Germany's allies. If the entry to the Black Sea could be achieved, then western supplies could equip the Russian armies. But to do that it would be necessary to force the Dardanelles.

Until then Churchill had not been very lucky in the Mediterranean. On the outbreak of war he had taken over the great battleship *Sultan Osman I* under construction for the Turks on the Tyne, and renamed her *Agincourt*. This was taken as an insult by the Turks, and at the same time the German battlecruiser *Goeben* and the cruiser *Breslau* evaded allied patrols to reach the Dardanelles, where they were presented to Turkey, reinforcing the wavering nation in declaring war against the allies. Perhaps there was a personal element in Churchill's desire to knock Turkey out of the war.

It had always been naval doctrine that ships could

not engage land forts directly unless they had overwhelming superiority, either in numbers or in technique and morale. The navy had been quite successful in bombarding Algiers and Alexandria in the past, and it is possible that they thought that the Turks, from a similar culture, would give in just as easily. Moreover, the modern battleship, with its huge guns and heavy armour, was a different animal from the old wooden walls. In March 1915 a large allied fleet had some success in knocking out the Turkish forts at the entrance to the strait, but soon ran up against mines. The battlecruiser *Inflexible* was damaged, three pre-Dreadnoughts were sunk and the attempt was abandoned.

OPPOSITE *U-131*, as painted by Wyllie. A late model of U-boat, this one was never completed and was broken up in Bremen after the war. Its high bows were useful as it spent most of its time on the surface.

BELOW British and French warships, including the *Inflexible*, attempt to force a passage through the Dardanelles in March 1915, against fierce gunfire from the Turkish forts.

It was decided to launch an amphibious operation on the Gallipoli Peninsula, using largely Australian and New Zealand, or ANZAC troops. There was no experience of an opposed landing on such a scale. George Butoft, a gunlayer in the pre-Dreadnought battleship *Queen*, watched in horror as the troops landed.

About three o'clock they were all lined up. We were afraid of the moon but it cleared all right. Not one soldier knew what he was going to meet when he got on shore. He didn't know the terrain. We had our telescopes. I could pick out all the ravines but that was all one could see at the front. When they got on top they hadn't a clue. Not a clue! It was chaos. But the Turks never fired. With the gun-sight telescope you could see everything. It was awe-inspiring. I've never had the feeling. But when the light came, it was just slaughter. There were not any of the Anzacs who would go home and tell about it.

There were fifty yards of beach and it was all open; their mates in front of them went down. They would drop down and wait for a little lull, using their mates which was the only guard they had. There were hundreds of them wounded in the backs of the legs where their feet were sticking out.[49]

After being bogged down for six months, the troops were withdrawn with heavy losses, and Churchill's political career seemed at an end as he was forced to resign from the Admiralty.

At around midnight on 31 May 1916 the ships of both sides left their North Sea harbours, the Grand Fleet from Scapa Flow and Invergordon, the battle-cruisers under Beatty from the Forth and the German High Seas Fleet under Admiral Scheer from Wil-helmshaven. The Germans hoped to trap a British squadron; the British had radio intelligence that the Germans were about to sail. Jellicoe's fleet had 24 Dreadnoughts with three battlecruisers attached; Beatty had the services of four ships of the *Queen Eliz-*

ABOVE The 'We want eight ...' campaign of 1908 was not the only one to be mounted on naval matters. Here, newspaper placards demand the return of Fisher to the Admiralty in 1916, after he resigned over the Dardanelles campaign.

abeth class, the most powerful warships in the world, to augment his six remaining battlecruisers. Early in the following afternoon, a neutral Danish merchant ship was sailing home when she was spotted by cruis-ers from both fleets. They both sent ships to investigate, and the cruisers spotted each other and reported back to their respective battlecruisers. Before she knew it, the innocent *N J Fjord* had huge shells passing over her from both directions, and the world's greatest sea battle had begun.

The two battlecruiser forces came quickly into action. Franz von Hipper, in command of the German force, tried to lure Beatty south onto his battleships. Beatty followed with full confidence, though due to a signalling error and lack of initiative the four great *Queen Elizabeths* did not follow at first. The Germans got the range quicker than Beatty's undertrained ships, and just after 4 o'clock the light deck armour of the battlecruiser *Indefatigable* was penetrated by shells and she blew up with a shattering explosion. Twenty minutes later the *Queen Mary* suffered a similar fate. Ernle Chatfield was Beatty's flag captain.

> I was standing beside Sir David Beatty when we both turned round in time to see the unpleasant spectacle. The thought of my friends in her flashed through my mind; I though how lucky we had evidently been in the 'Lion'.
>
> Beatty turned to me and said, 'There seems to be something wrong with our ships today,' a remark which needed neither comment nor answer.[50]

Worse was to come, as the main body of the German fleet appeared though the mist and Beatty had no alternative but to flee towards Jellicoe's ships. The main body of the Grand Fleet was some miles to the north, still in its cruising formation comprising six columns of four ships each. Jellicoe now had to decide on which side to deploy in line of battle. Despite poor reporting from his reconnaissance cruisers, he was able to select the port, northern side, which would allow him to 'cross the T' of the enemy – to deploy a large proportion of his broadside gunpower against the enemy van, which would only be able to make a feeble reply and would be pulverised. It was the Germans' turn to be shocked; they had not cut off Beatty's battlecruisers but had been led into a trap. The whole fleet had to go through 180 degrees, each ship turning at the same time and releasing smoke as she did so –a manoeuvre that the British had not expected. Jellicoe went in pursuit, but the British misfortunes had not ended. Just after 6.30 in the evening the *Invincible*, one of the battlecruisers attached to Jellicoe, was hit by fire from the *Derfflinger* and *Lutzow* and blew up. Royal Marine Bandsman A C Green was in the battleship *Hercules*.

> I saw the Invincible in two halves, I passed her in the water as the Hercules with the Fleet went by, and the lads on the upper deck were shouting and cheering and the Skipper called out from the bridge, 'Stop that cheering – that's one of our ships!' Course we never dreamed that a German could sink a British ship – that's the attitude we'd all got ...[51]

Scheer was now cut off from his bases and turned to the east, perhaps hoping to pass astern of the British. Instead he found himself about to have his T crossed again, and executed another 'battle turnaway'. This time he launched his destroyers and torpedo boats towards the Grand Fleet. Jellicoe, with typical caution, turned away and let the High Seas Fleet escape. The fighting was confused, as seen by the lower deck.

> It was a weird and wonderful business. You only saw the square mile you were in, but I have never seen anything so quick as the way a Destroyer would appear, fire a torpedo and go up in a sheet of flame and there'd be no Destroyer. Everything was at super speed; they would be overcome by enemy fire and where you looked there was a patch of troubled water but no Destroyer and that was a couple of hundred men.[52]

Night fell and brought with it a number of destroyer actions. The British sank a few German cruisers and the 12th Destroyer Flotilla sank the pre-Dreadnought battleship *Pommern*, an old ship that should never have been included in such a fleet. The greatest German loss was the fine battlecruiser *Lutzow*, which sank under tow after receiving heavy damage in the action.

The Germans passed astern of the Grand Fleet and thankfully headed home. They were quick to claim a victory, for they had sunk three battlecruisers and 11 other ships, with 6,000 dead; in return they

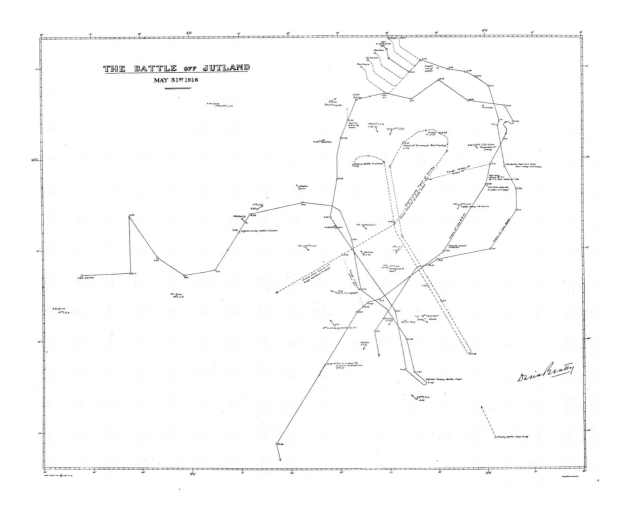

THE BATTLE off JUTLAND
MAY 31st 1916

had lost one battlecruiser, one aged battleship and nine others, with 2,500 dead. Their gunnery, damage control and perhaps their seamanship had been better, and their ships were far better equipped to take punishment and survive. On the other hand, many of them were too damaged to put so sea for many weeks, whereas the British were ready again the following day. More important, the Germans had to give up any hope of trapping a British squadron and return to the idea of submarine warfare, whatever the risks. After the failure of an attempt to lure the Grand Fleet into a submarine trap, they announced unrestricted submarine warfare, 'sink on sight' in February 1917.

It was an enormous gamble, for it was clear that the United States would declare war. German calcu-

ABOVE Beatty's plan of the Battle of Jutland. His battlecruisers come in from the left-hand side and turn south before heading north chased by the German fleet into the path of Jellicoe's Grand Fleet which can be seen deploying from five columns into one.

OPPOSITE Two of the three battlecruisers lost at Jutland. *Queen Mary* blows up (above); and (below) the wreck of *Invincible*, split in two by the force of the explosion of her midships magazine.

lations showed that Britain could be starved, and the heart knocked out of the alliance, before Americans had time to build up an army and ship it to France; moreover, the Russians were close to collapse on the other side of Europe and revolution would soon break out there. This time the German fleet comprised 105 U-boats in service. The British had developed the hydrophone to pick up the sound of a

submarine, but that was virtually useless in a ship at sea making its own noises. Soon merchant shipping was suffering catastrophic losses, half a million tons of shipping each in February and March, rising to 860,000 in April, for the loss of only nine submarines. The Americans did indeed declare war on 6 April, but the British were running desperately short of food and raw materials. They responded by laying mines to keep the U-boats in their bases, but struggled to find a more comprehensive answer.

The tactic of escorting merchant ships in convoys had been used in all wars of the age of sail, but conventional naval doctrine regarded it as useless with steamships, and especially against submarines. It would be difficult to find enough escorts, convoys would have to meet at specific points and wait for assembly, ships would be of unequal speed and difficult to control, and there would be severe congestion at a port when a convoy of ships arrived all at once. Nevertheless, the navy was already operating convoys on selected routes, with troopships, the coal trade to France and to neutral Norway. Under heavy pressure from the government, convoy was adopted as the general policy at the end of April. The Prime Minster, David Lloyd George, himself attended a meeting of the Board of Admiralty on the last day of the month to enforce it, though by that time the decision had already been taken.

The mainstream navy had to supply destroyers for long-range escort, but new classes of sloop and patrol craft were built to supplement them. Much of the inshore work was performed by members of the Auxiliary Patrol, former fishermen or non-seamen who at last found a key role in the wartime navy. Often they operated in converted trawlers or large yachts. The convoy system relied on a certain amount of bluff; as yet there was no fully effective means of dealing with a submerged U-boat. Asdic,

which used the echo from a 'ping' to detect a submarine, was not ready until the end of the war. The depth charge was already in use and was increasing in efficiency. It sank two submarines in the first two years of the war, six in 1917, and 22 in 1918. Combined with airship patrols to force the submarines to keep their heads down, this was enough to turn the tide of the U-boat campaign. Losses were falling by

the end of the year, and soon the greatly-expanded United States Army was on the way to Europe.

The Royal Naval Air Service (RNAS) had been formed in 1912 and was greatly supported by Churchill. It proved to be a very innovative service which operated well beyond the boundaries implied in its title. Unlike the mainstream navy it took on large numbers of outsiders as airmen and mechanics, and the regular navy claimed that the initials of the acronym stood for 'Really not a sailor'. But the combination of their new ideas with naval discipline led to many experiments. The RNAS can claim to have originated tanks, fighter defence, the aircraft carrier and heavy bombing, all key weapons systems of the next war. The service could claim one decisive success in anti-submarine warfare.

Naval Aviation

By about 1910 it was clear that aircraft could be useful over the sea in reconnaissance, bombing and torpedo attack, and the range of an aircraft could be greatly increased if it was launched from a ship. The American pilot Eugene Ely was the first to do this from a platform in the bows of the USS *Birmingham* in 1910, and this was repeated by HMS *Hibernia* in the mouth of the Medway in 1912. The cruiser *Hermes* was fitted with aircraft and had some success in the naval exercises of 1913. An alternative was to lower seaplanes, fitted with floats, into the water and several fast merchant ships were converted to do this when war broke out in 1914. They launched a pioneering if rather ineffective raid on German airship sheds at Cuxhaven in 1914, but seaplanes were often difficult to operate except in smooth seas, and their floats reduced their performance.

There were some successful attacks by torpedo, mainly in the Mediterranean theatre, but bombs were generally too small to do much damage and air reconnaissance was ineffective without good radio communication and navigation; it failed to have any effect at Jutland despite the launching of a seaplane from HMS *Engadine*.

For fighter defence, capital ships and cruisers were equipped with a few single and two-seater aircraft, which could take off from gun turrets pointing into the wind. The great problem was getting an aircraft back on board again. With war in the restricted area of the North Sea, it was just possible that a plane might find its way ashore. If not, it could ditch in the sea close to the fleet so that the pilot could be picked up. Even with the simple, cheap aircraft of 1916, that was an expensive way to operate. In that year the eccentric battlecruiser *Furious* was converted with a landing deck forward of the superstructure and Commander Dunning succeeded in landing on it once, with men grabbing handles attached to his wings, but he was killed in a second attempt. The afterdeck of the *Furious* was then converted to a landing platform but that proved impossible under weigh due to the air currents.

The only solution was a completely flat deck and that was provided by HMS *Argus*, converted from a liner and completed in 1918. She conducted trials in the Firth of Forth and raised hopes that a great torpedo attack might be launched against the High Seas Fleet in its harbours; the war ended before it came to anything but the concept of the aircraft carrier, which would dominate the Second World War in the Pacific, was already in existence.

The British were a long way behind the Germans in airship development, but the Royal Naval Air Service built several classes of non-rigid and semi-rigid airships for patrol mostly in the North Sea, where they had a certain amount of success against submarines.

LEFT Squadron Commander Dunning lands his Sopwith Pup on the forward deck of HMS *Furious* at Scapa Flow in August 1917, while naval personnel rush out to grab straps attached to his wings. It was the first successful British landing of an aircraft on a ship under way, but an attempt to repeat it a few days later resulted in Dunning's death.

ABOVE A Sea Scout naval airship coming down to her moorings on the after deck of *Furious* in 1918. The pilot is in the aircraft-type cockpit.

Airships were in company with convoys during dark as well as daylight hours, and were undoubtedly very valuable scouts. During the summer months of 1918 continuous air patrols of airships and seaplanes were (weather permitting) maintained throughout the whole passage of the convoys. The presence of aircraft has not always prevented successful attacks being made by enemy submarines, but, the attack being made, the submarine's subsequent movements have been followed and direct action taken by the aircraft, which afterwards directed the surface craft in their depth-charge offensive.[53]

When the RNAS was merged into the RAF in 1918, it was great blow to naval prestige and the service chiefs would spend nearly two decades fighting over it, while Britain fell far behind Japan and the United States in the development of the aircraft carrier.

For all four years of war the Royal Navy had operated a distant blockade of Germany. Once the war had ended the First Lord of the Admiralty paid tribute to the Tenth Cruiser Squadron.

The blockade is what crushed the life out of the Central Empires. That blockade was exercised by a little-advertised power – the 10th Cruiser Squadron. That Squadron, from 1914 to 1917, held the 800 mile stretch of grey sea from Orkney to Iceland. In those waters they intercepted thousands of ships taking succour to our enemies ...[54]

This was a little overstated. Germany had not been a net importer of food before the war and it was the drain on labour from the war fronts that had reduced her agricultural output. Germany began to collapse towards the end of 1918, with food riots and naval mutinies. In November, when the Kaiser fled and Germany requested an armistice, it was an Admiral, Sir Rosslyn Wemyss, who was sent by the British Government to negotiate the terms in the Forest of Compiègne. He was concerned mainly with the surrender and immobilisation of the German fleet, and did not object to the savage restrictions that the French General Foch imposed on the defeated enemy. One of the terms of armistice was that the most important ships of the High Seas Fleet should be interned and in the first instance they were sent to the Firth of Forth. They anchored there and Admiral Beatty addressed his men. 'They are now going to be taken away, and placed under the guardianship of the

Grand Fleet at Scapa, there they will enjoy (laughter) as we have enjoyed, the pleasures of Scapa. (laughter)' Then he made the signal which in effect ended the naval war. 'The German flag will be hauled down at sunset today, Thursday, and will not be hoisted again without permission.'[55] But six months later the German skeleton crews scuttled their ships at Scapa Flow, where some of the wrecks remain to this day, commemorating an ambiguous victory.

No-one was saying it out loud in a mood of national rejoicing, but the navy's performance during the war was a great disappointment. Instead of a new Nelson, it had produced the over-cautious Jellicoe and the slapdash Beatty. Instead of Trafalgar it had produced the stalemate of Jutland. Huge amounts of money had been lavished on the navy before the war, with very little to show in concrete results. Its officers had proved unimaginative and rigid. On two other fronts it had not distinguished itself either. It had failed twice at the Dardanelles due to faulty doctrine. And in the submarine war, it had only been successful in the end due to outside pressure and the widespread use of converted civilian vessels and non-naval seamen. Moreover, this was the first European war since Marlborough's time in which the army was seen as the main British force. While the navy was mostly anchored in Scapa Flow, the army was losing tens of thousands of men in the Somme, Ypres and other battles. Whether or not this was a result of military incompetence did not matter at the time and the army commander, Field Marshal Haig, was treated as a hero. The navy had suffered no great defeat, it had contributed decisively to the allied victory through the blockade, but its days as the supreme world force were now over. In 1922 the government agreed to the Washington Treaty, in which Britain had parity with the United States in warship numbers. It was a bitter pill for officers who were made redundant with no other skills to fall back on, and they felt they had done nothing to deserve it. Germany had been defeated without losing a major battle, and punished by the Treaty of Versailles without committing any clear and indictable crime, sowing the seeds of the next war. The Royal Navy, also unsatisfied after the Great War, would find new glory and affection in the second conflict.

LEFT King George V, in the centre of the picture, jokes with Admiral Beatty and two American officers during a visit to an American ship after the surrender of the High Seas Fleet, while the Prince of Wales, in army uniform, looks on.

Notes

Introduction and Part 1

1 B Lavery, ed., *The Royal Navy Officers Pocket Book*, London, 2007, p. 9

2 Garrett Mattingly, *The Defeat of the Spanish Armada*, London, 1961, pp 114–5

3 Michael Lewis, *Armada Guns*, London, 1961, p. 73

4 Colin Martin and Geoffrey Parker, *The Spanish Armada*, London, 1988, p. 153

5 Harold Hodges and Edward Hughes, *Select Naval Documents*, Cambridge, 1922, p. 22

6 Sir Julian Corbett, *Drake and the Tudor Navy*, London, 1899, vol. 2, p. 286

7 Michael Oppenheim, *A History of the Administration of the Royal Navy*, London, 1996, p. 384

8 Navy Records Society, *The Defeat of the Spanish Armada*, ed. J K Laughton, vol. 1, 1895, p. 190

9 Ibid., vol. 2, pp 96–7

10 Oldys and Birch, ed., *The Works of Sir Walter Raleigh*, Oxford, 1820, vol. 8, p. 344

11 Ibid., p. 346

12 Navy Records Society, *Sir William Monson's Naval Tracts*, 1902, ed. Oppenheim, vol. 2, p. 383

13 Historical Manuscripts Commission, *The Manuscripts of F J Savile Foljambe*, London, 1897, p. 69

14 Navy Records Society, *The Jacobean Commissions of Enquiry*, ed. A McGowan, 1971, pp 259, 288

15 Oppenheim, op cit, pp 223–4

16 C D Yonge, *The History of the British Navy*, London, 1863, vol. 2, p. 101

17 Oppenheim, op. cit., p. 231

18 Yonge, op. cit., p. 112

19 Nabil I Matar, *Britain and Barbary, 1589–1689*, Gainesville, Florida, c. 2005, p. 55

20 C Stephenson and F G Marcham, *Sources of English Constitutional History*, New York, 1937, p. 456

21 British Library, Harlean Manuscripts 684, f141, *Calendar of State Papers, Domestic, 1635*, p. 363

22 John Smith, *A Sea Grammar*, ed. Goell, London, 1970, p. 78

23 Navy Records Society, *The Autobiography of Phineas Pett*, ed. W G Perrin, 1917, p. 156

24 Thomas Heywood, *A True Description of His Majesty's Royall Ship*, ed. Alan R Young, New York, 1990, pp 20, 25, 26

25 Granville Penn, *Memorials of the Life of Sir William Penn*, London, 1833, vol. 1, p. 19

26 Edward Earl of Clarendon, *The History of the Rebellion and Civil Wars*, vol. II, Oxford, 1849, pp 262–63

27 British Library Pamphlets, E95 (8)

28 Navy Records Society, *Letters and Papers Relating to the First Dutch War*, ed. S R Gardner and C T Atkinson, vol. 3, 1905, pp 7, 94

29 Ibid., pp 340–1

30 Ibid., Vol. 5, 1912, p. 109

31 Navy Records Society, *British Naval Documents, 1204–1960*, ed. J B Hattendorf *et al*, 1993, p. 257

32 Edward Barlow, *Barlow's Journal*, ed. Basil Lubbock, London, 1934, vol. 1, p. 43

33 *British Naval Documents*, op. cit., p. 257

34 Samuel Pepys, *Diary*, 24 October 1662, 15 May 1663, 30 July 1667

35 Pepys, *Diary*, 1 October 1661

36 Eric Homberger, *The Historical Atlas of New York City*, New York, 1994, p. 168

37 Pepys, *Diary*, 1 July 1666

38 Bruce S Ingram, ed., *Three Sea Journals of Stuart Times*, London, 1936, pp 48–9

39 Barlow, op. cit., pp 118–9

40 Ingram, ed., op. cit., p. 54

41 Pepys, *Diary*, 30 June 1667

42 Andrew Marvell, *Last Instructions to a Painter*, 1667

43 Pepys, *Diary*, 20 October 1666

44 Navy Records Society, *The Tangier Papers of Samuel Pepys*, ed. Edwin Chappell, 1935, p. 122

45 Harold Hodges and Edward Hughes, op. cit., pp 72–3

46 Navy Records Society, *Samuel Pepys's Naval Minutes*, ed. J R Tanner, 1925, pp 71–2

47 J R Tanner, ed., *Pepys's Memoires of the Royal Navy, 1679–1688*, Oxford, 1906, pp 10–11

48 E B Powley, *The English Navy in the Revolution of 1688*, Cambridge, 1928, pp 87–8

49 Linda Colley, *Britons, Forging the Nation, 1707–1837*, London, 1992, p. 53

Part 2

1 Peter Marsden, *The Story of the* Anne, Hastings, 1992, p. 15

2 Samuel Jeake, *An Astrological Diary of the Seventeenth Century*, ed. Michael Hunter and Annabel Gregory, Oxford, 1988, p. 204

3 John Charnock, *Biographia Navalis*, vol. 1, London, 1974, p. 361 note

4 Historical Manuscripts Commission, *Manuscripts of the House of Lords*, New Series, 1, 1900, p. 220

5 Navy Records Society, *Queen Anne's Navy*, ed. R D Merriman, 1961, pp 254–5

6 Ned Ward, *The Wooden World*, ed. Callender, Society for Nautical Research Occasional Publications, 1929, pp 14–5

7 Bridget Cherry and Nikolaus Pevsner, *The Buildings of England, London 2, South*, London, 1990, p. 262

8 Navy Records Society, *The Naval Miscellany*, vol. 5, ed. N A M Rodger, 1984, pp 173, 187

9 *The Life and Adventures of Matthew Bishop*, London, 1744, p. 20

10 Ibid., p. 21

11 Quoted in T C Smout, *Scottish Trade on the Eve of Union*, London, 1963, p. 275

12 Lord Belhaven, *Speech in the Scotch Parliament*, 1706, p. 3

13 Marcus Rediker, *Villains of all Nations; Atlantic Pirates in the Golden Age*, London, 2004, p. 143

14 Quoted in Keevil and Coulter, *Medicine and the Navy*, vol. 4, Edinburgh, 1963

15 Richard Walter, *Anson's Voyage Round the World*, New York, 1974, p. 78

16 Ibid., xlvi

17 Brian Lavery, *Ship of the Line*, vol. 1, 1983, p. 90

18 Ibid., p. 93

19 Quoted in John S Gibson, *Ships of the '45*, London, 1967, p. 2

20 Scottish History Society, Vol. 21, 1895–6, *The Lyon in Mourning*, Vol. II, pp 99, 253; Vol. III, op. cit., p. 12

21 Ibid., p. 79

22 Olaudah Equiano, *The Interesting Narrative of the Life ...*, London, 2003, p. 55

23 A N Ryan, 'The Royal Navy and the Blockade of Brest, 1689–1805', in *Les Marines de Guerre Européennes*, Paris, 1985, p. 182

24 David Erskine, ed., *Augustus Hervey's Journal*, London, 1953, p. 227

25 N A M Rodger, *The Articles of War*, Homewell, c. 1982

26 Lavery, *Ship of the Line*, op. cit., vol. 1, p. 109

27 N A M Rodger, ed., *The Narrative of William Spavens*, London, 1998, pp 4, 74–5

28 Melvyn Bragg, *The Adventure of English*, London, 2003, p. ix

29 Erskine, op. cit., p. 329

Part 3

1 Linda Colley, *Britons*, London, 1994, p. 99

2 David Cordingly, *Marine Painting in England, 1700–1900*, London, 1974, pp 121–2

3 Richard B Morris, ed., *The American Revolution, 1763–1783, A Bicentennial Collection*, New York, 1970, p. 124

4 David Syrett, *Shipping and the American War*, London, 1970, pp 243, 236

5 Eric Homberger, *The Historical Atlas of New York City*, New York, 1994, op. cit., p. 51

6 W B Clark, (ed.), *Naval Documents of the American Revolution*, Vol. 1, Washington,

1964, p. 356

7 US Navy, Bureau of Naval Personnel, *Naval Orientation*, 1945, p. 373

8 N A M Rodger, *The Insatiable Earl*, London, 1993, p. 161

9 Navy Records Society, *The Letters and Papers of Charles, Lord Barham*, ed. J K Laughton, vol. 1, 1906, pp 66–7

10 Benjamin Silliman, *Journal of Travels in England, Holland and Scotland*, Newhaven, 1812, pp 58–9

11 Michael Duffy, *Soldiers, Sugar and Seapower,* Oxford, 1987, pp 8–13, B R Mitchell, *Abstract of British Historical Statistics,* Cambridge, 1962, p. 312

12 Robert Hughes, *The Fatal Shore*, London 1987, p. 63

13 Ibid., pp 145–146

14 G E Manwaring and Bonamy Dobrée, *The Floating Republic*, London, 1935, p. 63

15 Ibid. p. 59

16 Ibid. pp 265–6

17 Ibid. p. 277

18 Basil Hall, *Fragments of Voyages and Travels*, London, 1860, p. 82

19 Jane Austen, *Persuasion*, London, 1998, p. 19

20 Navy Records Society, *Shipboard Life and Organisation*, ed. B Lavery, 1998, p. 451

21 Rudolf Ackermann and Thomas Rowlandson, *Loyal Volunteers of London*, London, 1972, p. vii

22 John Ehrmann, *The Younger Pitt*, vol. 3, *The Consuming Struggle,* London, 1996, p. 263 footnote

23 Quoted in Janice Murray, ed., *Glorious Victory, Admiral Duncan and the Battle of Camperdown, 1797*, Dundee, 1997, p. 20

24 Navy Records Society, *The Letters of Admiral Markham*, Vol. XXVIII, 1904, p. 398

25 C S Forester, ed., *The Adventures of John Wetherell*, London, 1954, pp 31–2

26 National Maritime Museum manuscripts, AGC/P/17

27 William Robinson, *Jack Nastyface, Memoirs of a Seaman*, Annapolis, 1973, p. 34

28 N H Nicolas, ed., *The Dispatches and Letters of Lord Nelson*, vol. VII, 1998, p. 60

29 Joseph Allen, *The Life and Services of Sir William Hargood*, Greenwich, 1861, p. 286

30 Ibid., pp 289

31 *The Nelson Dispatch*, vol. 5, part 11, July 1996, p. 398

32 Navy Records Society, *Shipboard Life and Organisation*, op. cit., pp 402, 355

33 Quoted in Ian Robertson, *A Commanding Presence*, Stroud, 2008, p. 51

34 Alexander Gordon, *A Cavalry Officer in the Corunna Campaign*, ed. H C Wylly, London, 1913

35 Quoted in Navy Records Society, *The Keith Papers*, ed. Christopher Lloyd, vol. 3, 1955, p. 259

36 W S Dudley, ed., *The Naval War of 1812, a Documentary History*, vol. 2, Washington, 1992, p. 48

37 Ibid., p. 183

38 Dudley, op. cit., p. 126

39 Frederick Lewis Maitland, *Narrative on the Surrender of Buonaparte*, 2nd edition, London, 1826, p. 83

40 Navy Records Society, *Five Naval Journals*, ed. H G Thursfield, 1951, p. 323

Part 4

1 British Library Additional Ms 38041

2 Roger Perkins and K J Douglas-Morris, *Gunfire in Barbary*, Havant, *c* 1982, p. 129

3 Louise King-Hall, ed., *Sea Saga, being the Diaries of Four Generations of the King-Hall Family*, London, 1936, p. 62

4 Christopher Lloyd, *The Navy and the Slave Trade*, London, 1949, p. 70

5 Ibid., p. 72

6 Henry Baynham, *From the Lower Deck,* London, 1969, p. 150

7 Quoted in Michael Lewis, *The Navy in Transition*, London, 1965, p. 195

8 See Peter Hore, 'Lord Melville, the Admiralty and the Coming of Steam Navigation', in *Mariners Mirror*, vol. 86, May 2000, pp 157–172

9 Henry Baynham, *Before the Mast,* London, 1972, p. 59

10 John G Wells, *Whaley, the Story of HMS Excellent*, Portsmouth, 1980, p. 202

11 Baynham, *Before the Mast*, op. ci.t, p. 61

12 C N Robinson, *The British Tar in Fact and Fiction*, London, 1909, pp 240–44

13 G B Endacott, *An Eastern Entrepot*, London, 1964, p. 96

14 Oxford *New Dictionary of National Biography*, article on Charles Darwin

15 Lewis, *The Navy in Transition*, op. cit., pp 186–7

16 Baynham, *Before the Mast*, op. cit., p. 111

17 Bonner-Smith and Dewar, ed., Navy Records Society, *Russian War, 1854*, 1943, p. 47

18 Mark Kerr, *The Navy in My Time,* London, 1933, p. 9

19 Naval Estimates, in Brassey's *Naval Annual*, 1887, p. 531

20 Sam Noble, *An Autobiography*, London, 1925, p. 2

21 Caledonia *Journal*, 1939, p. 23

22 National Archives, ADM 1/6084

23 Baynham, *Before the Mast*, op. cit., p. 179

24 John Wells, *The Immortal* Warrior, London, 1987, p. 125

25 John Winton, *Hurrah for the Life of a Sailor*, London, 1977, p. 196

26 Antony Preston and John Major, *Send a Gunboat*, London, 1967, *passim*

27 Lionel Yexley, *The Inner Life of the Navy*, London, 1908, pp 90–91

28 National Maritime Museum Manuscripts, MSS/73/669

29 Baynham, *Before the Mast*, op. cit., pp 127–8

30 National Archives, ADM 1/6388, para 86

31 Frederic Whyte, *The Life of W T Stead*, New York, 1925, pp 145–152

32 Roy Jenkins, *Gladstone,* London, 1996, p. 610

33 Henry Baynham, *Men from the Dreadnoughts*, London, 1976, p. 54

34 Winston S Churchill, *The River War*, London, 1973, p. 263

35 Navy Records Society, *The Papers of Admiral John Fisher*, ed. P K Kemp, vol. 1, 1960, p. 12

36 Jon Sumida, *In Defence of Naval Supremacy*, London, 1993, p. 50

37 Randolph S Churchill, *Winston S Churchill*, Volume II, Companion Part 3, London, 1969, p. 1836

38 National Archives, ADM 116/1182

39 Hansard, 16 March 1903, col. 866

40 National Archives, ADM 7/941

41 Baynham, *Men from the Dreadnoughts*, op. cit., p. 128

42 William James, *New Battleship Organisations*, Portsmouth, 1916, p. 81

43 Anthony Carew, *The Lower Deck of the Royal Navy, 1900–38*, Manchester, 1981, pp 64–5, 207–10

44 Louise King-Hall, op. cit., pp 366–7

45 Navy Records Society, *The Papers of Admiral John Fisher*, op. cit., vol. 1, p. 12

46 Stephen King-Hall, *My Naval Life*, London, 1952, p. 106

47 Angus Cunningham Graham, *Random Naval Recollections*, Gartocharn, 1979, p. 35

48 *Brassey's Naval Annual*, 1906, p. 1

49 Baynham, *Men from the Dreadnoughts*, op. cit., p. 231

50 Lord Chatfield, *The Navy and Defence*, London, 1942, p. 143

51 Baynham, *Men from the Dreadnoughts*, op cit, p. 236

52 Ibid., pp 237–8

53 Admiralty (Civil Engineer in Chief), *The Technical History and Index*, Vol. 8, *Scandinavian and East Coast Convoys*, p. 59

54 *Journal of the Royal United Service Institution,* February 1923, p. 2

55 Navy Records Society, *The Beatty Papers*, ed. B McL Ranft, 1989, Vol. I, pp 562–574; Paul G Halpern, *A Naval History of World War I*, London, 1994, p. 448

Bibliography

General History

Melvyn Bragg, *The Adventure of English*, London, 2003

Edward Earl of Clarendon, *The History of the Rebellion and Civil Wars*, Oxford, 1849

Linda Colley, *Britons, Forging the Nation, 1707-1837*, London, 1992

K Theodore Hoppen, *The Mid-Victorian Generation*, Oxford, 1998

G Kitson Clark, *The Making of Victorian England*, London, 1963

Paul Langford, *A Polite and Commercial People*, Oxford, 1989

Piers Mackesy, *The War for America*, London, 1964

B R Mitchell, *Abstract of British Historical Statistics*, Cambridge, 1962,

Naval History, Primary Sources

William James, *New Battleship Organisations*, Portsmouth, 1916

John Smith, *A Sea Grammar*, (ed. Goell), London, 1970

Lionel Yexley, *The Inner Life of the Navy*, London, 1908

Our Fighting Seamen, London, 1911

Naval History, Secondary Sources

Anthony Carew, *The Lower Deck of the Royal Navy, 1900-38*, Manchester, 1981

John Charnock, *Biographia Navalis*, 6 vols, London, 1794-8

Sir Julian Corbett, *Drake and the Tudor Navy*, London, 1899, 2 vols

J D Davies, *Pepys's Navy*, Barnsley, 2008

John S Gibson, *Ships of the '45*, London, 1967

Paul G Halpern, *A Naval History of World War I*, London, 1994

Arthur Herman, *To Rule the Waves*, New York, 2005

Michael Lewis, *Armada Guns*, London, 1961
The Navy in Transition, London, 1965

Christopher Lloyd, *The Navy and the Slave Trade*, London, 1949

Christopher McKee, *Sober Men and True*, Cambridge, Massachusetts, 2002

G E Manwaring and Bonamy Dobrée, *The Floating Republic*, London, 1935

Colin Martin and Geoffrey Parker, *The Spanish Armada*, London, 1988

Garrett Mattingly, *The Defeat of the Spanish Armada*, London, 1961

Michael Oppenheim, *A History of the Administration of the Royal Navy*, London, 1896

Hemut Pemsel, *Atlas of Naval Warfare*, London, 1977

Roger Perkins and K J Douglas-Morris, *Gunfire in Barbary*, Havant, *c.* 1982

E B Powley, *The English Navy in the Revolution of 1688*. Cambridge, 1928

Antony Preston and John Major, *Send a Gunboat*, London, 1967

Marcus Rediker, *Villains of all Nations; Atlantic Pirates in the Golden Age*, London, 2004

C N Robinson, *The British Tar in Fact and Fiction*, London, 1909

N A M Rodger, *The Wooden World*, London, 1986
Safeguard of the Sea, London, 1997
Command of the Ocean, London, 2004

Jon Sumida, *In Defence of Naval Supremacy*, London, 1993

Brian Tunstall, *Naval Warfare in the Age of Sail*, London, 1990

John G Wells, *Whaley, the Story of HMS Excellent*, Portsmouth, 1980

John Winton, *Hurrah for the Life of a Sailor*, London, 1977

C D Yonge, *The History of the British Navy*, London, 2 vols, 1863

Shipbuilding and Technical Subjects

D K Brown, *Before the Ironclad*, London, 1990
Warrior to Dreadnought, London, 1997

Frank Fox, *Great Ships*, London, 1980

Robert Gardiner, ed., *Conway's All the World's Fighting Ships, 1860-1905*, London, 1979
Conway's All the World's Fighting Ships, 1906-1921, London, 1985
The Line of Battle, London, 1992
Steam Steel and Shellfire, London, 1992
The Eclipse of the Big Gun, London, 1992

Robert Gardiner, *The First Frigates*, London, 1992
Frigates of the Napoleonic Wars, London, 2000

Thomas Heywood, *A True Description of His Majesty's Royall Ship*, (ed. Alan R Young), New York, 1990

Andrew Lambert. *The Last Sailing Battlefleet*, London, 1991

Brian Lavery, *Ship of the Line*, 2 vols, 1983-4
Nelson's Navy, London, 1989

David Lyon, *The Sailing Navy List*, London, 1994
The First Destroyers, London, 1996

Peter Marsden, *The Story of the Anne*, Hastings, 1992

Peter Padfield, *Guns at Sea*, London, 1973

Rif Winfield, *British Warships in the Age of Sail, 1793-1817*, Barnsley, 2005

Memoirs by Seafarers

Edward Barlow, *Barlow's Journal*, ed. Basil Lubbock, London, 2 vols, 1934

The Life and Adventures of Matthew Bishop, London, 1744

Henry Capper, *Aft from the Hawsehole*, London, 1927

Lord Chatfield, *The Navy and Defence*, London, 1942

Basil Hall, *Fragments of Voyages and Travels*, London, 1860

Augustus Hervey's Journal, (ed. David Erskine), London, 1953

Mark Kerr, *The Navy in My Time*, London, 1933
Sea Saga, being the Diaries of Four Generations of the King-Hall Family, (ed. Louise King-Hall), London, 1936

Stephen King-Hall. *My Naval Life*, London, 1952

N H Nicolas, ed., *The Dispatches and Letters of Lord Nelson*, 7 vols, 1998

Sam Noble, *An Autobiography*, London, 1925

Granville Penn, *Memorials of the Life of Sir William Penn*, London, 2 vols, 1833

The Works of Sir Walter Raleigh, ed. Oldys and Birch, Oxford, 8 vols, 1829

William Robinson, *Jack Nastyface, Memoirs of a Seaman*, Annapolis, 1973

The Narrative of William Spavens, ed. N A M Rodger, London, 1998

Richard Walter, *Anson's Voyage Round the World*, New York, 1974

The Adventures of John Wetherell, ed. C S Forester, London, 1954

Regional and Topographical

Bridget Cherry and Nikolaus Pevsner, *The Buildings of England, London 2, South*, London, 1990, and many others in the series

Michael Duffy, *Soldiers, Sugar and Seapower*, Oxford, 1987, pp 8–13,

G B Endacott, *An Eastern Entrepot*, London, 1964

Eric Homberger, *The Historical Atlas of New York City*, New York, 1994

Robert Hughes, *The Fatal Shore*, London 1987

Nabil I Matar, *Britain and Barbary, 1589-1689*, Gainesville, Florida, *c.* 2005

Other Topics

E H H Archibald, *Dictionary of Sea Painters*, Woodbridge, 1980

John Blake, *The Sea Chart*, London, 2009

David Cordingly, *Marine Painting in England, 1700-1900*, London, 1974

Norman Friedman, *British Carrier Aviation*, London, 1988

Keevil and Coulter, *Medicine and the Navy, 1200-1900*, 4 vols, 1957-63

Brian Lavery and Simon Stephens, *Ship Models*, London, 1995

P M Rippon, *Evolution of Engineering in the Royal Navy*, vol. 1, Tunbridge Wells, 1988

Dava Sobel, *Longitude*, London, 1995

Collections of Original Documents

Henry Baynham, *From the Lower Deck*, London, 1969

Before the Mast, London, 1972

Men from the Dreadnoughts, London, 1976

W B Clark, ed., *Naval Documents of the American Revolution*, Vol. 1, Washington, 1964

Historical Manuscripts Commission, *The Manuscripts of F J Savile Foljambe*, London, 1897

Manuscripts of the House of Lords, New Series, 1, 1900

Harold Hodges and Edward Hughes, *Select Naval Documents*, Cambridge, 1922

Three Sea Journals of Stuart Times, ed. Bruce S Ingram, London, 1936

B Lavery, ed., *The Royal Navy Officers Pocket Book*, London, 2007

Richard B Morris, ed., *The American Revolution, 1763-1783, a Bicentennial Collection*, New York, 1970

C Stephenson and F G Marcham, *Sources of English Constitutional History*, New York, 1937

Ned Ward, *The Wooden World*, (ed. Callender), Society for Nautical Research Occasional Publications, 1929

Other Memoirs and Biography

John Ehrmann, *The Younger Pitt*, vol 2, *The Reluctant Transition*, London, 1986, vol 3, *The Consuming Struggle*, London, 1996

Olaudah Equiano, *The Interesting Narrative of the Life ...*, London, 2003

Samuel Jeake, *An Astrological Diary of the Seventeenth Century*, ed. Michael Hunter and Annabel Gregory, Oxford, 1988

Roger Knight, *The Pursuit of Victory*, London, 2005

N A M Rodger, *The Insatiable Earl*, London, 1993

Benjamin Silliman, *Journal of Travels in England, Holland and Scotland*, Newhaven, 1812

Frederic Whyte, *The Life of W T Stead*, New York, 1925

Pepys's Memoires of the Royal Navy, 1679-1688, ed. J R Tanner, Oxford, 1906

The Diary of Samuel Pepys, ed. Robert Latham and William Matthews, 11 vols, London, 1970-83

Navy Records Society Volumes

The Defeat of the Spanish Armada, ed. J K Laughton, vol. 1, 1895

Sir William Monson's Naval Tracts, vol. iv, ed. Michael Oppenheim, 1913

The Letters of Admiral Markham, ed. Sir Clements Markham, 1904

The Letters and Papers of Charles, Lord Barham, ed. J K Laughton, vol. 1, 1906

The Autobiography of Phineas Pett, ed. W G Perrin, 1917

Samuel Pepys's Naval Minutes, ed. J R Tanner, 1925

The Tangier Papers of Samuel Pepys, ed. Edwin Chappell, 1935

Russian War, 1854, Ed Bonner-Smith and Dewar, 1943

Five Naval Journals, ed. H G Thursfield, 1951

The Keith Papers, ed. Christopher Lloyd, vol. 3, 1955

The Papers of Admiral John Fisher, ed. P K Kemp, vol. 1, 1960

Queen Anne's Navy, ed. R D Merriman, 1961

The Jacobean Commissions of Enquiry, ed. A McGowan, 1971

The Naval Miscellany, vol. 5, ed. N A M Rodger, 1984

British Naval Documents, 1204-1960, ed. J B Hattendorf et al, 1993

Shipboard Life and Organisation, ed. B Lavery, 1998

The Milne Papers, ed. John Beeler, 2004

Picture Credits

Anova Books Ltd is committed to respecting the intellectual property of others. We have taken all reasonable efforts to ensure that the reproduction of all content on these pages is done with the full consent of the copyright owners. If you are aware of an unintentional omissions please contact the company directly so that any necessary corrections can be made for future editions.

Index

Figures in *italics* indicate captions.

2nd Cruiser Squadron *248*
12th Destroyer Flotilla 257
Abbot, Midshipman Charles 192
Abbot, Lemuel *181*
Aboukir 251
Aboukir Bay 166
Achilles, HMS 222
Ackermann, Rudolf 159
Addington, Henry 168
Admiral class 220
Admiralty 203, *203*, 204, 211
    administration of 68
    and ship design 96
Admiralty Board 49, 65, 68, 105, 117
Admiralty Charts 209, *209*
Adventure 133
Africaine 184
Agamemnon 166, 180
Agamemnon (steam battleship) 204, 224,
    225
Agincourt (previously *Sultan Osman I*)
    254
aircraft carriers 11, 263
airships 263, *263*
Ajax 204, *248*
Alarm (frigate) 141
Albemarle 67
Albert, Prince Consort *236*
Albert Edward, Prince of Wales 217
Alecto 203, *203*
Alexandria, bombardment of (1882) 227,
    228, 240, 255
Alfred 186
Algiers *34*, *196*, 197, 199-200, 255
Allin, Sir Joseph 117
America *see* United States
American Civil War (1861-5) 202, 220,
    224
American Revolutionary War (1775-83)
    91, *131*, 134-40, 142-5, 166, 180, 205
Amiens, Treaty of (1802) 168, 181
Anglo-Dutch Wars
    1st (1652-4) 45-7
    2nd (1665-7) 50, 54-7, 56, 103
    3rd (1672-4) 54, 60-61, 63
Anglo-Spanish War (1585-1604) 19-29,
    33
Anglo-Spanish War (1718-19) 98, (1726-
    7) 98, (1762-3) 125
Anne 76-7, *76*
Anne, Queen 69, 86, 93
Anne Royal 34
Anson, Admiral Lord George 11, 91, 105,
    106, *106*, 110, 111, *111*, 115, 117, 118,
    118, 119, 121, 165
Anthony Roll 18
Antwerp, fall of (1585) 24-5
ANZAC troops 255-6
Archimedes 203
Ardent 137
Argus, HMS 262
Argyll, Earl of 66
Arnauld, George 167
Arne, Thomas *124*
Articles of War 11, 46, 48-9, 114-15, 119
Asdic 241, 260
Asiento slave contract 89, 94, 109
Association 89
Audacious 248

Austen, Jane 157, 159
Auxiliary Patrol 260

Bacon, John *142*
Badger 180
Baker, Matthew 19, *19*
Bank of England 81, 94
Banks, Sir Joseph 132
Barbados 34, 43, 100, 143
Barbary corsairs *34*, 36, 190
Barfleur, Battle of (1692) *74*, 78, *78*
Barham, Lord *see* Middleton, Sir Charles
Barlow, Edward 48, 55
Barrow, Sir John 209
Bastia siege 151
Battle Cruiser Fleet 252
Beachy Head, Battle of (1690) *74*, 76-7,
    76, 80, 96, 137
Beagle 209, 211
Beatty, Vice-Admiral Sir David 252, 256-
    7, *259*, 263-4, *264*
Beaufort, Sir Francis 209
Becher, A B 200
Bechervaise, John 205, 206
Bedford, Duchess of 117
Bedford, Duke of 110
Beechey, Sir William *125*
Bell, Henry 210
Belleisle 175, 178
Bellerophon 192, *193*
Bellona 141
Bellona class 117
Benbow, Admiral 86, 88
Beresford, Admiral Sir Charles *228*, 240,
    241
Berlin Decrees (1806) 183
Bettesworth, George 171
Birch, Thomas *189*
Bishop, Edward 88
Bismarck, Prince Otto von 237
Black Joke 201
Blackbeard 94, 95
Blake, General-at-Sea Robert 11, 45, *45*,
    46, 47
Blakeney, General William 113
Blane, Dr Gilbert 91
Blenheim, Battle of (1704) 88
Bligh, Captain William 11, 133, 152
Blomefield, Thomas 40
Board of Longitude 89
Board of Trade 211, 226
Boer War, 2nd (1899-1902) 236-7
Bonhomme Richard 137, *137*
Boreas 180
Boscawen, Admiral Edward 113, 120
Boscawen, HMS 220
Bougainville, Louis-Antoine de 134
Boulogne 170, 171, 181
    blockade of *170*
Bounty 11, 151-2
Bourbons 86, 89
Boyne 80
Boyne, Battle of the (1690) 77, *80*
Brassey, Lord 253
Breda 67
Breslau 254
Brest, France 110, 137, 151, 170
Bretagne 136
Briggs, Henry Perronet 45
Britannia 64
Britannia (formerly *Prince of Wales*) *214*,

215
Britannia Royal Naval College,
    Dartmouth 246, *247*
British Empire 11, 13, 33, 34, 86, 88,
    125, 226, 228, 229, 237
Brixham 70, *71*
Broke, Captain Philip 192
Brooking, Charles 96, *97*
Brunel, Marc Isambard 183, *183*
Brunswick 150
Bry, Theodore de *21*
Buckingham, Duke of 34, 36
Bunker Hill, Battle of (1775) 135
Burghley, Lord 18
Burgos, siege of 189
Bute, Lord 125
Butoft, George 255-6
Byng, Admiral Sir George 98, 104, 113,
    114, 137, 165
Byng, Admiral John 113, 114-15, *114*, *115*,
    117, 119
Byron, Captain 134

Ça Ira 164
Cadiz 171, 173, 174, 178, 181
    Battle of (1587) 20, *21*, 22
    expedition (1625) 34, 36, 37
Calder, Admiral 171
Caledonia, HMS 157, 159
Callaghan, Sir George 251, *251*
Calliope 207
Calvi, Siege of 151, 180
Camperdown, Battle of (1797) *156*, 159,
    165, 166
Camperdown *235*, 236
Cape Finisterre, Battle of (1805) 171
Cape Passeto, Sicily 98
Cape St Vincent, Battle of (1797) 151
Capper, Henry 246
Captain 180, 220
Carcass 180
Carmichael, John Wilson *212*
Carron Iron Works, Scotland 140
Carteret, Lieutenant Phillip 134
Censeur 164
Centurion 105, *106*
Centurion (battleship) *248*
Chamberlain, Joseph 229
Chambers, George *80*, *196*
Channel Fleet *71*, 153, 155, 170, 171
Charles Edward Stuart, Prince (Bonnie
    Prince Charlie) 106, 108
Charles I, King 11, 34, 36, 37, 39, 41, 42,
    43, 47, 67
Charles II, King *38*, 42, 48, 49, 50, *52*, 53,
    54, 56, 60, 61, 63-6, 68, 81, 83, 84, *93*,
    96, 98
Charles II, King of Spain 86
Charles III, King of Spain 89
Charleston, blockade of (1717) 94
Chatfield, Ernie 257
Chatham Dockyard 41, 56-7, 65, 67, 99,
    140, 180, 222
Chatham, Earl of 186
Chaucer, Geoffrey 12, 84
Cherub 192
Chesapeake 192, 205
Chesapeake Bay, Battle of (1781) *138*,
    139
Choiseul, Duc de 136
Chrystie, Lieutenant Thomas 197

Churchill, Sir Winston 9, 179, 236, 241,
    242-3, *243*, 246, 248, 253-4, 256, 261
Chuson, taking of (1840) *206*
Clerk, John 165
Clermont 210
Cleveley, John 96
Clive, Robert 120
Clyde (frigate) 129
Cochrane, Captain Arthur 224
Cochrane, Admiral Thomas, Earl of
    Dundonald 12, 186-7, *186*, 206
Cockburn, Admiral 192
Colbert, Jean Baptiste 75-6
Collard, Lieutenant 247
Collingwood, Admiral Cuthbert *173*, 174,
    175
Collins, Greenvile 69
Combined Fleet 137, 139
Comet 210
Commonwealth 6, 47, 48, 50, 63
Condor 227, 228
Conflans, Admiral 121
Constable, John 131
Constant Reformation, The 43
Constitution, USS *189*, 190, 191
Continental Navy 137, 190
Continental System 183, 186
convoy system 260
Cook, Captain James 13, *89*, 91, 132-3,
    133, 149, 209, 211
Cooke, E W 220
Cooke, T P 205, 206
Cope, General 108
Copenhagen, Battle of (1801) 167-8, 181
coppering 139, *140*, 141, *141*
Corbet, Captain Robert 183-4
Corn Laws, abolition of (1846) 225
Cornwallis, General 139, 170
Corresponding Societies 150, 159
Corsica *149*, 151, 180
Corunna, Battle of (1809) *185*, 186, 187
Covent Garden Theatre, London *204*,
    206
Cressy 251
Crimean War (1853-6) *13*, 211-13, *212*,
    220, 226, 237
Cromwell, Oliver 11, *43*, 47, 48, 60, 152
Cruizer class 183
Cunningham-Graham, Lieutenant Angus
    252
Curtis, Captain Edmund 47-8

Dakar, West Africa, capture of (1758)
    120
Dalrymple, Lieutenant 108
Dampier, William 86, *87*, 95
Dardanelles campaign (1915) 241, 254,
    255, *256*, 264
Dartmouth 200
Dartmouth, Earl of 69-70
Darwin, Charles 209
De Grasse, Admiral 139, 144
De la Jonquière, Marquis 110-11
de Lesseps, Ferdinand 226
De Winter, Admiral Jan Willem 156
Deane, Anthony 50, 76
Deane, Richard 47
Declaration of Independence (1776) *134*
Declaration of Indulgence (1687) 67
Defoe, Daniel: *Robinson Crusoe* 12, 95,
    96, 105

Derfflinger 257
Devastation 220, *220*, 221
Dibdin, Charles 87
Digby, Captain 63
Dighton, Denis *175*
Disraeli, Benjamin 226, 227
Dolphin 215
Doughty, Thomas 22
Douglas, General Sir Howard 144, 205
Dover, Treaty of (1670) 60
Downs, Battle of the (1639) 39
Drake, Sir Francis 9, 11, 13, 18, 19, 20, *21*, 22-3, *23*, 24, 61, 94, 105, 137
Dreadnought 239, *239*, *243*
Dreadnoughts 11, 239, 240, 241, *248*, 249, 251, 256, 257
Dreyer, Lieutenant Frederick 242
Dreyfus, Captain 240
Drisus, Reverend Samuel 54
Duchess 67
Duke of Argyle 109
Duncan, Admiral Adam 155, *156*, 159, 165, 166
Dunning, Squadron Leader 262, *26*
Dutch navy 64, 75, 76

Edward, Prince of Wales (later Edward VIII, then Duke of Windsor) *264*
Edward VI, King 17, 19
Edward VII, King *217*
Eliot, Sir John 37
Elizabeth I, Queen 17-18, *17*, 19, 22, 24, 25, *27*, *28*, 29, 33, 37, 42, 70
Elliot, Captain Charles 209
Elphinstone, George (later Admiral Lord Keith) 109
Ely, Eugene 262
Enchantress 243
Endeavour 132
Engadine, HMS 262
English civil war (1641-51) 41
English language 13, 119, 121, 123, 139, 149
Equiano, Olaudah 110
Espiritu Santo, New Hebrides 134
Essex 192
Evelyn, John 53
Excellent, HMS 205, *216*, *219*, 229, 240, 246
Exmouth, Lord *196*, 197, 199, 200

Fair Rosamund 201
Fenian Ram 237
Fergusson, Captain John 108
Ferme 136
Fighting Instructions 47, 48, 105, 111, 166
Figuera da Foz, Portugal *185*, 186
Finisterre, First Battle of (1747) 110-11, *111*, 144, 165
Finisterre, Second Battle of (1747) 111, 144
First World War 11, 241, 251-64
Fisher, Admiral Sir John, Baron of Kilverstone 9, 229, 239-40, 246, 251-2, *256*
Fitzpatrick, Lieutenant 153
FitzRoy, Robert 209, *209*, 211
Foley, Captain Thomas 166, 168
Forester, C.S. 12-13, 206
Formidable 121, *145*
Fort Charles, Port Royal, Jamaica *4*
Fort Duquesne 113
Fort Marabout, Egypt 228
Fort Trinidad, Rosas Bay, Spain 187

Four Days Fight (1666) 55
Fox, Charles James 155, *160*
Franco-Dutch War (1672-8) 64
Franklin, Sir John 211
French navy 60-61, 64, 75, 88, 96-7, 113, 136, 150, 184
French Revolution (1789-99) 149-50, 152
French Revolutionary Wars (1792-1802) 150-51, 159-60, 166-8
Frigate Bay, Battle of, St Kitt's (1782) *142*, 144
Frobisher, Sir Martin 19, 22
Fullarton, Lieutenant John 197
Fulton, Robert 210
Furious, HMS 262, *262*, 263

Gambier, Sir James 185, 187
Gannet 227
Garibaldi, Giuseppe 226
Garrick, David 131
Gaspee 135
Genoa 202
George I, King 93, 98
George II, King 98, 125
George III, King 99, 125, *125*, 129
George V, King *217*, *264*
German fleet 237, 263
German High Seas Fleet 256, 257, 262, 263, *264*
Gibraltar 88, 89, 113, 114, 143, 147, 173
Gilbert, Sir Humphrey 19
Gillray, James *160*, *168*, *181*
Giltra 253
Gladstone, William Ewart 207, 226, 229, 235
Gloire 220
Glorious First of June, Battle of the (1794) 129, *150*, 151
Glorious Revolution (1688) 70, 93
Glory 153
Gloucester 119
Glover, Richard 101, *101*
Goeben 254
Golden Hind 22, *23*
Golden Lion 26
Goliath 166
Gorgon 200
Gouden Leeuw 61
Goudan 214
Goya, Francisco 186
Grace Dieu 17
Grand Fleet 251, *251*, 252, 253, 256, 257, *259*, 259, 264
Grand Turk replica *9*
Gravelines, naval battle of (1588) 22, 24-5
Graves, Vice-Admiral Samuel 136
Graves, Rear-Admiral Thomas *138*, 139
Great Britain 203
Great Eastern 224
Great Michael 17
Great Fire of London (1666) 56, *56*, 80
Great Turk — Greek War of Independence (1821-9) 202
Green, Royal Marine Bandsman A C 257
Greenwich Hospital (later Royal Naval College) *51*, 83, *83*, 86, 87, 96
Griffier, Jan, the Elder *51*
Griffiths, Captain Anselm 184
'grog' 103, 105, 219
Guadeloupe 120, 125
guerre de course 79, 83, 235
Guerriere 189, 191
Gulf of Tonkin affair 134
Gulliver's Travels (Swift) 96

gunpowder 40, 207, *207*
guns
    range of 11, 20, 242
    breech loading 30, 40
    reloading 39
    gun crews 39, *40*
    muzzle loading 40
    gunnery 1620-1850 40, *40*
    cast 40
    broadside 47
    carronades 140
    training in naval gunnery 205, 242
    Hotchkiss 239
    modern 30mm 9

Hakluyt, Richard 29
Hall, Captain Basil 157
Hall, Captain William 207
hammocks 18, 215
Hampden, John 39
Hancock, John *134*, 135
Hardwicke, Lord 118
Hardy, Sir Charles 137
Hardy, Vice Admiral Sir Thomas (as Captain) 165, *175*
Harrison, John 85, 89
Hase, George von 249
Hawke, Admiral Sir Edward 111, 121, 165
Hawkins, Sir John 17, 18-19, 22, 23, 24, 94
Hay, Lord Arthur 213
Hazard (sloop) 106
'Heart of Oak' naval anthem 121
Heights of Abraham, Quebec 120, *120*
Henri Grace à Dieu 17, *18*
Henrietta Anne, Duchess of Orléans 55
Henry V, King 17, 42
Henry VII, King 42
Henry VIII, King 11, 17, *18*, 19, 24, *31*, 41, 42
Herbert, Admiral 76
Hercules 257
Hermione mutiny 159, *159*, *170*
Hervey, Captain Augustus 113, 125
Hibernia, HMS 262
Hicks, Lieutenant 153
Hindustan 214
Hipper, Franz von 256
Hodges, William *133*
Hogue 251
Holland, John Philip 237
Holland No 1 237
Holman, Seaman Thomas 227
Holmes, Sir Robert 56
Hong Kong 209
Hood, Admiral Sir Samuel *142*, 144
Hoppner, John *152*
Hornby, Sir Geoffrey Phipps 226
Hornigold, Captain Benjamin 94
Horton, Admiral Sir Max 12
Hosier, Rear-Admiral Francis 101, *101*, 104
Hotham, Admiral William 151, *164*, 166, 180
Houblon, John 81-2
House of Commons 11, 49, 51, 64, 103, 219, 243
House of Lords 241
Howard of Effingham, Lord 22, 24, 25, 26-7
Howe, Admiral Richard 121, 135, *150*, 151
Howe, General Sir William 135

Hughes, Admiral Sir Edward 139
Hume, David 119
Humphreys, Charles 220
Huntley, Lieutenant 201
hydrography 132
hydrophone 259-60
Hyndman, H M 229

Illustrious, HMS 215
Impregnable 219, *219*
Income Tax Act (1789) *12*, 159-60
Indefatigable 257
Inflexible 255
Inglefield, Lieutenant E F *199*
Inscription Maritime 76
Invincible 111, *111*, 219, 257, *259*
Invincible class 240
Iron Duke 251

Jacobite Rebellion (1715) 93
Jacobite Rebellion (1745) 104, 106, 108, 113
Jacobites 75, 77, 95-6, 104
Jamaica 43, 47, *142*, 143
James, Commander William 243, 247
James I, King (VI of Scotland) 19, 33, 34, 43
James II, King (VII of Scotland; also as Duke of York) 51, 53, 55, 61, *63*, 66-7, 69, 76, 77, 79, 106, 206
James IV, King of Scotland 17
James Stuart (the Old Pretender) 93
Java 191
Jeake, Samuel 82
Jeffreys, Judge 66
Jellicoe, Admiral Sir John 251, 252, 256, 257, *259*, 264
Jenkin, Petty Officer William 226
Jenkins, Captain Robert 103
Jerrold, Douglas: *Black Ey'd Susan* 204, 205, 206
Jervis, Sir John *see* St Vincent, Earl of
John, King 17
Jones, John Paul 137, *137*, 190-91
Juan Fernandez island 95, 105, 118
Justitia (prison hulk) 148
Jutland, Battle of (1916) *259*, 264
Juverna (slave schooner) 109

Keith, Admiral Lord 170
Kendall, Larcum 89
Kent 108
Keppel, Admiral Augustus 136, *136*, 137
Kerr, Mark 215
Keyham, Plymouth dockyard 222, 227
Kiel Regatta Week (1914) *248*, 249
King George V 248
King-Hall, Lieutenant Stephen 249, 252
Kip, Thomas 83
Kirkby, Captain Richard 86, 88
Kitchener, General: Nile expedition (1898) 236, *236*
Kneller, Sir Godfrey *51*

la Galissionère, Admiral 113
La Hogue, Battle of (1692) 78-9
La Hougue, Cotentin peninsula 77
La Rochelle expediton (1627) 36
Ladysmith, Siege of (1899-1900) 237
Lagos Bay 78, 80
Lake Erie, Battle of (1813) *191*, 192
Lambarde, William 25
Lancaster (frigate) *9*
Larne 207
Lawley, John, of Dartmouth *12*

Lawrence 191
Lawrence, Captain James 192
Leake, Admiral Sir John 89
Leake, Samuel 77
Leander 166
Leeward Islands 143, 180
Lely, Sir Peter 48
Lely, Thomas 39
Lenox 108
Leopard 39
Lepanto, Battle of (1571) 20, 235
Lestock, Admiral 105
Liberty (sloop) 135
Lind, Dr James 91
Lissa, Battle of (1866) 220
Livingstone, Dr David 226
Lloyd George, David 241, 260
London 199
longitude 85, 89
Lord High Admiral 68
L'Orient 166, 167, 207
Louis XIV, King of France 13, 55, 60, 74, 75, 77, 93
Louisbourg fortress, Canada, capture of (1758) 120
Loutherbourg, Philip de 131
Lowe, Sir Hudson 192
Lowestoft 98
Lowestoft, naval battle of (1665) 55
Lucas, Captain 175
Lucas, Lieutenant C D, VC 213
Luny, Thomas 129, 131, 145
Lusitania 254
Lutwidge, Captain Skeffington 180
Lutzow 257
Lyons, Rear Admiral Sir Edmund 211

Macedonian 191
McPherson, Seaman Charles 202
Magnanime 121
Mahon, Minorca 89, 100, 100
Maitland, Captain Thomas 192
Majestic class 236
Malaga, Battle of (1704) 88, 104
Malta 166, 167, 168
Manila, Philippines 125
Marine Society 119
Mariner's Mirror, The 29
Markham, Rear-Admiral Albert 236
Marlborough, Duke of 88, 264
Marryat, Captain Frederick 12, 156, 159, 206
Martello tower 149
Marvell, Andrew 57, 60
Mary 53
Mary I, Queen 17, 19
Mary II, Queen 51, 67, 69, 70, 76, 77, 83
Mary of Modena 69
Mary Queen of Scots 19
Mathews, Admiral Thomas 105-6, 114, 137, 165
Matthew replica 4, 31, 85
Maurepas, Comte de 96
Maynard, Thomas 142
Mediterranean Fleet 181, 240
Medway raid (1667) 56, 56
Melville, Lord 202-3, 205
merchantmen, merchant ships 24, 37, 41, 43, 79, 80, 180, 253, 260
Middleton, Sir Charles (later Lord Barham) 139, 141, 141, 171
Milton, John 51
Minorca 89, 100, 100, 113, 113, 114, 118, 147, 167, 168, 187
Monamy, Peter 96, 102, 108

Monck 55
Monck, Richard, Lord Albemarle 47, 48, 55
Monmouth, Duke of 66
Monson, William 29
Montagu, Edward, Earl of Sandwich 48, 50
Moore, General Sir John 185, 187
Mordaunt, Lord 53
Morgan, Sir Henry 93, 94
Morice, Humphrey 94
Morineau, Pierre 97, 111
Mutine (a brig) 166
mutiny 12, 26, 34, 36, 151-3, 155-6, 155, 159
Mutiny Act 11

N J Fjord 256
Napier, Sir Charles 211
Napoleon 204
Napoleon Bonaparte 151, 159, 166, 167, 170, 171, 174, 183, 190, 192, 193, 193
Napoleonic Wars 12, 40
Naseby 48
Nash, John 96
national debt 82
Nations, Battle of the (1813) 192
naval architects 202
naval arms race 235, 240
naval aviation 262
Naval Defence Act (1889) 11, 222, 235
navigation 84-5, 85, 134
Navigation Acts 45, 49, 180, 211
Navarino, Battle of (1827) 200, 202
Navy Board 18, 49, 50, 53, 66, 68, 180, 202
Navy League 238, 240
Nelson, Admiral Lord Horatio 9, 11, 13, 164, 180-81, 181, 206, 217, 229
    and close-range action 166
    boarding party on the San Josef 153
    favours decisive, annihilating action 166
    Battle of the Nile 166, 181
    Battle of Copenhagen 167, 168
    blockade of Toulon 170-71, 181
    at Trafalgar 173-5, 175, 178, 181
    death 178, 179
Nelson class 202
Nemesis 207, 207
Neptune 243
Nereide 183
New York 54, 54, 135
Newcomen, Thomas 210
Newton, John 109-10
Niagara 191
Nicol, John 206
Nicolas, Lieutenant Paul 175
Nile, Battle of the (1798) 166-7, 167, 168, 181
Nine Years' War (1688-97) 69-71, 74-83
Nore mutiny (1797) 155, 156, 156
North government 140
North Sea 45, 70, 132, 253, 254, 262
North Sea Fleet 155, 159, 170
Nuestra Señora de Covandonga 106
Nuestra Señora de la Concepción 22

Oates, Titus 65
O'Brian, Patrick 13, 206
Ogle, Captain Chalenor 95
Ollivier, Blaise 97
Opium Wars (1840-60) 206, 207, 207, 209
Orford 108

Orion class 241
Orme, Daniel 156
Osborne, Isle of Wight 207
Ossory 78

Pacific 132, 133, 180
Palmerston forts 221
Pankhurst, Sylvia 240-41
Panther 248
Paoli, Pasquale 151
Paris, Peace of (1783) 145
Paris, Treaty of (1763) 125
Parker, Sir Hyde 167, 168, 181
Parker, Richard 156, 156
Parker, Rear-Admiral Sir William 206
Parma, Duke of 21, 25
Parsons, Charles 237, 238
Paul I, Czar of Russia 168
Payne, Sir John 39
Pelican 22
Peninsular War (1807-14) 185, 186-7, 189-90
Penn, William 66
Pepys, Samuel 11, 47, 48, 48, 49, 50-51, 50, 53-7, 60, 61, 63-6, 67, 75, 76, 78, 81, 96, 118, 202
Perry, Captain Oliver Hazard 191, 192
Pett, Henry 102
Pett, Peter 38, 39, 57
Pett, Phineas 39
Phillip, Captain Arthur 149
Phillip I, King of Spain 19-21
Phillip II, King of Spain 66
Phillips, Charles 104
Phoebe 192
Phoenix 4, 91, 188
Pigot, Captain Hugh 159, 170
Pitt, William, the Elder 118, 119, 125
Pitt, William, the Younger 151, 152, 160, 168, 171
Plassey, Battle of (1757) 120
Player's Navy Cut 219, 219
Pocock, Nicholas 129, 150, 175
Pollen, Charles 242
Pommern 257
Popham, Sir Home 184, 189-90, 205
Popish plot (1679) 51, 65
Port Jackson, Australia 147
Portland, Battle of (1653) 47
Portobello (in modern Venezuela) 101
    capture of (1739) 102, 103, 104
Portsmouth 115, 128, 196, 247
Powell, John 171
Praslin, Duc de 136
President 190
'President's House', 191, 192
press gangs 11, 48, 54-5, 76, 119, 168-70
Prestonpans, Battle of (1745) 106
Pride, Colonel 47
Prince of Wales class 202
Prince Royal 32, 33
Princessa 105, 108
prison hulks 147, 148
Privy Council 57
Puerto Cabello, Venezuela 159
Pugin, Augustus Welby Northmore 68, 204

Q-ships 254
Quebec, capture of 120, 121, 123, 135
Queen 255
Queen Charlotte 150
Queen Elizabeth class 241, 256
Queen Mary 243, 257, 259

Queen's House, Greenwich 51, 83, 150
Quiberon Bay, Battle of (1759) 120, 121, 129, 144, 165
Quota men 155-6

Raby, H J, VC 213
Raisonable 180
Raleigh, Sir Walter 19, 27, 29
Ramsay, Lieutenant 201
Ranger 95
Ranger (sloop) 137, 137
Rasay, Isle of 108
Rattler 203-4, 203
Rebecca 103
Redoubtable 175, 175
Renown, HMS 236
Republicans 48
Resolution 133
Retribution 210
Reynolds, Sir Joshua 136
Roanoke, Virginia 22
Roberts, Bartholomew 94, 95
Robinson, William 171, 206
Roch, Captain Jeremy 55
Rodney, Admiral Sir George 142, 143, 144, 145, 165, 166
Roebuck 86, 87
Rogers, Woodes 95
Rolfe, John 34
Rooke, Admiral Sir George 79, 80, 88, 104
Rosario 22
Ross, James Clark 211
Roteley, Lieutenant Louis 174
Rowlandson, Thomas 68, 204
Royal Academy, London 129, 131
Royal Charles 48, 56, 56
Royal Dockyards 68, 141, 147, 222
    Deptford 49
    Portsmouth 183
Royal Fortune 95
Royal George 121, 145
Royal Marines 17, 246
Royal Naval Air Service (RNAS) 261, 262, 263
Royal Naval Volunteer Reserve 253
Royal Navy
    births and rebirths 17
    power of 9, 11, 26
    discipline 11, 170
    financing of 11
    mutiny see mutiny
    impressment 21, 24, 27, 29, 41, 47-8, 119
    commission's report (1618) 33
    pay 41, 89, 98, 119, 153, 155, 197
    English Naval Revolt (1648) 41
    reforms of 1652 46
    England's greatest naval crisis (1667) 49
    Pepys' reforms 51
    officers 63-4, 86, 94, 98, 152-3, 156-7, 159, 183-4, 197, 215-16
    shipbuilding (1670s) 64-5
    and the Glorious Revolution 70
    industries supporting 82
    seamens' diet 82, 91, 153, 205, 219
    formal career structure 94
    and slavery 109, 200-202
    uniforms 117, 117, 216-17, 217
        Anson's reforms 117, 118
    lack of race distinction 156, 157, 159
    fleet tacticals 165-6
    and the Berlin Decrees 183
    reaches the high point in its life 192-3